Keys To Teaching Elementary School Music

by
CARL O. THOMPSON
and
HARRIET NORDHOLM

SCHMITT, HALL & MCCREARY COMPANY
Minneapolis

Grade School Chorus
Seymour Public Schools, Seymour, Wisconsin

DEDICATION

Dedicated to the thousands of elementary school teachers who play such an important part in building a Musical America.

TABLE OF CONTENTS

FOREWORD

The teaching profession has long been calling for a practical and inspirational book which will guide elementary school teachers in the processes of presenting music to children. The authors have met this challenge so adequately that now all grade teachers can provide a well-balanced and richly creative program of musical experiences for children by applying their own creative resources to this most helpful volume.

The co-authorship which made this book possible is a fortunate and significant combination indeed, because each author brings a strong and unique background of training and experience to the reader. Carl O. Thompson, who has been a leader in teacher education as Chairman of the Division of Fine and Applied Arts at the State Teachers College, Bemidji, Minnesota for many years, has also demonstrated invaluable ability and insight as a prominent official in the Minnesota Music Educators Association for many years. His students, scattered throughout the nation, have reflected and dispersed his human and practical philosophy of music education to thousands of rural, town, and city school children.

Harriet Nordholm shares with the reader her many fruitful years of daily contact with elementary children in all kinds of musical situations. Miss Nordholm is an artist-teacher in every sense. She is both inspirational and practical in her approach to the teaching of music, and her work as Director of Elementary Music Education at Austin, Minnesota has been the successful proving-ground of her contributions to this book. Moreover, Miss Nordholm has deep insight concerning problems of teacher education through her inspiring work as President of the Minnesota Music Educators Association and as director of summer workshops at the University of Minnesota, Winona State Teachers College, and other teacher-training institutions.

Significantly, both Miss Nordholm and Mr. Thompson played major roles in the writing, organization, and the state-wide adoption and use of the *Guide for Instruction in Music* published by the State Department of Education, September 1948. Indeed, both authors are highly qualified to offer guidance and suggestions to all those who wish to enrich the lives of American children through music.

They have succeeded in presenting specific and varied methods, procedures, and materials in such a way that both the student teacher in-training as well as the teacher in-service may profit by the contents of this volume.

The authors have as their chief aim the improvements of musica opportunities for all children with the hope that their book will stimulate, suggest, and guide teachers in building programs of music education which will evoke great joy and sustained appreciational attitudes toward music. This philosophical approach is developed throughout the book in such a practical, straight-forward presentation that any reader who is actively interested in elementary music education, regardless of training and musical background, will be able to adapt its contents to the musical interests, needs, and capabilities of boys and girls in any community.

Robert W. Winslow
Associate Professor of Music Education
University of Minnesota

INTRODUCTION

This book is an outgrowth of experiences the authors have had in the teaching of music education courses in teacher training institutions and in public school music work. The primary concern in setting forth definite teaching plans has been to make them as practical as possible for the teaching of elementary school music, both in the urban elementary schools, as well as in the small village or rural school. The use of the book will be briefly described under the following headings:

a. For Teacher Training

Successful music teaching must be developed through the teacher training institutions. It has been the experience of the authors that many students do not have the necessary background in music fundamentals to do effective music teaching, and some are not able to sing artistically or to play the piano acceptably. Therefore, it was felt that a chapter on music fundamentals and music teaching skills should be included in this book, as well as actual teaching methods on different grade levels. This book is a comprehensive coverage of requirements for college students who wish to become elementary teachers.

b. For In-service Training

There is a growing tendency on the part of school administrators to require teachers who are deficient in the knowledge and skills in music teaching to take in-service training until effective teaching in music is accomplished. The music consultant, charged with this responsibility, will find this book a valuable guide. It is a common practice in many states, for this type of instruction to be affiliated with teacher training institutions so college credit can be given toward academic degrees. There is sufficient material in the book if all phases of the work are studied, to cover approximately one full year of music education study. It is possible to shorten the course by eliminating some assignments and spending less time on other portions of the study material. However, the authors strongly recommend that if possible, an entire year be devoted to the study of the contents of this book.

c. For Individual Study

There are many grade school teachers who have excellent backgrounds in music, but who wish to keep abreast of modern practices in music teaching. The authors have attempted to make all teaching plans so definite that teachers with a good music background may use the book as a guide to improve their music teaching. The numerous stories about compositions and lists of phonograph records, with the outlines of listening lessons should be of special value. There are also many practical helps for the introduction of creative music into the music program on each grade level.

d. For Administrators

Many administrators wish to know what standards and objectives should be reached by the teachers under their supervision. These have been constantly kept in mind and have been expressed in non-technical terms so that the administrators who do not have strong music backgrounds, may be able to evaluate the progress of music teaching in their schools.

e. For Graduate Students

As a book on practical teaching helps, and as a source book studied for the evaluation of all music activities, this book should prove helpful.

f. For the Rural Teacher

If Appendix I is studied rather carefully, it will be seen that the entire book may be used by teachers in one, two, three, and four room rural schools. Lists of books are given, suggestions for conducting county festivals are outlined, and references to other sections of the book are made to give practical helps on all phases of the teaching of rural music.

ACKNOWLEDGEMENTS

Our thanks to Miss Beatrice Barry, Miss Thresa Garry, and Mrs. Frances Christiansen for their valuable contributions; to Dr. Winslow for writing the Foreword; and to many others who helped in the preparation of this book.

Chapter I

WHAT THE URBAN AND RURAL ELEMENTARY
TEACHER SHOULD KNOW ABOUT
MUSIC FUNDAMENTALS

It is imperative that the student of Public School Methods has a foundation course in Music Fundamentals. In order to give the rural and urban elementary teacher a readily accessible source for study or reference, a brief chapter devoted to the fundamentals of music is included in this book. The following basic facts are necessary for the teacher to know in order to teach music effectively, and should be mastered by everyone teaching or planning to teach music to elementary school children.

I. THE STAFF

The music staff consists of five lines and four spaces. Notes are placed on the staff to indicate pitch, which is the highness or lowness of tone.

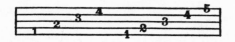

II. LETTERS

The first seven letters of the alphabet, (A B C D E F G) are used to name the lines and spaces.

III. CLEFS

There are eight clefs that may be used in writing music. Those in most common use are the treble, alto, tenor and bass. For vocal and piano music the treble and bass clefs are used almost exclusively. You will find it most practical to remember that "middle C" has the same pitch in each of these clefs.

When the treble and bass clefs are placed together in the following form, it is called the Great Staff:

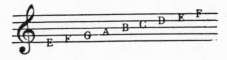

A. Treble Clef

The treble clef is used for notes written for women's, children's, and tenor male voices; also for the higher instruments of the band, orchestra, and for the piano. The treble clef sign turns around the G line and it is often called the G clef. The treble clef letter names are as follows:

B. Bass Clef

The bass clef is used for notes written for men's voices, for the lower instruments of the orchestra and band, and for the piano. The bass clef sign originally was the letter *F*, and therefore the bass clef is sometimes called the *F* clef. The two dots above and below the fourth line indicate where *F* is found. The bass clef letter names are as follows:

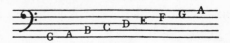

Some instruments with a very wide range play music written in both clefs. Piano music, for instance, is written in both treble and bass clefs.   baritone, viola, cello, piano,

IV. LEGER LINES

Sometimes notes must be written that are too high or too low to be contained in the staff. Short lines may be added above or below as needed to increase the range. These lines are called *leger lines*. There is theoretically no limit to the number of *leger lines* which may be written but for the present purposes, three will be used.

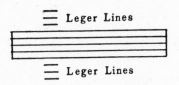

The sign "8va" over a note indicates that it should be played one octave higher than written. "8va" written below indicates that the note should be played one octave lower than written.

V. BAR AND DOUBLE BARS

Lines drawn vertically through the staff are called *bars*. The double bar consists of two vertical lines placed close together. They are used at the beginning and end of a strain or section of a composition.

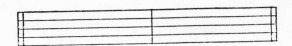

VI. THE MEASURE

Bars serve to divide the music into measures of equal duration. The distance between bars is called a *measure*.

VII. NOTES AND RESTS

Modern music uses eight different types of notes to indicate the length of time a tone should be held. Each of these eight notes has a corresponding rest.

◖O◗ is a double whole note	▬▬ is a double whole rest
o is a whole note	▬ is a whole rest
♩ is a half note	▬ is a half rest
♩ is a quarter note	ƺ is a quarter rest
♪ is an eighth note	⁊ is an eighth rest
♬ is a sixteenth note	⁊ is a sixteenth rest
♬ is a thirty-second note	⁊ is a thirty-second rest
♬ is a sixty-fourth note	⁊ is a sixty-fourth rest

Notes are as large as the space between the lines of the staff. Usually when they lie above the third line, the stems point down; when below, they point up. Stems pointing down are on the left side of the note, while those pointing up are on the right side.

VIII. METER SIGNATURES

Meter signatures are numerical indications of the regular recurrence of a beat or pulse. They are composed of two numbers, one above the other. The upper figure indicates the number of beats in a measure and the lower figure, the kind of a note which receives one beat. For example, in 4/4 meter, there are four counts per measure and each quarter note receives one count.

All groups of notes usually fall into three types of meter: duple, triple, and quadruple. There are several combinations of these three. The following meter signatures are the most commonly used in music today. Each measure has been filled by notes as indicated by the meter signature.

The meter signatures in which the quarter note receives one count:

The meter signatures in which the eighth note receives one count:

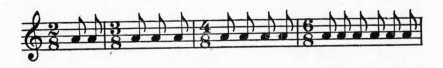

Eighth notes may be written individually or grouped together by beams or lines:

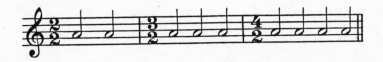

The meter signature giving the half note one count:

Sometimes the letter "C" is used to indicate 4/4 meter:

When a line is drawn through the "C", the half note receives one count instead of the quarter. This is called ala breve or "cut time."

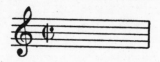

IX. ACCENTS

A. Primary Accent

The first beat of the measure is usually accented, regardless of the meter signature.

B. Secondary Accents

In each measure, there are lighter or secondary accents.

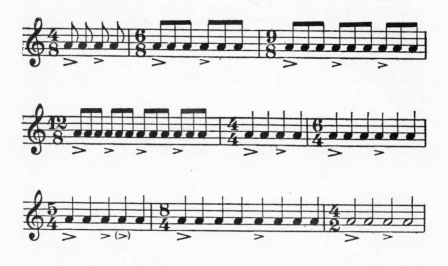

C. Syncopation

When the accent falls on the usually unaccented beat, the music is said to be *syncopated*. Examples:

X. PIANO KEYBOARD

A knowledge of the piano keyboard is a valuable aid in understanding and learning the different types of scales.

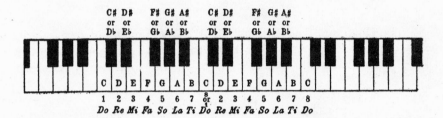

We can see from the above picture of part of a piano keyboard that from one key to the next is a half step; that is, from a white key to the neighboring black one. From E to F is also a half step since there is no black key between these two white ones. The same is true of B and C.

XI. SHARPS AND FLATS

The best way to study the musical scale is to use the piano keyboard. In order to build major scales other than C, it is necessary to use one or more black keys of the piano. These black keys are indicated by using sharps or flats.

A. **Step**—A step is a unit for measuring distance in music.

1. Half Step—The tone nearest to any given tone, either above or below, is a half step from the given tone.

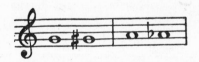

The half steps which occur normally on the staff are between B-C and E-F.

2. Whole step—A whole step consists of two half steps.

B. **Sharp**—A sharp is a character used to indicate a tone one half step higher than the normal pitch of that tone.

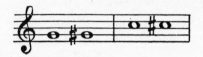

C. Double Sharp—The double sharp is a character used to indicate a tone one whole step above the normal pitch of that tone or one half step above the pitch of the tone indicated by the sharp.

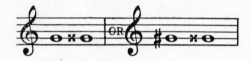

D. Flat—A flat is a character used to indicate a tone one half step lower than the normal pitch of that tone.

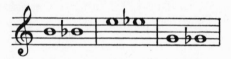

E. Double Flat—The double flat is a character used to indicate a tone one whole step below the normal pitch of that tone or one half step below the pitch of the tone indicated by a flat.

F. Cancel or Natural—A character which is used to remove the effect of a sharp or a flat is called a cancel or natural. The sharp or flat cancelled may be in the original signature or just previously inserted. For example:

1. Placed before a flatted note, the cancel or natural has the same effect as a sharp and raises that tone one half step higher

than the pitch represented by the flatted note.

di   mi   so   la   te   la   ti

2. Placed before a sharped note, the cancel or natural has the same effect as a flat and lowers a tone one half step below the pitch represented by the sharped note.

le   do   sol   mi   fi   fa   mi

3. In the case of a double flatted note, the cancel restores that note to the pitch of the normal tone. Likewise in case of the note flatted, the cancel is used to restore the note to the normal pitch.

4. In the case of a double sharped note, the cancel restores that note to the pitch of the normal tone. Likewise in the case of the note sharped, the cancel is used to restore the note to the normal pitch.

When sharps, flats, or naturals are used in a measure of music, they affect only the same note when repeated in the same measure, as distinguished from sharps and flats appearing in the signature.

XII. SCALES

A. Tetrachords—A tetrachord is a series of four tones on consecutive staff degrees. The pattern for the major tetrachord is: one whole step; one whole step; one half step. The example below indicates this pattern.

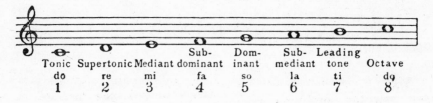

Lower tetrachord   Upper tetrachord

B. The Major Scale

If on the piano, we number the white keys beginning with C, we find that there is a whole step from 1 to 2; also from 2 to 3; from 3 to 4 is a half step; 4 to 5—a whole step; 5 to 6—a whole step; 6 to 7—a whole step, and from 7 to 8—a half step.

The major scale steps are therefore in the following order:

This arrangement of steps is called the major scale.

1. Theory names, syllables and numbers of the major scale.

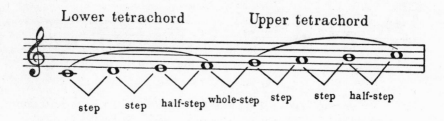

C. The Minor Scale

A minor scale starts on the sixth note of the major scale and uses the same signature.

Three forms of the minor scale are used.

The Normal Minor

The normal minor scale ascends and descends using the same notes as its relative major, but starting on the sixth note, or "la."

The Harmonic Minor

The harmonic minor is like the normal, except that the seventh note is raised one half step both ascending and descending.

The Melodic Minor

In the melodic scale, the sixth and seventh notes are each raised one half step in the ascending scale. It descends exactly as the normal minor.*

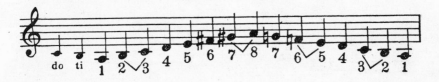

*There is a tendency in some schools to call this scale the mixed minor, and to call the scale with the raised 6th and 7th degrees both ascending and descending, the melodic minor.

any scale that ascends & descends by half step

D. The Chromatic Scale (ascending and descending)

If all the white and black notes starting on C on the piano are played consecutively, twelve equal half-steps or semitones to the octave will be played. This is called the chromatic scale. Each chromatically altered tone has been given a syllable name as follows:

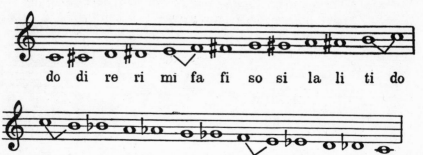

do   di   re   ri   mi   fa   fi   so   si   la   li   ti   do

do   ti   te   la   le   so   se   fa   mi   me   re   ra   do

XIII. SIGNATURES

The sharps and flats in the staff immediately following the clef sign form what is known as the key signature. When a sharp is in the signature, it is played a half tone higher throughout the staff unless altered by another sign. A flat in the signature causes that note to be played one half tone lower throughout the staff unless altered by another sign. The following signatures are used:

(Major Key Signatures)

Treble Clef														
KEY OF	C	G	D	A	E	B	F#	C#	F	Bb	Eb	Ab	Db	Gb	Cb
Bass Clef														

(Minor Key Signatures)

	a	e	b	f#	c#	g#	d#	d	g	c	f	bb	eb

Each major scale has a relative minor. There is a short-cut to learning the minor signatures. If the student will think of the signature for the major key with the same name and then add three flats or take away three sharps, he will have the parallel minor key signature with the same name. Examples:

C Major (plus 3 flats)—c minor   E Major (less 3 sharps)—e minor

XIV. INTERVALS

An interval is defined as the distance between two tones; it is always read upwards from the lower tone. The major scale is adways used as the measurement for intervals. In order that a teacher of public school music may hear whether or not two, three, and four part singing is "in tune," she must train herself to recognize all intervals.

Taking the tonic, or *do* as a starting point, there will be four types of intervals to be learned.

A. Perfect Intervals

The distance between *do* and *do* (two voices singing the same pitch), *do* and *fa*, *do* and *so*, and *do* and *do* (octave above), form perfect intervals. These tones should be sounded separately and then simultaneously. They are written as follows:

Perfect Intervals (Key of C)

Perfect Prime   Perfect Fourth   Perfect Fifth   Perfect Octave

B. Major Intervals

The distance from *do* to *re*, *do* to *mi*, *do* to *la*, and *do* to *ti*, are called major intervals. The tones are written as follows:

Major Intervals (Key of C)

Major Second   Major Third   Major Sixth   Major Seventh

C. Augmented Intervals

When major or perfect intervals are extended one half step, either by raising the upper tone or lowering the bottom tone, the interval is said to be augmented.   Example:

Perfect Fifth   Augmented Fifth   Augmented Fifth

For the sake of brevity, only one set of augmented intervals, those with the raised upper tone, will be presented in the following illustrations:

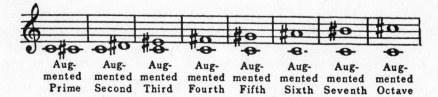

Aug-   Aug-   Aug-   Aug-   Aug-   Aug-   Aug-   Augmented   mented   mented   mented   mented   mented   mented   mented
Prime   Second   Third   Fourth   Fifth   Sixth   Seventh Octave

D. Minor Intervals

When a major interval is made smaller by one half step, it becomes minor.   For example, the interval of a major third from C to E may be made smaller, either by lowering the upper or raising the lower note.   Example:

Major Third   Minor Third   Minor Third

If *do* is stationary, the following minor intervals, formed by lowering the upper note one half step, will be written as follows:

Minor Second   Minor Third   Minor Sixth   Minor Seventh

E. Diminished Intervals

When perfect intervals are made smaller by one half step, they become diminished. When major intervals are made smaller by a whole step or when minor intervals are made smaller by one half step, they become diminished. Examples:

| Perfect
Fifth | Diminished
Fifth | Diminished
Fifth | Major
Sixth | Minor
Sixth | Diminished
Sixth |

The following abbreviations are used in the chart below: maj. — major, min. — minor, perf. — perfect, aug. — augmented, dim. — diminished, chrom.—chromatic.

Chrom.
Semi-tone, Min. 2nd, Maj. 2nd, Aug. 2nd, Min. 3rd, Maj. 3rd, Perf. 4th, Aug. 4th — Unison

Dimin. 5th, Perf 5th, Aug. 5th, Min. 6th, Maj. 6th, Aug 6th, Min. 7th, Maj. 7th, Perf. Oct.

XV. CHORDS

A combination of three or more sounds heard at the same time is called a chord. The following single tones would sound as follows (play them on the piano and sing them with syllables):

When sounded simultaneously, they form a chord as follows:

Note: Divide the class into three sections and have them sing *do, mi, so.*

XVI. TRIADS

A triad is a chord made up of three tones. If the root (the fundamental tone) is on a line, the next two tones will be on the next two lines. Likewise, if the root is in a space, the next tones will be in the next two spaces. Examples:

 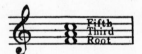

Triads get their names from the degree of the scale on which they are built. If they are built on the tonic, they are called the tonic triad, etc.

A. Triads in Major Keys

1. Major Triads

There are four types of triads. The major triad is formed when the distance between the root and third is a major third (two whole steps), and a minor third (one and a half steps) from the third to the fifth.   In the major scale there **are three** major triads, found on the tonic, subdominant, and dominant.

Note: Intervals of 1½ steps in a triad are often called a *small block,* indicated by (S). The interval of two whole steps is called a *large block,* indicated by *(L).*

Key of C

I	IV	V
TONIC	SUB-DOMINANT	DOMINANT

2. Minor Triads

The minor triad has a small block (S) between the root and the third, and a large block (L) between the third and the fifth of the triad.   There are three minor triads found in the major keys.

Examples:

Key of C

II	III	VI
SUPERTONIC	MEDIANT	SUBMEDIANT

3. Diminished Triads

There is only one diminished triad.   It is found on the leading tone and is made up of two small blocks.   A Roman numeral with an ° after it indicates a diminished triad.   Example:

Key of C

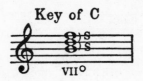

VII°

B. Triads in Minor Keys

1. Major Triads

The minor scale triads are written using the harmonic minor scale. The seventh tone of the scale, "so," is raised a half step to become "si." A major triad then is formed on the dominant. The two major triads found in minor keys are on the dominant and on the submediant. Examples:

Key of A Minor

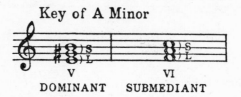

2. Minor Triads

Minor triads are found on the tonic and on the subdominant in minor keys. Examples:

Key of A Minor

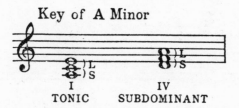

3. The Augmented Triad

One triad will have two large blocks. This triad is found on the mediant in minor scales and is called the augmented triad. It is marked by a large Roman numeral III+. Example:

Key of A Minor

4. The Diminished Triad

The diminished triad is found on two degrees of the minor scale: the supertonic and the leading tone. The diminished triad is marked with a small (^{0}) after the Roman numeral. Example:

Key of A Minor

II^0 VII^0
SUPERTONIC   LEADING TONE

C. Inversions of Triads

When the third of the chord is the lowest tone, the chord is in the first inversion and the second position. When the fifth of the chord is in the lowest tone, the chord is in the second inversion and the third position. Example:

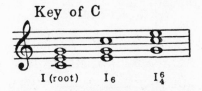

Key of C

I (root)   I$_6$ I$_4^6$

Note: The first inversion is marked with an arabic numeral 6 after the Roman numeral. If one counts from the bottom tone, the steps are 3 and 6. The common practice is to leave off the 3 indicating a triad of the first inversion.

Likewise, in the second inversion, the steps counted from the bottom tone are 4 and 6. These numbers, following the Roman numeral, always indicate the second inversion of the triad.

XVII. SEVENTH CHORDS

Seventh chords are formed by adding a third, major or minor depending upon the signature, to the triads.

A number 7 is added to the triad numeral to indicate a seventh chord. (Example 1.)

Note: It must be kept in mind that seventh chords, like triads, are written in the harmonic minor in minor keys.

The first inversion of the seventh chord has the third of the chord as the lowest tone. If the steps are counted from the lowest tone, they will be 3, 5, and 6. (Example 2.)

The second inversion of the seventh chord is written with the fifth as the lowest tone. The steps, counted from the lowest tone will be 3, 4, and 6. (Example 3.)

The third inversion of the seventh chord has the seventh as the lowest tone. The steps from the lowest tone are 2, 4, and 6. (Example 4.)

Tonic Seventh Chord, Key of C

Dominant Seventh Chord(V⁷) in key of C

(1)   (2)   (3)   (4)

BIBLIOGRAPHY

Jones, Archie N. and Barnard, Floyd P. *Introduction to Musical Knowledge.* Paul A. Schmitt Music Co., Minneapolis, 1935.

Rohner, Traugott, and Howerton, George. *Fundamentals of Music Theory.* Gamble Hinged Music Company, Chicago, 1943.

Smith, Ralph Fisher. *Elementary Music Theory.* Oliver Ditson Company, Philadelphia, 1930.

Swift, Frederick F. *Fundamentals of Music.* Belwin, Incorporated, New York, 1943.

Robinson, O. E. *Music Fundamentals.* Hall-McCreary Company, Chicago, 1936.

Smith, and Krone. *Fundamentals of Musicianship,* Volume I, Volume II. M. Witmark Company, New York, 1940.

Chapter II

ESSENTIAL MUSIC SKILLS

I. THE USE OF THE PITCH PIPE

There is often a lack of knowledge on the part of the elementary teacher in the use of the pitch pipe. Any teacher who knows thoroughly the materials set forth in the first chapter of this book can easily develop this skill. The following suggestions should prove helpful.

A. It is usually advisable for children to sing the song in the key in which it is published. If a song is written in the key of *D*, it should be sung in that key. The editors of our standard music text books are experienced music teachers and their judgment regarding voice range should be respected.

Note: Singing a song higher than pitched is less injurious to voices than singing a song lower. In fact, if there is a tendency toward sluggishness or poor intonation, pitching a song higher will improve the tone.

B. Whenever a teacher wishes to have the children sing a song, whether in a major or minor key, the pitch given should always be *do* for that song. If the song begins on *mi* or *so*, the teacher or the children should find the correct pitch for the note, either by going up the scale diatonically—*do, re, mi, fa, so,* or by means of the tonic triad skips—*do, mi, so.*

C. There are simple rules for finding *do.* If there are sharps in the signature, the last sharp to the right is *ti.* The next note above is *do.* Example:

Key of D

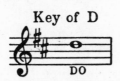

DO

D. If the song to be sung starts on a note of the triad below high *do,* a quick way to find low *do* is to count down lines or spaces on the syllables *ti, so, mi, do.*

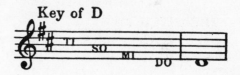

E. If the song to be sung has flats in the signature, the teacher may count down from the last flat to the right, *fa* to *do.* Example:

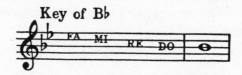

A quicker way would be to go from *fa* to *mi* and skip a line or space to *do.* Example:

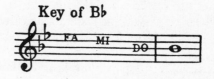

F. If the song to be sung has no sharps or flats in the signature, it is written in the key of C Major or a minor. In either case, the pitch should be either high or low *do,* depending upon where the first note of the song is found. Example:

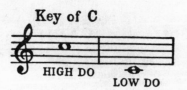

G. Recommendations for the Care and Use of the Pitch Pipe.

1. Keep the pitch pipe in a box or cloth sack.

2. Before putting the pitch pipe away, gently tap the moisture from it to prevent rusting.

3. A pitch pipe should be used by only one person.

4. Do not tap pitch pipe on desk.

5. Use a chromatic pitch pipe with which the tone is produced by blowing only.

Note: There are some pitch pipes where the tone comes from both blowing and drawing. The former are preferable.

6. Blow softly.

7. To secure absolute accuracy, the teacher, after blowing the pitch, should hum it. Next, have the class hum the same tone and then sing "*do.*"

8. The teacher must be able to find beginning tones quickly and accurately.

9. The pitch pipe must be blown frequently while the class is singing to insure accuracy.

Assignments

1. Beginning with the first song in any community song book, have each student successively take each succeeding song, naming the key-note or *do,* until each member has named several keys.

2. On the blackboard, each student is to write the clef and key signature as dictated by the teacher; then write the keynote or *do* on the proper line or space.

3. To become familiar with the pitch pipe, the instructor may give suggestions as follows:

    a. "Blow *do* for 2♯–3♭–5♭, etc.

    b. This is *mi;* it is g♯; blow *do.*"

4. Another way of becoming familiar with the pitch pipe is to learn to play *America* on it. Practice until the song may be played accurately and in correct tempo. The melody line is as follows:

F F G E F G A A B♭ A G F G F E F

C C C C B♭ A B♭ B♭ B♭ B♭ A G

A B♭ A G F A B♭ C D B♭ A G F

The same plan may be followed with "Twinkle, Twinkle Little Star"

F F C C D D C B♭ B♭ A A G G F
F F C C D D C B♭ B♭ A A G G F
C C B♭ B♭ A A G C C B♭ B♭ A A G
F F C C D D C B♭ B♭ A A G G F

II. THE ABILITY TO TRANSPOSE

It becomes necessary very often for a teacher of public school music to have music sung higher or lower as the need may be. Writing music higher or lower than it was originally written is called transposition. It must first be determined how much higher or lower the music is to be written, and then if the syllable names of the notes will be kept in mind the problem of transposition can be very easily mastered. If, for example, *America* is to be transposed one whole step higher, the procedure would be as follows (the melody is written in the key of F, the conventional key):

Procedure:

A. Make a staff of the same number of measures as the song to be transposed.

B. Write in the signature of the new key which is a whole tone higher; in this example, G.

C. Write the correct syllable names as in the original song. (See example above.)

D. Now write in the notes corresponding to the syllable names; observe note values.* Example:

America (Key of G)

do do re ti do re mi mi fa mi re do
1 1 2 7̄ 1 2 3 3 4 3 2 1

Assignment

1. Finish the transposition of *America*.

2. Transpose *America* into the keys of E, E♭, and A.

3. Select other melodies and transpose them higher and lower.

4. Transpose all four parts of a hymn or folk tune.

*See scales in Chapter I.

Note: For additional help, refer to p. 41 of *My Music Book, Volume II*, by Margueritte House, or *Transposing Tunes*, by Elmer Uggen. Both books are published by the Paul A. Schmitt Music Co.

III. THE ABILITY TO TAKE MELODIC DICTATION

In order to carry out a program of creative music in the classroom, the teacher must be able to notate unfamiliar melodies accurately. This skill can be acquired only through practice and the study of fundamentals. A way in which one can become more skillful in notating a melody is to use a familiar tune, such as *America*, and attempt to write it from memory. If the teacher is adept at writing syllables, the tune may first be written using the syllables, *do, re*, etc., and then later, the notes may be put into their proper places on the staff. When a number of songs can be written accurately following the above plan, the teacher is ready to notate songs created by the children.

Note: Consult sections on creative music from Chapters III through X.

Assignments

1. Play a record such as Brahms' *Lullaby* V 4435 and write down the melody. The entire record, or parts of it, can be played as many times as necessary to write the melody correctly.

2. Write down other melodies from records until skill in melodic dictation is acquired.

IV. THE ABILITY TO PLAY THE PIANO

Many feel that the requirement that every elementary teacher must learn to play the piano is an impossible demand. Is it? Modern educational philosophy demands that we must educate the *whole child.* We should not allow him to go through the elementary grades without experiencing the joy of singing beautiful songs with piano accompaniment. We should give him the satisfying experiences of responding with large, bodily movements to such rhythms as running, skipping, swaying, walking; also, of participating in dramatizations and mimetic play, to appropriate music played on the piano by the teacher. With the aid of the piano, part singing may be more easily introduced, and a sense of chords developed. Using the phonograph is a possibility of giving these experiences to the child, but it never can serve as adequately as the piano. It is well to train the child to sing with and without the piano. Each teacher, then, should make an earnest effort to acquire adequate skill in playing the piano. The teaching of class piano is now accepted as an essential part of the elementary music program, and the teacher should be able to demonstrate the materials used. The methods for teaching class piano to children are given in Chapter V of this book.

> Note: Many teacher training institutions that require the ability to play the piano as one of the requirements for graduation, find it possible to give this basic knowledge and skill through the class method of teaching. No more than eight students should be in a class, so each one may have an opportunity to perform during the lesson period. If possible, piano study should be without extra cost to the student.

Assignments

1. Observe successful piano classes on college level as well as those taught to elementary school children.

2. Demonstrate a class piano lesson with the college class participating. Use books and methods suggested in Chapter V.

V. THE ABILITY TO IMPROVISE

It is helpful in their teaching if both the urban and rural teachers have developed skills for improvising. This ability to "play by ear" is thought of by some as being an impossible skill to acquire; however, this is not true if the fundamentals of music (with special emphasis on chords) have been thoroughly studied.

Using *America* as an example again, it will be found, if analyzed, that the three chords used most frequently are the tonic, the dominant, and the sub-dominant.

To get the "feel" for chording, play these three chords in the Key of F on the piano many times in the positions found below:

Key of F **Key of F**

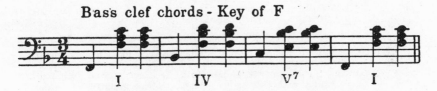

Bass clef chords - Key of F

I   IV   V⁷   I

Taking the Key of C as a starting point, *transpose* the chords into keys having more and more sharps and flats:

Keys Having Sharps								Keys Having Flats						
C♯	F♯	B	E	A	D	G	C	F	B♭	E♭	A♭	D♭	G♭	C♭
7	6	5	4	3	2	1		1	2	3	4	5	6	7

When this can be done with ease, play the melody of *America* with the right hand and *chord* with the left hand. Try to make it sound "right." If it does not, analyze the song to determine what chords to use. There may be other chords used occasionally—the mediant, sub-mediant, etc. Try to include those in their proper places.

Assignments

1a. After the key has been established by the teacher, have the class write the numbers of the chords as they are played on the piano.

1b. Write the notes of each chord as they are played by the teacher on the piano.

2. As the entire class sings "Twinkle, Twinkle," have one member of the class play the correct chords on the piano.

3. Analyze chords in songs selected by the teacher. Then sing them, indicating the numbers of the chords with the fingers.

Example—*Billy Boy*

Oh, where have you been Billy Boy, Billy Boy,
I   I   I   I

Oh, where have you been charming Billy?
I   I   V

I have been to seek a wife, She's the joy of my life,
V   V   I   I

She's a young thing and cannot leave her mother.
I   V   I

4. If an autoharp is available, have each student play the accompaniment for the same songs, sung by the class.

Note: The skill of chording may be applied directly to such instruments as the autoharp and the guitar. The use of these instruments serves a useful purpose in the music teaching program and their study and use should be encouraged. The popularity of ballad singers, (who invariably use guitar accompaniment) on the radio, attest to the popularity of this folk instrument.

VI. THE SKILL TO SING ARTISTICALLY

For the child, singing is a satisfying emotional experience. There is but one way for him to learn to sing, and that is by imitating others. Many children enter kindergarten and first grade without this ability. Many never hear singing in the home by either parent. There is only one means by which all children in a classroom can learn the necessary singing skill, and that is by imitating the teacher.

Teachers, therefore, must learn to sing artistically. Their voices must be clear, their diction good, their pitch accurate, and they must have a feeling for the proper phrasing. The study of great song literature under competent instructors should be a part of a program for self improvement of every teacher.

Note: The study of voice is required for graduation at most teacher training institutions. An economical and effective method of voice training is through the voice class. In addition to the techniques of tone production, articulation, breathing and phrasing, each teacher should learn a large repertoire of folk and art songs. An easy schedule would be to learn one folk and art song each week.

Assignments

1. Make one list of 50 folk songs and one of 50 art songs that should be memorized; check them off as they are learned.*

2. Measure the voice range of the good speakers that you hear on the radio or speaker's platform, and report to the class.

3. Learn to recognize 20 operatic arias (use radio, records and music) and list them as you learn them.

4. Read the stories of the operas of which they are a part, and be prepared to report in class.

*See the book: 55 *Art Songs,* by Spaeth, Sigmund and Thompson, Carl O., published by C. C. Birchard and Co., Boston.

VII. THE PRACTICAL KNOWLEDGE OF MELODY INSTRUMENTS

There are several inexpensive melody instruments on the market that are quite satisfactory for classroom use. It is advisable that every intermediate or rural school teacher learn to play at least one so that she can give to her students the experience of playing. Such instruments as tonettes, song flutes, flutophones, xylophones, recorders and harmonicas are very satisfactory for group instruction. Because each instrument has definite pitch and is capable of playing all the notes in the diatonic scale, hundreds of simple songs may be learned by the children. The main advantage of this type of instruction is, that if properly taught, the children learn to read music more accurately. Most public school instrumental teachers encourage the grade school teachers to develop melody bands in the intermediate grades, since this pre-band activity serves to lay an excellent foundation for note reading, to arouse interest in band and orchestra instruments, and to call attention to unusual musical talent.

Assignments

1. Learn to play ten songs on a wind melody instrument and ten songs on a xylophone.

2. Visit your local music store, or write for a list of books available for teaching tonettes and other melody instruments.

3. Observe a grade school class that is being taught a lesson on melody band instruments.

4. One member of the class should teach the others a beginning lesson on a melody band instrument.

VIII. THE ABILITY TO CONDUCT

One of the most useful skills any teacher can develop is the ability to conduct. The primary teacher may use it in connection with rhythm band work. In the intermediate grades, when part singing is begun, it is even more essential. In the upper grades, when boys' voices begin to change, the use of three and four part music for mixed voices makes it imperative that the teacher can conduct gracefully and effectively.

In the rural school and rural community, the teacher has many opportunities to use conducting skills. He or she not only has to be able to conduct the rhythm band and school singing, but the opportunity for community service is almost unlimited. Teachers will be the ones most likely to be called upon to lead community singing at all school and community functions. Every rural community looks to the teacher for leadership in the conducting of 4H club choruses and church choirs.

It is imperative to have a knowledge of music fundamentals before beginning work in conducting. The knowledge of music theory, outlined in the first chapter of this book, is definitely essential. One must know rhythmic patterns in 2/4, 3/4, 3/8, 4/8, 6/8, 12/8, 2/2, 3/2 and 4/2 meters. The teacher must also know intervals in order to be able to judge proper tone relationships in two, three and four part singing. It is necessary also to have a knowledge of the proper relationship of the tones in the various positions of the triads and seventh chords.

There are several ways of getting the necessary experierce in conducting. One method is to listen to phonograph records playing music of different meter signatures. Another method is to conduct the class, beginning first with simple unison songs, then gradually getting experience in conducting two, three and four part music. A third method is to have someone play music having different meter signatures until the class can conduct all the conducting beats gracefully. Lists of songs, records, and piano music are given for each of the meter signatures and conducting beats on the following pages. It is advisable for the students to practice in front of a large mirror before conducting the class. Try to develop graceful and flowing beats that are at all times very definite and easy to follow.

A. Baton Technique

One who is beginning the study of conducting should by all means use a baton. Each conducting beat should be practiced until the movement is entirely automatic. When each beat has been mastered, only practice in actual conducting will make for progress. One or more of the following plans may be used in developing baton technique.

1. The teacher, or one of the students, may play selections on the piano in the various tempi to be studied; the rest of the class should practice the proper conducting beat as suggested by the teacher.

Note: The book *Elementary Rules of Conducting*, by Bakaleinikoff (Boosey Hawkes Belwin, Inc.), has examples of all the conducting beats illustrated with music to be played on the piano.

2. The entire class, collectively and individually should practice conducting to phonograph records. (Recordings are listed below for this purpose.)

3. With the teacher or one student playing the accompaniment, one student may conduct familiar songs while the class sings.

4. Students should avail themselves of every opportunity to study baton t e c h n i q u e of experienced conductors in rehearsal and concert.

5. Much individual conducting before a large mirror will help the student develop poise in conducting.

6. Students should study the books listed in the *bibliography* at the end of this chapter for additional suggestions on conducting.

B. The Preparatory Beat

It is very important to give the singers in a chorus an opportunity to take a deep breath before starting the first tone. It is also important to give some indication of the tempo of the music to be sung. (This also holds true in conducting instrumental groups.) Conductors make this possible by what is known as the preparatory beat. This beat usually begins on the count preceding the one on which the singers and players are to begin. The principle holds true regardless of the time signature. In ¾ meter, if the performers are to begin on the first beat of the measure, the preparatory beat must begin on the third beat as in the following diagram:

Example 1

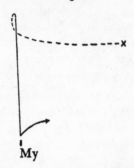

My

Note: Practice conducting the preparatory beat by singing the first word in the song *America*.

Whenever possible, the preparatory beat should be made larger than the ordinary beat to make it easier for the performers to follow.

Very often, songs begin on other beats of the measure rather than on *one*. The same principle holds true as in the above diagram—the preparatory beat is made larger than the usual conducting beat. The song *The Star Spangled Banner* is in ¾ meter and begins on the third beat of the measure. Students may practice, either as a class or individually, by conducting the first two words of the song.

Example 2

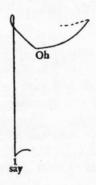

Oh

say

C. Attacks and Releases

Precision on the part of the conductor is essential for securing attacks and releases. Good attacks are secured by a definite preparatory beat and a definite beat on the count of the measure on which the song begins. (See previous example.) A good release is equally important. The nature of the composition will determine how vigorous the release should be. A gentle close to a composition will most likely call for a release near the body. A loud ending is effected by a vigorous movement of the hands and arms in a circular motion, either toward or away from the body. It is customary when ending a fermata within a composition, to end the beat with the hands away from the body. When indicating a release after a fermata at the end of a composition, the hands are usually brought towards the body. The following illustrations give two of the most common releases used by conductors.

Example 3   Example 4

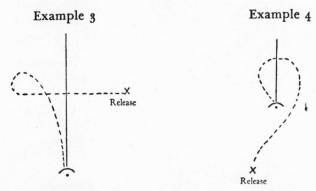

Example three shows the release away from the body with a quick motion of the wrists as the arms are extended.

Example four shows the movement of the arms toward the body. In either case, the movement must be rapid and decisive so that the performers will never be in doubt when the release is wanted.

When the conductor has acquired ease and facility in the use of the baton, he may, on occasion, abandon it and use only his hands. This is particularly true if the group is not too large. It is often easier to give certain dynamic effects if the hands are used in preference to the baton. Although conducting beats should be simple and direct, grace may be acquired by merely turning the palm of the hand in the direction of the beat. Always avoid ostentation.

D. Conducting Beats

1. The Two Beat Measure

The meter signatures 2/8, 2/4, 2/2, rapid 6/8 and ₵ (alla breve or cut time) are conducted with two beats per measure. All quickstep marches fall into this category. Here a definite *one* is important. The second count must also be definite, although somewhat lighter than the first. Two of the most common conducting beats for the two beat measure are illustrated below. Example 5 is often used for slow tempi; Example 6 for fast.

Example 5   Example 6

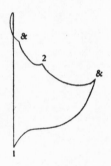

Illustrations

Songs (Found in nearly all community song books)

     Dixie Land (2/4)

     Marching Along Together (Rapid 6/8 time)

     Anchors Aweigh (Cut time—₵)

Records—Victor Album No. E-74 (Unbreakable records for elementary schools)

     March (from "Il Trovatore") Verdi.................No. 45-505

     Soldiers' Chorus (from "Faust") Gounod...........No. 45-505

     March (from "Aida") Verdi......................No. 45-505

Piano selections—from Rhythmic Games and Dances, by Hughes. Am.
Bk. Co., 1942)

Ballet Music (from *"Rosamunde"*) Schubert........... (p. 112)

Morris Dance by E. German........................ (p. 114)

Rustic Song by Schumann......................... (p. 138)

Note: Use metronome and follow markings carefully.

Assignments

1. Practice conducting the above selections individually and as a
   class. Playing a variety of selections having different tempos
   will help to prevent monotony.

2. Find other songs, records and piano pieces that can be conducted
   with two beats to the measure.

3. Study the conducting beats diagrammed in the books listed in
   the bibliography at the end of this chapter. How do they differ?
   Is there a different method for conducting a slow two beat
   measure?

2. The Three Beat Measure

The three beat measure is one of the most commonly used.
The meter signatures 3/8, 3/4, 3/2 and rapid 9/8 are all
conducted as follows:

Example 7

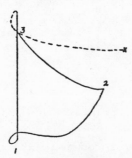

Illustrations

Songs from America Sings

America....................... (Begins on first beat) p. 104

Come Thou Almighty King........ (Begins on first beat) p. 112

The Star Spangled Banner........ (Begins on third beat) p. 102

Note: Recorded on Victor Album E-91.

Records—Victor Album E-74 (Unbreakable records for elementary schools).

The Skaters Waltz by Waldteufel..................V 45-5012

Minuet by Mozart...........................V 45-5012

Waltzes by Schubert ....V 45-5012

Piano selections from Rhythmic Games and Dances by Hughes.

German Dance by Beethoven.........................p. 108

Valse Sentimentale by Schubert.......................p. 120

Minuet by Mozart................................p. 157

Assignments

1. With the entire class and individually, practice conducting the three beat measure while singing, listening to the phonograph, or listening to music played on the piano.

2. Study the three beat measure as illustrated in the books at the close of this chapter.

3. Try to observe while an experienced conductor conducts a song having three beats to the measure. Notice how he increases the size of the beats as he conducts the louder passages.

   Note: Beginning conductors often slow down the beat of 3/2 meter and take the 3/8 meter faster. To avoid this mistake, follow metronome markings very carefully.

4. Practice conducting in front of a large mirror and try to improve poise and posture.

3. The Four Beat Measure

One of the most common and the most useful conducting beats is the four beat measure. The primary accent falls on *one,* as with the previous conducting beats outlined, but in addition there is a *secondary accent* on *three.* The sweep to the right makes it possible to emphasize this secondary accent. The conductor must be careful to make all four beats clear and definite, but with extra emphasis on its first **and third.**

The traditional four beat measure is conducted as follows:

Example 8

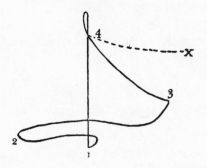

The following meter signatures are conducted with the four beat measure:

C   4/4   4/8   4/2 and rapid   12/8

Illustrations

Songs from America Sings.   Robbins Music Corp.

Old Folks at Home................. (Begins on first beat) p. 15

Auld Lang Syne.................. (Begins on fourth beat) p. 12

Londonderry Air......... (Begins on *and* after third beat) p. 65

Note: When a song begins on the and, or second half of the beat, it is
necessary to indicate the notes of the divided beat with the baton.
The following illustration may be of help: (*Would God I Were
a Tender Apple Blossom.*)

Example 9

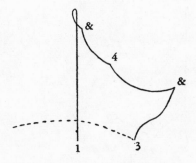

Records—Victor Album E-91 (Unbreakable records for elementary schools).

America the Beautiful...........................No. 45-5080
Battle Hymn of the Republic....................No. 45-5082
Battle Cry of Freedom..........................No. 45-5082

Piano Selections from Rhythmic Games and Dances, by Hughes. American Book Co.

Chorale by Chopin.....................................p. 123
Tarantara by Sullivan ....p. 137
Coronation March by Meyerbeer......................p. 144

Assignments

1. Use the metronome to find exact tempo composer intended whenever possible.
2. Practice conducting the four beat measure using the examples listed above.   This may be done individually or as a class activity.
3. Learn to conduct other songs that begin on counts other than one.
4. Study the conducting beat for the four beat measure as illustrated in the books listed in the bibliography.
5. Try to observe as experienced conductors conduct the four beat measure.

4. The Six Beat Measure

Some of our most graceful music is written in 6/8 and 6/4 time.   It is therefore necessary for the conductor to develop a graceful conducting beat for this meter. Here, also, the secondary beat is important and the sweep of the arm from three to four will bring out this accent. The two most common beats for these signatures are as follows:

Example 10a

Example 10b

Rapid 6/8 meter is conducted with the conducting beat used in the two beat measure as diagrammed in example ten b. Many marches are written in 6/8 meter and are always conducted with two beats per measure.

Illustrations

Songs from America Sings

Records

Piano selections from Rhythmic Games and Dances by Hughes

Assignments

1. Notice how naturally the 6/8 meter becomes two beats per measure when the tempo is increased. Start counting the six beats slowly; gradually increase tempo until the counts one, two seem natural. Now gradually slow down to six beats.

2. Look through many songs having 6/8 meter. It will be noticed that a great number have rapid metronome markings. These must be conducted with two beats per measure.

3. Practice conducting the above selections with both types of conducting beat.

5. The Nine Beat Measure

The nine beat measure is less commonly found. When the music flows along rather rapidly, 9/8 meter is conducted as three beats per measure.

Example 11

Example 12

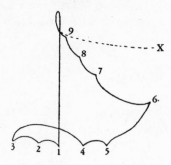

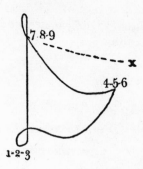

Illustrations

Songs

Beautiful Dreamer

Beautiful Isle of the Sea

Piano selections

from the book, Elementary Rules of Conducting

Example No. 11, p 50

from the book, Everybody's Favorite Piano Pieces, Amsco Music Sales Co., 1600 Broadway, N. Y.

Notturno, by Grieg.....................................p. 117

Assignments

1. The change from nine beats per measure to three can easily be felt if the count is gradually made more rapid. Practice until the change becomes automatic.

2. Practice conducting to the music listed above.

6. The Twelve Beat Measure

12/8 meter is sometimes encountered in music. In slow 12/8 time, the twelve beats per measure are definitely felt. However, when the tempo becomes more rapid, the feeling of four beats per measure predominates.

Example 13   Example 14
Slow 12/8   Rapid 12/8

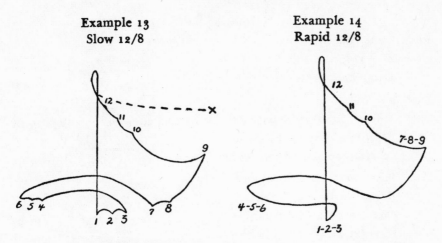

Note: For practice in conducting, have a member of the class play
      Example No. 12 from the book Elementary Rules of Conducting.
      Observe how the conducting beats become four instead of twelve
      if the tempo is increased.

7. The One Beat Measure

There is no meter signature in common use today that calls
for one beat per measure. Occasionally, however, music
written in 3/4 and 3/8 meter has to be taken so rapidly
that it is impossible to beat three counts per measure. It is
necessary then for the conductor to beat one count per
measure. Since it is always important to have a definite
down beat as the first beat of each measure, the one beat
measure will be conducted as follows:

Example 15

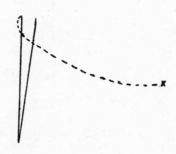

Illustrations

Songs from America Sings

Records

Piano selections from Rhythmic Games and Dances

Assignments

1. Practice conducting the one beat measure with the music listed above. Try to make the baton beat graceful; there should be a bounce to the baton after each beat so the beat will not become stilted.

2. Find other selections like the above that may be used for practicing the one beat measure.

8. The Eight Beat Measure

One of the less common beats is the eight beat measure. It follows the general outline of the four beat measure and is conducted as follows:

Example 16

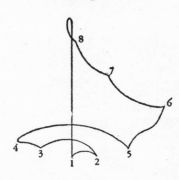

Illustrations

An example of the eight beat measure that may be used as an illustration for class conducting will be found on page forty-nine in the book *Elementary Rules of Conducting.*

Occasionally music written in 4/4 meter has to be conducted so slowly that a divided beat is necessary. *Behold the Lamb of God* and *Surely He Hath Borne Our Griefs* from The Messiah by Handel are well known examples.

9. The Five Beat Measure

Although the five beat measure is not as common, the conductor must be prepared to conduct it when the occasion arises. The secondary accent is very important as it determines the type of beat the conductor must use. Some music in 5/4 time has a secondary accent on three and some on four. The conductor must study the score to determine which secondary accent the music calls for. The conducting beat is merely a combination of the two and three beat measures. If the secondary accent falls on three, the music will be conducted with two beats plus three beats, as follows:

Example 17

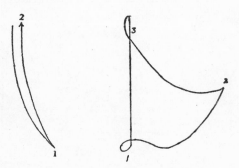

When the secondary accent falls on the *fourth* beat, **the five beat** measure will be conducted as follows:

Example 18

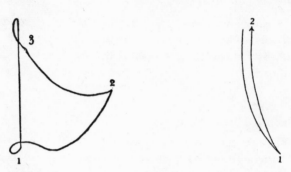

Assignment

In the book *Elementary Rules of Conducting* will be found examples of the five beat measure that can be played by a pianist while the class conducts. Page 43 illustrates music that is conducted with the two, three beat combination; page 44 illustrates the three, two. Practice these two selections until the beats become automatic.

10. The Seven Beat Measure

The seven beat measure is not very common, but since it will occasionally be encountered, it is well to be prepared to conduct it. 7/4 meter will have a secondary accent either on four or five. If it falls on four, the conducting beat will be a combination of three and four.

Example 19

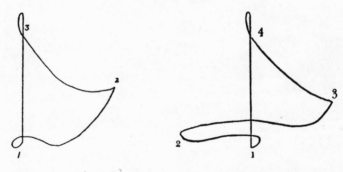

When the secondary accent falls on five, the conducting beat is a combination of four and three.

Example 20

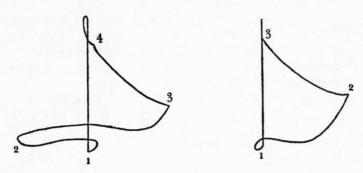

Assignments

For practice in conducting the seven beat measure, use music from *Elementary Rules of Conducting,* pp. 47 and 48.

E. The Movement of the Baton

A good conductor never lets the baton come to a complete stop at any one time as long as the music continues, unless he is striving for special effects. The baton "flows" with the music. To secure smoothness of the beat, he will secure a rebound with the baton after it has indicated the exact point where the beat occurs. The following diagram may help to clarify the point:

Example 21

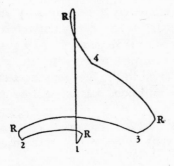

The baton does not stop at 1, but proceeds without a stop toward 2. Sometimes a quick movement of the wrist at the beat will give a more definite indication of the exact time of the beat.

F. Conducting the Fermata or Hold

It is important for the conductor to beat all the counts in the fermata, beating all the counts with one hand while indicating the hold with the other. He must judge the length of time he wishes to hold the note, and space the beats accordingly, giving each one approximately the same value.

Note: The fermata is often used in the climax of a composition; also, to indicate a pause or cessation of time while a soloist performs a cadenza.

Illustrations

Songs from America Sings

Taps ....p. 30

Sailing ....p. 35

Flow Gently, Sweet Afton...p. 49

Assignments

1. Practice conducting the songs listed above, and others, which have the fermata indicated. Notice its importance in giving expression to music.

G. Placing the Voices in the Proper Section

It is essential for the conductor to become well acquainted with the voice quality of each singer in his chorus. It is just as important to consider the quality of the voice as the range in deciding which part a person should sing. A female voice of heavy timber should never sing first soprano even though the singer has adequate range. Using a heavy voice on high notes gives the section too thick a quality and has a tendency to make the section sound flat. There is a tendency in amateur choruses to put all singers who can read on the inner parts and to have all the others sing the melody. If too many voices are placed in the first soprano section, that section will predominate and poor balance will be the result.

H. Placing the Sections Properly

There are many differences of opinion as to the best arrangement of the sections of a chorus. For good intonation, it is important for the singers carrying the melody and the sections furnishing the root of the chord structure to be placed where they can easily hear one another. With this idea in mind, the following section placements should provide for the best possible intonation:

1. Unchanged Voices

It will be noticed in the following diagrams that the first soprano section, which usually carries the melody, and the second alto section, which usually furnishes the root of the chord structure, are in the center of the chorus:

Two Part Choir

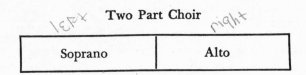

Soprano	Alto

Three Part Choir

Second soprano	First soprano	Alto

Four Part Choir

Second soprano	First soprano	Second alto	First alto

2. Mixed Voices

Mixed voice groups are those that have both masculine and feminine voices. Because men are usually taller, they are placed in the rear. The following diagrams will indicate the usual section placement:

Three Part Choir

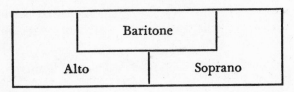

Four Part Choir

Bass	Tenor
Soprano	Alto

The Eight Part Choir

There will be an occasional demand for teachers to conduct choirs in larger churches and large 4H Club choruses. In this type of chorus, there will be opportunities to conduct eight part music. The following seating arrangement has been found very satisfactory:

First bass	Second bass	First tenor	Second tenor
Second soprano	First soprano	Second alto	First alto

There are several advantages to the above seating arrangement. Much of the music sung will be the ordinary four-part music. The choir is then seated in the four-part choir plan as illustrated above. Very often in eight-part singing the men have to sing alone. As the first tenors usually have the melody, the intonation will be better if they are next to the second bass section. In the above diagram, it will be noticed that this is possible. Occasionally, also, the women's voices sing alone. The same arrangement of the first soprano next to the second alto part is possible in this arrangement.

Composers frequently write for the "inner choir" of altos and tenors. It will be noticed that the above seating arrangement makes for good blending by this group of the choir.

I. Intonation

Good intonation in a choir doesn't just happen; it must be developed. Here are some suggestions for the beginning conductor to follow:

1. Whenever possible, select chorus personnel by giving aptitude tests and by testing voices.

2. Have the lighter voices sing the higher parts and the heavy voices sing the lower parts, regardless of the ability of the singers to sing other parts.

3. Select voices for each section that have similar voice quality or tone color.

4. Work for good tone quality. No group sings with good intonation if the quality is bad.

5. To develop good breath control, singers may practice some of the following exercises:

    a. Have the singers try to feel the expansion of the lower ribs as they inhale. Placing their hands to their sides may be of help.

    b. Have the group sing a unison tone with the common vowels a, e, ah, oh, oo. Now sing the opposite. Lengthen the tones as the group improves.

    c. Have them sing scales and tonic triad skips on each of the vowels listed above.

6. Try to get the group to think the intervals correctly. Almost invariably, when a group flats, the singers think the steps in the ascending scale too small and in the descending scale, too large. They should be especially careful to sing the seventh tone (ti) high.

7. Try to get the group to listen to other members within the choir to make their voices blend. Uniform vowel color within a section tends to make the voices blend.

8. Use music of high quality so a background of, and taste for good literature will be established. Listen to good choirs and collect programs of successful ones.

J. Diction

Good diction in a choir depends upon two factors: good tone quality and clear articulation of the consonants. The conductor must remind the singers that the consonants, as well as the vowel sounds, must carry to every part of the auditorium.

K. Rehearsals

Listed below are a few suggestions for the beginning conductor. Whether or not he can hold the respect of the group depends upon his ability to develop good rehearsal technique.

1. Start on time and end on time.

2. Be cheerful and pleasant at all times.

3. Sing music that is not too difficult, yet music that will challenge the group.

4. Do not speed tempi. Try to correct the tendency of most choirs to sing at a fast tempo when the music is loud, and likewise, the common error of slowing down when the music is soft.

5. Sing only music of good quality: our heritage of classics by great composers; good arrangements of folk songs of all nations; and the best of present day compositions.

6. Always provide an incentive by arranging programs and concerts well in advance.

7. Try to secure good balance between parts. It is better to have a smaller, well-balanced group than one that is large but poorly balanced.

8. Teach new music by the whole method as much as possible. Singers learn to read by reading much new music. Unless the music is very difficult, have them read through the entire composition before too much attention is paid to details.

9. The conductor should memorize the music before the rehearsal. He should mark out phrases, entrances, and dynamics, with red pencil while studying the score. Practice in conducting the number while singing the entrances will help in memorizing. Conducting before a large mirror will help the conductor to evaluate his conducting.

10. Be sure to cue in the sections that have individual melodic lines. It will give them confidence.

11. Avoid tapping the foot and using awkward motions when conducting. The feet should not be too far apart.

12. Use the left hand only to help in securing the desired* dynamics, moods, entrances, fermatas, attacks, and releases.

13. Be very considerate of the accompanist. He is usually the best musician in the community.

14. Have the group elect officers to run the business of the organization.

15. Social gatherings after the rehearsal in a community chorus will help to stimulate interest.

16. Good discipline is absolutely essential. This is secured by

keeping the group very busy at the enjoyable task of learning an abundance of good music, and by expecting from them at all times, their maximum in cooperation and attention.

L. How to Secure Music of Good Quality

Much of the music on the market is not great music. The competent director spends much time looking for good music that is proper for his organization. As most chorus budgets are very small, the conductor must use the utmost care in selecting his music. He can usually get most for his money by buying music in choral collections compiled by outstanding choral conductors. He should attend choral schools, clinics, summer sessions, professional meetings, etc., whenever possible.

M. The Use of the Metronome

It is extremely important for the beginning conductor to use the metronome while learning how to conduct. In order to have a starting point from which to judge tempi, he should practice marching to the metronome marking 128, the standard marching tempo for the U. S. army. If he knows from marching experience what m.m. 128 is, he can easily judge m.m. 64, etc. Changing tempi of compositions sometimes completely change the mood. Beginning conductors should be very careful, therefore, to follow the metronome markings accurately. Metronomes that are electrically operated are the most satisfactory.

Assignments

1. Study the conducting beats in the books listed in the bibliography at the end of the chapter. Practice drawing them, then select the ones most natural for the permanent conducting beat if the ones diagrammed in this chapter do not seem natural.

2. As a review in developing conducting technique, start with the one beat measure and conduct each one up to twelve as outlined in the chapter. Now start with the twelve beat measure and conduct each one back to the one beat measure.

3. Each member of the class should have practice in conducting the fermata where one voice is held while the other voices move. (For method see p. 44.) An example of this may be found in

the last measure of the song, *Up the Mountain,* p. 206 in Sing Out, (C. C. Birchard & Co.).

4. Each member of the class should make a list of six compositions of good quality for each of the following types of choruses; SA, SSA, SAB, SATB.

BIBLIOGRAPHY

Bakaleinikoff, Vladimir, *Elementary Rules of Conducting.* Boosey-Hawks, Incorporated, New York, 1938.

Bodegraven, Paul Van, and Wilson, Harry Robert, *School Music Conductor.* Hall-McCreary Company, Chicago, 1942.

Cain, Noble, *Choral Music and Its Practice.* M. Witmark and Sons, New York, 1942.

Finn, William Joseph, *The Conductor Raises His Baton.* Harper and Brothers, New York, 1944.

Waters, Fred E., *Practical Baton Technique.* Gamble Hinged Music Company, 1948. M.P.H.

Tkach, Peter, *Vocal Technique.* Neil A. Kjos Company, Chicago, 1947.

Moore, Gerald, *The Unashamed Accompanist.* MacMillan Company, New York.

CHAPTER III

MUSIC IN THE KINDERGARTEN AND FIRST GRADE

The appreciation of music as well as the performance of it, is the goal of music education. It is, therefore, necessary and natural that the foundation of the child's musical education be laid in the kindergarten and first grade. The many phases of music which play a vital part in kindergarten activity, such as rhythm band, creative music, singing, music dramatization, and listening, should give the child a happy, interesting, and satisfying experience, as well as an educational adventure.

After completing the first grade, a child should have improved in intonation, in rhythmic sense, in creative expression, and should show even greater pleasure in music.

Although singing, tone drills, rhythms, creativity, and listening, go hand in hand, the far-sighted teacher will plan her lessons so that the group is exposed to as many phases of subject matter as possible with a well-organized lesson still maintained. The changes in arrangement will vary with moods and needs of the children and the subjects that are to be considered, both in music and in other classes. In an integrated program, the teacher will find that planning her music is an easy and natural thing.

The importance of pupil planning (with the help of the teacher) needs careful consideration. The teacher might plan certain procedures for each day, but her plans should be flexible enough to allow pupil planning.

Reading a story or poem about fairies in reading class might lead to drawing imaginative fairies in art class; to learning a group of fairy songs in singing class; to using fairy echo calls for tone drill work with the out-of-tune singers, and to creative rhythmic response to accompanying fairy music. One first grade girl who had taken part in such a fairy unit created a dance to fairy music. When asked just what she had been doing, she replied, "I flew home to sleep in my bright buttercup." She had used a line from the song, "The Fairy" (Listen and Sing), learned in singing class, to interpret an illustrative dance in a rhythms class.

The program, with emphasis on the fun and beauty of music, should include:

53

A. Listening: (This may be done during rest periods, at specified times, or at any time when an activity or mood suggests it.)
1. To singing
2. To the piano
3. To the phonograph

B. Performing
1. By singing, alone or in the group (at least twenty-five minutes each day)
2. Through rhythmic interpretations, dramatizations, mimetic play
3. By playing rhythmic games
4. By playing rhythm instruments

C. Creating
1. Through songs
2. Through rhythms
3. Through the making of instruments
4. Through drawing pictures

I. GENERAL METHODS FOR TEACHING SINGING

A. The Rote Song

1. **The Importance Of Rote Singing**
Rote singing is singing by imitation.
It should be the general objective of the kindergarten and first grade teacher to teach many fine rote songs. These should be reviewed until the children have a large repertoire of well chosen beautiful songs.

Note: The number of songs learned each week depends entirely upon the group. An occasional kindergarten or first grade may be found which can master a new song each day. If a song is well learned it often requires more than one day's singing lesson.

2. **Objectives Of Rote Song Singing**
   a. To foster the love of beautiful songs.
   b. To develop self expression through singing.
   c. To develop the ability to respond to rhythms and moods.
   d. To provide happy group activity.

3. **How To Select The Rote Songs**
   a. The songs should be short.

Rhythm Band
Minneapolis Public Schools

[handwritten margin notes: kindergarten almost always phrase method; start whole song 1st gr; if not too long; no note reading starts end of 2nd yr.]

b. They should have skips based on the tonic triad, simple diatonic progressions, or repeated tones.

c. The range should be limited within the treble staff.

d, They should be melodically beautiful, and should include some folk songs.

e. The subjects should be within the interest of the child and should possess appropriate vocabularies.

4. How To Teach The Rote Song

There are two methods of teaching the rote song:

The Whole Song Method

The Phrase Method

The whole song method is considered the better for simple songs, the phrase method for the longer, more difficult ones. However, in modern schools of thought regarding learning procedures in general, the method of learning as a complete unit, or as a whole, is becoming more widely used. Also in music, many teachers are using the whole song method for their rote work.

The phrase method is learning the song by phrases, and in the case of more difficult songs, groups of phrases. Because the phrase method has to be used for some of the more difficult songs, it can readily be seen that both the phrase and the whole song methods have their place in rote teaching procedure. Some songs lend themselves well to the phrase method, and other songs to the whole song method. The following outlines should clarify the teaching procedures.

a. Whole song method

(1) Motivate the song through use of pictures, stories, or questions which will arouse the child's interest.

(2) Sing the song artistically to the group, using beautiful tone, careful diction, logical phrasing, and good interpretation.

(3) Ask questions of the children regarding their understanding and enjoyment of the song.

(4) Sing the song again. As imitation is the essential feature of rote singing, be careful to sing the song each time the same way and with good interpretation.

(5) Gradually and naturally lead the children to join in the singing. Little by little, withdraw until the children can sing the song independently.

(6) Have the children sing the whole song, giving them help only on the more difficult portions of the song.

(7) Let them try to sing the whole song alone.

b. The phrase method

(1) Memorize the song so as to be able to teach it without a book.

(2) Motivate the song through pictures and stories related to the subject matter of the song.

(3) Sing the entire song as a work of art, with good tone, phrasing, diction, and interpretation.

(4) Let the pupils discuss the text and ask questions about the song.

(5) Sing the entire song again.

(6) Sing one phrase at a time, and have the children repeat each phrase.

(7) Sing the entire song through in the same manner as the first presentation, but have the class sing this time.

(8) Let the class sing the entire song alone; give help only when necessary.

c. Additional suggestions on teaching the rote song

(1) Always pitch the song in the original key.

(2) Children will never learn to sing high unless they use light, clear tones.

(3) Because of a very limited attention span, the children should have frequent short participation periods, both individually and as a group.

(4) Do much individual work to improve out-of-tune singers.

Note: Individual singing should be done with the in-tune singers as well, to help develop special abilities.

(5) Poor response on the part of the pupils may be due to indistinct singing on the part of the teacher, poor choice of songs, or outside distractions.

(6) Kindergarten children will not be expected to master a song in one lesson.

(7) In order to create more interest in the lesson, the children should suggest ways of acting the song whenever it suggests dramatic possibilities. This should not be attempted until the song has been well learned.

(8) To encourage singing at home, let the children teach songs in class which they have learned at home.

(9) For a second day's work on the same song, or as an additional step in teaching the song, have individual children sing solos on some of the easier phrases.

(10) Sometimes interest in a song can be stimulated by singing it to the class the day before it is to be learned.

5. How To Phrase A Rote Song

Since children of kindergarten age are too young to begin phrasing, this activity should begin in the first grade. It should be conducted only occasionally, since not all songs lend themselves to phrasing, and the teacher needs only to phrase songs often enough to develop the habit of thinking in terms of phrases.

a. The children may sit or stand erectly and phrase several familiar nursery rhymes. This arm phrasing can be best explained to the children by making them think in terms of phrases as circles. The hands should be placed at the hips before the phrasing begins. When they begin speaking the words or singing, they should think of the first phrase as a complete circle, which they will make by raising their arms up above their heads and coming back to the waist again at the end of the phrase. The other phrases of the song are done in the same way. Sometimes the children may get a clearer picture of phrasing, if they are told that their arms, as they move them from the hips over their heads, and back again to their hips, will be in the shape of an apple.

Twinkle	twinkle	little	star
How I	wonder	what you	are
Up	above the	world so	high
Like a	diamond	in the	sky

b. Sing several familiar songs while the children try to phrase them. One child who does it correctly should be chosen to demonstrate for the group.

c. The children may have other ideas for phrasing, such as:
   1. Raise right arm above the head to make a half circle and then back again to the waist. Left arm may do the same.

   2. Or, one arm at a time may be extended from the waist to the front and back again; then do the same with the other arm.

   3. Use both arms together for the two above motions.
Note: Allow the children to make up their own phrase actions.

d. As the group sings the song *Ducks,* which they have previously learned as a rote song, draw curved lines on the board to represent the phrases of the song.*

Ducks

German Folk Song

*Beattie, J. W., et al., *American Singer, Book I.* American Book Company, Chicago, 1946.

When the entire song is sung and phrased the figure will look as follows:

See the lit-tle duck-lings

Swim-ming here and there,

Heads are in the wa-ter,

Tails are in the air.

    e. When other songs are sung and phrased, let the children have frequent participation in drawing the phrases on the blackboard.

   6. A Typical Lesson Plan For Teaching The Rote Song

Pretending

I wish I were a fair - y
I wish I were a po - ny

trip - ping and skip - ping,
run - ning and trot - ting,

A daint - y lit - tle fair - y
A black and shin - y po - ny,

danc - ing here and there.___
trot - ting here and there.___

a. General aims
  1. To create a desire to sing.
  2. To provide an opportunity for individual self-expression through singing and through bodily motion.
  3. To develop a phrase sense.
  4. To develop the ability to sing well.

b. Child's aims
  1. To hear a new song.
  2. To learn a new song.
  3. To play fairies.

c. Motivation
  1. Yesterday Jerry told us that flying a kite is the thing that he likes best to do. I think that almost everyone has something he likes to do better than anything else. I know a song that tells what a certain little girl and little boy like to do best of all. Before I sing the song for you, would each of you like to close your eyes and think of the thing you like to do? Then we will see if any of you like the same things that the children in the song like. . . . Now listen to the song.
  2. Were you surprised to discover what the children in the song like? Do you like the same things they do?

d. Procedure
  1. Sing the song again for the children.
  2. Allow discussion of the text of the song.
  3. Sing the song once more, with the children phrasing it as you sing. Teacher draws picture of phrases on the board.
  4. Sing one phrase of the song. Have the children sing it. Repeat with each phrase until the entire song has been sung.
  5. Sing the entire song again with the children.
  6. Have the children sing the song alone. Help them only when necessary.
  7. Suggest that the children might like to pretend that they are really playing fairies. Give them an opportunity to sing and dramatize the song. Let the boys pretend that they are riding ponies.

e. Expected outcomes

1. A keener appreciation of the dramatic possibilities in a song.
2. A better sense of phrasing.
3. A feeling of pleasure through accomplishment.
4. An increased ability to sing simple songs correctly and artistically.

7. Reading References

Annet, Thomas. *Teaching Music in the Rural School.* Boston Music Company, Boston, 1939. pp. 17-19.

Beattie, J. W., et al. *American Singer, Book I.* American Book Company, Chicago, 1946. pp. 1-2.

Cundiff, Hannah M., and Dykema, Peter. *School Music Handbook.* C. C. Birchard Company, Boston, 1936. pp. 72-80.

Gehrkins, Karl. *School Music Teaching.* C. C. Birchard Company, Boston, 1938. p. 21.

Nohavec, Hazel. *Normal Music Methods.* University Publishing Company, Lincoln, Nebraska, 1926. pp. 15-19.

Wright, Frances, *Elementary Music Education.* Carl Fischer, Inc., New York, 1941. pp. 118-133.

B. THE CHILD VOICE

The music education of every child should begin with singing. It is the natural medium for self-expression. Therefore, music educators should be concerned first with the voice—the instrument of song.

1. Tone Quality

The first thing to be considered in studying the child voice is tone quality, although the child himself should not be conscious of it. If the desire to express the beauty of music is awakened in children, if they are reminded of the thought in each song, and if they are aware of the importance of interpreting that thought, the light, high quality will come naturally. Most children, if sitting "tall" or standing erect, will breathe correctly, thereby using the right kind of tone. Indeed, good posture, whether sitting or standing cannot be overemphasized. The children need to be reminded often to sit erect, with their feet flat on the floor, their backs away from the chair, and their chests high. If the chest is sunken, the shoulders forward, and the waist bent, a heavy tone is produced. A positive reminder, telling them how much better they sound when sitting tall, is very effective encouragement.

The teacher must do much individual work with each child to be able to single out and diagnose bad quality. If she does find harsh or strident tone, it is her duty to do everything in her power to correct it. A child might have bad tone because:

a. He is using his heavy, playground voice to sing.
b. His singing is loud, causing him to strain his voice.
c. His posture habits are poor, his jaw tight or he possesses physical defects (nasal).

The last of these we have discussed. For the first we can only stress the importance of singing with a light, beautiful tone.

The second is not rare. Most children like to sing loudly. Childish enthusiasm is likely to carry over into loud singing. The teacher need only remind the group that sweet voices, not loud voices, are desirable. The class (not any particular individual) should be impressed with the importance of opening the mouth wide in singing. Tight lips, a tight throat, or a stiff jaw prevent free movements of the tongue and result in much strain on the voice, although these facts need not be told to the children. Some helps for such a problem are:

a. Open mouths wide . . . let the mouth fall open, especially on high tones.
b. A smiling face makes for sweet, "joyous" tones.
c. Make sure that the songs are not pitched too high or too low. The range for small children is from first line "E" to fifth line "F." Most songs in the singing books are pitched correctly. (See list.)

2. Seating Plans

Rather than seating the children according to their abilities, most music educators agree that it is more pedagogically sound to follow a more informal plan, having the children seated on chairs or on the floor around the piano. This heterogeneous plan eliminates any feeling of ability consciousness.

3. Improving the "Out-of-tune" Singers

One of the first and most serious problems confronting the teacher is the training of the out-of-tuners. There are few real monotones. The word really should be applied only to children who can sing *but one tone*. A poor sense of pitch is rare, and very few children, if guided correctly by the teacher, ever get beyond the second or third grade without being able to carry a tune. Such training for the defective singers should begin immediately in the kindergarten or first grade.

4. Why Many Children Cannot Sing

Know

It is not only important for the teacher to ascertain which children are non-singers, she must also sense *why* they cannot sing in tune. There are many causes and most of them are only temporary. A child may be out of tune for any of the following reasons:

a. He is shy, perhaps too frightened to sing.

b. He has difficulty in speaking clearly, and therefore cannot sing well. *(Baby talk)*

c. He lacks family cooperation.

d. He has not yet found his singing voice. *Important*

e. He is inattentive to pitch; he does not yet recognize pitch.

f. He lacks coordination of the vocal muscles.

g. He has never had any musical experience and therefore lacks understanding.

h. He has some physical defect.

The first seven of the above reasons can be helped early in the kindergarten years, but the eighth, needs to be referred to a physician. It is natural for children and people to be able to sing, and it is a safe statement to say that almost everybody can learn to sing.

One of the first things the teacher must do is give each child, singer or out-of-tuner, many opportunities to sing alone. She must not slight the less musical ones, neither must she allow any child to ridicule these children. She must listen carefully and diagnose each case. Thus, also, does each child build up more self-confidence. He should be given constant encouragement and praise for his efforts.

Of the eight listed, the first that should concern the teacher is number four. The importance of the child's singing voice has already been discussed. The teacher will find that most of her out-of-tune singers can develop beautiful, clear, true voices under careful guidance.

By starting to sing on a high pitch and bringing the voice down most children will avoid throaty tones and they will maintain a high voice quality.

5. Suggestions for the Out-of-tune Singer

When the following devices are used, the tone matching should be done by octave or tonic triad skips.

a. Imitating a train whistle—"too-too."
b. Imitating the wind—"oo."
c. Squeaking like a mouse—"whee."
d. Calling "yoo-hoo."
e. Singing like a bird—"tweet-tweet."
f. Imitating a fire siren—"oo."
g. Meowing like a cat—"meow."
h. Barking like a dog—"bow-wow."
i. Imitating a sheep—"baa."
j. Using short motives or phrases of a song.
k. Beginning with the pitch the child gives and extending the range higher or lower as the individual case requires.
l. Singing "hello."
m. Singing "goodbye."
n. Calling names of playmates in octaves—"Joan."
o. Imitating large and small clocks—"tick-tock."
p. Imitating bells—"ding, dong."
q. Standing on tiptoes, reaching up, singing high.
r. Playing informal games, as singing conversation over play telephones.
s. As his hands make the motion of going upstairs, the child sings "up we go."
t. The teacher may use her own ingenuity in devising tone drills from familiar songs learned by the group.

u. The following selections from *The American Singer,*
Book I, American Book Company, are good for the use
of "out-of-tuners":

Cows and Sheep	p. 75	(moo and baa)
Little Boy Blue	p. 166	(toot-toot)
Transportation	p. 27	(choo-choo)
		(too-too)
		(whoo-whoo)
		(zoom-zoom)
The Cuckoo Clock	p. 164	(cuck-OO)

The selection below, from *New Music Horizons*, Books I
and II, Silver Burdett Company, are also good:

My Little Pony	p. 26	(hop-hey) Book I
Birthday Song	p. 24	(scale-wise progressions)
Witches Are Calling	p. 18	(yoo-hoo) Book II
The Echo	p. 22	(hello)

The selections following from *Our Songs*, C. C. Birchard
Company, are good for this work:

Little Bunny Hops	p. 31	(nibbling)
Hello	p. 35	(hello)
Down and Back	p. 91	(Tommy)
March Wind	p. 97	(oo)

6. Song Materials

The following basic and supplementary texts have been
found to be particularly adapted for class use:

a. Basic texts

Armitage, M. T. and others. *Our First Music.* Singing
School Series. Birchard, 1941.

Beattie, J. W. and others. *American Singer*, Book I.
American Singer Series. American Book, 1944.

Glenn, Mabelle and others. *Listen and Sing.* World of
Music Series. Ginn, 1943.
Sing a Song. World of Music Series, Ginn, 1936.

McConathy, Osbourne and others. *New Music Horizons*,
Book K. New Music Horizons Series. Silver, 1944.

b. Supplementary texts

Armitage, M. T., and others. *Our Songs.* Singing
School Series. Birchard, 1939.

Boesel, A. S. *Sing and Sing Again*. Oxford Univ., 1938.

Bryant, Laura. *More Sentence Songs for Little Singers*. Willis Music Co., 1939.
Especially fine for out-of-tune singers.

Carter, Laura. *Twenty Little Songs*. Ginn, 1936.
Especially fine for out-of-tune singers.

Coit, L. E. and Bampton, Ruth. *Tone Matching Tunes for Singing and Playing*. Flammer, 1940.

Coleman, S. N., and Thorn, A. G. *Singing Time*. Day, 1938.

. . . .*Another Singing Time*. Day, 1939.

Cumpson, Helen. *Step a Song*. Simcoe Pub., 1930.
Especially fine for out-of-tune singers.

Dalton, Alene. *My Picture Book of Songs*. Donohue, 1947.

Davis, K. K. *Cradle Songs of Many Lands*. Summy, 1936.

Elkan, Belle. *Songs for Today's Children*. Summy, 1941.

Norton, June. *Sing-It-Again Book for Small Children*. Snellgrove pub., 1935.

Renstrom, Moiselle. *Rhythm Fun for Little Folks*. Pioneer Music Press, 1938.

Siebold, Meta. *Happy Songs for Happy Children*. Schirmer, 1936.

. . . .*More Happy Songs for Happy Children*. Schirmer, 1938.

Wiechard, A. C. *Today's Tunes for Children*. Paul A. Schmitt Music Co., 1941.

Wiechard, A. C. *Little Singers Song Book*. Birchard, 1931.

Wright, Agnes. *Singing Round the Year*. Barnes, 1940.

Assignments

1. Have several students teach a rote song to the class using:
(a) the whole song, (b) the phrase plan.

2. Do the exercises for out-of-tune singers with all members of the class as well as the individuals, to help the out-of-tune singers.

3. Find songs on the kindergarten and grade I level that have possibilities for doing remedial work. List the song, page, and book.

4. Make a collection of pictures of all things that would be of interest to kindergarten and first grade children. This might in-

clude animals, birds, toys, circus activities, etc. Paste the pictures on card board.

5. Visit a kindergarten or first grade singing class, to observe the activities.

6. Examine and evaluate many song books, keeping in mind such things as:

    a. Are the songs suitable?

    b. Are the illustrations good?

    c. Are the books well-bound?

C. Rhythm Band or Toy Orchestra.

1. Meaning

    a. Rhythm band work is working with simple percussion instruments, such as drums, rhythm sticks, sand blocks, tambourines, jingle sticks, cymbals, bells, triangles, castanets, and wood blocks.

2. Values of Rhythm Band Work in kindergarten and first grade may be summed up as follows:

    a. It is a delightful approach to music appreciation.

    b. It stimulates an interest in instrumental music.

    c. It becomes a medium for rhythmic response and develops rhythmic skills for future study.

    d. It provides an additional and interesting avenue of self-expression and creative work.

    e. It teaches the necessity and value of cooperation, teamwork, independence, leadership, and general competence.

    f. It is desirable for the less musical children.

    g. It results in a greater enjoyment of music.

3. Instruments Used in Rhythm Band —description and how to play them.

    a. Rhythm sticks. These are about one foot long; they are round and resemble a long, unsharpened pencil. They should be held firmly, but with the arms relaxed. The sticks should be struck near the ends, right over left, then left over right. Little more than a quick wrist movement is necessary.

b. Sleigh Bells. These usually have a strap, but it is best not to fasten them around the wrist. Play with a quick downstroke.

c. Tambourines.   These can be played with tap and a shake movement.   The tap is executed by holding the instrument in the right hand and striking it sharply against the closed left fist.   The shake is done by bringing it back with a swing and a short snap.

d. Jingle stick.   These are sticks shaped like a spatula with bells or pieces of metal, which will rattle, fastened to them.   The back of the stick is rapped against the palm of the left hand.

e. Triangle.   The triangle is suspended by string and played, preferably with a wooden stick for a soft tone.

f. Wood block. A block of wood which has been hollowed out in the center to produce a resonant sound.   Through a hole drilled in one end, the block is suspended with a string and played with a drumstick.

g. Drum.   The drum is played with alternating taps.   It is played best if the left stick is held palm up, the right, palm down.   (See drum method for proper position.) The drum should never be played louder than the other instruments.

h. Cymbals.   These are correctly struck by bringing the right hand down, the left hand up, just a little off center. They should never be brought directly together as in clapping the hands.

4. **Things to Remember When Purchasing Instruments:**

a. They should be easy to manipulate.   Rhythm band instruments for the kindergarten and first grade should be strictly percussion, that is, the teacher should not attempt to have her primary group work with instruments which have different tones, or can produce a melody.   A possible exception to this might be the xylophone.

b. Instruments should be of good quality and in perfect playing condition.   They should be durable and have good tone quality.

5. Suggestions for Making Rhythm Band Instruments

a. Drums made from hatboxes or tin cans with shellacked cloth, inner tubes, cheese-cloth, or drumheads stretched over the top.

b. Drums made from chopping bowls with either cloth or rubber inner-tube for heads.

c. Indian rattles. Boxes made of paper or wood, filled with tiny balls or pebbles. These can be painted bright colors.

d. Sand blocks—wooden blocks about four inches square and one inch deep covered with sandpaper, which may be attached with thumb tacks. They are played with an up and down stroke in the same manner as the cymbals so that they will make a soft "swishing sound."

e. Jingle sticks can be made by attaching ordinary bottle caps near the end of a wooden stick 5 inches long, 1 inch wide, 1/3 inch thick. These require at least two caps which will rattle against each other.

f. Horseshoes or large nails may be used for triangles.

g. Round chair-spindles or broom handles can be painted bright colors and used for rhythm sticks.

h. Tin pan covers can be substituted for cymbals.

i. Rattles can be made by piercing a hole in the bottom of a gourd, putting in a few seeds or pebbles, and then sealing up the hole. These can also be painted bright colors.

j. Clam or oyster shells can be filled with shot and sealed with adhesive tape.

k. Tambourines can be made from paper plates and bottle caps.

6. Balance of Instruments

a. Comparative numbers of each instrument—in band of thirty players:

   1 drum

   2 tambourines

   4 jingle sticks

   6 bells

   2 pair cymbals

   2 wood blocks

    10 pair rhythm sticks, or six pair of rhythm sticks and four pair of sand blocks

    3 triangles

b. Seating arrangements
Tambourines, Castanets, Drum, Cymbals,
Bells, Wood blocks, Jingle sticks,
Triangle, Sand blocks, Rhythm sticks.

7. Method of Introducing the Rhythm Band

a. Preparatory work

1. Show all instruments, giving their names and how they are held to be played. The similarity between the rhythm band instruments and the instruments in a real band might be discussed if the children have had an opportunity to hear an adult or school band.

2. Distribute instruments among the children. Explain that each child will have a chance to play every instrument later, so there need be no particular choices for certain instruments now.

3. Ask the children to refrain from playing their instruments until told to do so.

4. Have the children listen to the selection played on the piano or phonograph.

5. As the selection is repeated, have the children play whenever they wish. Gradually they will play on the accented beats.

b. Development

1. Clapping even beats to a familiar rote song.

2. Arm phrasing with familiar songs (see unit on phrasing the rote song).

3. Introduction of the rhythm sticks

    a. Play every beat 4/4.

    b. Play every other beat.

    c. Play only the first strong beat in each measure.

4. Introduction of other instruments

    a. Drum takes strong beat while rhythm sticks take weak beats:

        2/4   ONE, two; ONE, two.

        4/4   ONE, two, three, four; ONE, two, three, four.

        3/4   ONE, two, three; ONE, two, three.

(It is perhaps inadvisable to begin this work until the children are in the first grade.)

   b. Instruments which can be adapted to other kinds of music

     1. Drums—bear growling, heavy tread of giants, soldiers marching, rolling of thunder.

     2. Bells—fluttering of butterflies, fairies dancing, rustling of leaves, etc.

     3. Tambourines—gypsy dancing, hurdy gurdy man, etc.

     4. Cymbals—thunder, etc.

     5. Rhythm sticks—marching.

5. Song approach—after considerable experience

   a. Have the children sing a familiar rote song.

   b. Decide on different instruments for the four phrases by:

     1. Letting the children choose the instruments to be used in a certain song.

     2. Letting the children choose the instruments to be played with each phrase.

   c. As the selection is sung again, have each child listen for his or her phrase.

   d. Now, when the selection is sung have each child raise his hand for the part which he is to play. In this way we can make sure that each child knows when to come in.

   e. Let the children play the song, each group playing on its own particular phrase.

6. Occasionally a child will be found who is absolutely unaware of the rhythmic pulsations in the music. Such a child can be easily noticed because, instead of playing regularly with the beats, he will play irregularly either too fast or too slow. The following plan might be used for such a child:

   a. Have the class sing a song like "A Game."

   b. Let them clap with the words of the song. Then let the child who has difficulty do this alone until he can do it well and independently.

c. Have another child tap with him, tapping the regular beats of the song, that is, in fours, if it happens to be a 4/4 song.

d. Now have the first child tap just the way the second one did.

e. Let the two children do this with instruments. Try to have the children think of this as a new and interesting experiment, with one particular child chosen to "try it out." If some children do not seem aware of the rhythm in the music, merely having another child demonstrate will usually be enough to help them.

A Game *

German Folk Tune

Let the feet go tap, tap, tap,

Let the hands go clap, clap, clap,

Let the head nod to and fro,

Now a - round the room we go.

*McConathy, Osborne. *The Music Hour Kindergarten and First Grade.*
Silver, Burdett Co., Chicago, 1938.   p. 19.

c. Illustrative lesson plan for the song approach
　1. Objectives of the Pupil
　　a. General
　　　1. To have fun.
　　　2. To develop a good sense of rhythm.
　　　3. To become more familiar with the rhythm band in-
　　　　struments.
　　b. Specific
　　　1. To plan an orchestration for a well-known rote song.
　　　2. To orchestrate the rote song.
　　　3. Procedure (this activity is suggested for first grade).
　　　　a. Have everybody sing the song.
　　　　b. Have the children act out the words of the song.
　　　　c. Let them phrase the song with their arms.
　　　　d. Ask them to listen to the music on the piano and think
　　　　　the words of the song while they listen.
　　　　e. Orchestration
　　　　　1. "What are the words to the first phrase?" (Let the
　　　　　　feet go tap, tap, tap.)
　　　　　2. "How do you think we could decide which instru-
　　　　　　ments should play that phrase?" (Some child will
　　　　　　say, "Those instruments that tap!")
　　　　　3. "What are our tapping instruments?" (drum,
　　　　　　rhythm sticks, wood sticks, wood blocks and tri-
　　　　　　angles).
　　　　　4. "Let's hear the triangles, drum, wood blocks, and
　　　　　　rhythm sticks play the first phrase."
　　　　　5. "What are the words to the second phrase?" (Let
　　　　　　the hands go clap, clap, clap). Some child will
　　　　　　again suggest that the clapping instruments play
　　　　　　the second phrase.
　　　　　6. "What are the clapping instruments?" (cymbals,
　　　　　　sand blocks, jingle sticks).
　　　　　7. Let the cymbals, sand blocks, jingle sticks, play
　　　　　　the second phrase.
　　　　　8. "How would it be if we have the rest of the in-
　　　　　　struments who haven't played yet, play the third
　　　　　　phrase?"

9. "Tambourines, castanets and bells now play the third phrase."

10. "Since everybody has had a turn, what do you think we should do with the last phrase?" (Somebody will suggest that the teacher choose somebody who is sitting tall, or that everybody play it together.)

11. Have everybody play the last phrase.

12. "Listen to the music. Raise your hand when your part is being played."

13. Now have the children play the piece, everybody playing his part. If some of the children do not come in on the right part, or if they forget to play when they are supposed to be playing, go over their parts again.

14. Repeat the piece.

15. Ask for suggestions and criticisms from the group.
    a. "Did everybody come in at the right time?"
    b. "Were we playing too loudly?"

16. One of the things that will keep the lesson going smoothly is to make sure that no one is playing unless he is asked to. All instruments should be under the chairs when not being played. Thus it is imperative that the teacher will tell the children when to play and when not to play so that there will be no confusion in their minds.

d. Instrumental accompaniment approach

Although there are no words to this music, the child's imagination will be stimulated by the mood and kind of music. He will want to imitate the things that go on in the music with the different instruments. Very short, simple, and well-phrased pieces should be chosen for children at this particular level. Some examples of pieces that lend themselves to this activity are:

1. *Pirates March*—The Music Hour for the Kindergarten and First Grade. p. 81.

2. *Andante* from the Surprise Symphony, Haydn. Music Hour for the Kindergarten and First Grade.

3. *Tiptoe March*. Play a Tune. p. 38.

4. *Norwegian Dance*. Ibid. p. 39.

5. *The Song of the Clock*—American Singer, Book I, p. 168.

6. *Soldiers March*—Schumann.   Ibid. p. 115.

7. *Minuet*—Mozart.   Rhythmic Games and Dances.   Hughes.

8. *The Secret*—Gautier.   Ibid.   p. 99.

8. **Other Suggestions on Teaching the Rhythm Band.**

   a. Send to your music or book store for catalogs on rhythm band music and instruments.

   b. Rhythm band work should be auxiliary to the music program and should not take the place of singing in the school.

   c. Public appearance of the rhythm band will provide an excellent opportunity to "sell" the idea of music to the parents. However, the teacher should be warned against exploiting a group of children because parents or luncheon club members think they are "cute".

   d. Do not let the same child play the same instrument too long just because he plays it well.   If the rhythm band practices about twice a week, the instruments should be changed about every two weeks.   Keep a record of the instruments each child has had a chance to play so that he will have an opportunity to play every instrument.

   e. The accompanying music (piano or phonograph) must be heard over the rhythm band.   Children should be told to play softly.

   f. Warn against noise . . . take the instruments away if the children make any noise with the instruments except during actual playing.

   g. The rhythm band should be pupil-planned as well as teacher-planned.   A band which has been organized and planned by the teacher will probably play better, but the children will not have advanced as far as through orchestrating. Children should have the experience of selecting the instruments to fit the music.

   h. Excellent rhythm training in pupil leadership may be developed by letting the children conduct.

9. **Books Containing Excellent Material.**

   Beattie, J. W.   *American Singer, Book I.*   American Book Co., Chicago, 1946.

Glenn, Mabelle, et al. *Play a Tune* from The World of Music Series. Ginn and Co., Chicago, 1936.

Hughes, Dorothy. *Rhythmic Games and Dances.* American Book Co., Chicago, 1942.

10. The Following Records are Excellent for Rhythm Band Teaching.

It is more satisfactory to teach rhythm band with piano, however, and phonograph records should be used only for diversion, or for the teacher who cannot play the piano.

Air de Ballet—Jadassohn	V E-72
Amaryllis—Ghys	V 21938
Badinage—Herbert	V 20164
Country Dance—Weber	V 20451
Waltzing Doll—Poldini	V 1981
El Capitan—Sousa	V 35805
March—Gurlitt	V 20401
March from Nutcracker Suite—Tchaikowsky	V 22168
Parade of the Wooden Soldiers—Jessel	C 35719
Rendezvous—Aletter	C 418-M
Skater's Waltz—Waldteufel	V 21938
Stars and Stripes Forever—Sousa	V 35805
Toy Symphony—Haydn	V 20215

A complete list of Victor records for rhythm band is given on page 17 (Album E90) in the Victor catalog of Records for Elementary Schools.

11. Reference Readings on Rhythm Bands:

Annet, Thomas. *Music in the Rural School.* The Boston Music Company, Boston, 1938. pp. 58-63.

Nohavec, Hazel. *Normal Music Methods.* University Publishing Co., Lincoln, 1926. pp. 19-21.

Perham, Beatrice. *Music in the New School.* Neil Kjos, Chicago, 1941. pp. 71-73.

Waterman, Elizabeth. *Book of Rhythms.* Barnes, New York, 1936. pp. 56-58.

Assignments

1. Make a set of rhythm instruments following directions as given on pages 67-68.
2. Organize the class into a rhythm band using the song approach and the instrumental accompaniment approach.

3. Each member of the class should demonstrate how to hold and play each instrument.

II. THE LISTENING PROGRAM

A. Music Appreciation

Every lesson should be one of appreciation.   There are a number of ways to develop appreciation, two of the best being singing many songs and listening to much good music.

B. The General Plan for Introducing the Listening Program:

1. Playing restful music while resting.
2. Listening occasionally to songs in singing class.
3. Listening to spirited music in rhythm band.
4. Listening to songs and records dealing with things familiar to the child's experience.

C. Procedures

1. Listening to Contrasting Moods

a. Lullabies and marches
   Rockabye Parade—de Leath ....C 4212-M
   Berceuse—Godard ....C 4212-M
   Rockabye Baby ....V 20174
   Sweet and Low ....V 20174
   Lullaby—Brahms ....V 20174
   March of the Toys—Herbert ....V 12592
   March Militaire—Schubert................V 4314

b. Elves and fairies (dainty, sweet, happy music) as compared with witches and goblins (harsh, weird, unhappy).
   Fairies—Schubert.........................V 19882
   Gnomes—Reinhold ....in. V E-71
   Witch's Dance—MacDowell ....in. V E-81
   Elfin Dance—Grieg......................in. V E-78
   The Witch—Tschaikowsky ....V 20399

c. Weather, nature, birds, animals
   Canaries ....V 25-0001
   To a Water Lily—MacDowell.............in. V E-79
   Butterflies—Schumann ....in. V E-73
   The Bee—Schubert ....V 20614
   At the Brook—Boisdeffre ....V 20344
   The Wild Horseman—Schumann ....V 20153
   Butterfly Etude—Chopin................. V 5 Listening

d. Story telling music

Peter and the Wolf—Prokofieff . . . . DM-566 or
CMM-477

Snow White—Disney VY33

Of a Tailor and a Bear—MacDowell . . . . V 20153

Hansel and Gretel—Humperdinck . . . . in. V E-80

Animal Fair MJV-59

e. Contrasts of major and minor moods

Funeral March of a Marionette—Gounod . . . . . C 7374M

Dance of the Sugar Plum Fairy from
Nutcracker Suite—Tschaikowsky . . . . . . in. V DM-1020

2. **An Instrumental Approach to the Listening Program**

There are many schools where the facilities are such that
the children have an opportunity to hear and observe bands
and orchestras of older children or adults. When this is
true, the study of the instruments of the band and orchestra
may be begun at a very early age. The following plan
may serve as a possible guide to such a study program.

a. Objectives

1. To develop an appreciation for good music through
   listening to and studying the various band and orchestral instruments.

2. To acquaint the child with orchestral instruments
   so that he will recognize them by sight and sound.

3. To teach the common use of the band, such as
   indoor and outdoor concerts, parades, and enter-
   tainment at athletic events; and the orchestra, for
   concerts, accompaniment to singing and instrumental solos.

4. To stimulate the desire to play an instrument.

5. To create and develop for the child a repertoire
   of familiar and well-loved music.

D. **General Suggestions for the Introduction of Instrumental
Study**

1. Approach the problem through music, not mechanics. It
   is important to have the children listen to good music
   played by good performers in order to make the lesson
   effective.

2. If possible, take the children to a concert by an older student or an adult band or orchestra; study the music before the concert.

3. An actual performance by a competent performer is much more satisfactory than the use of pictures and phonograph records. Make use of the high school players in your vicinity.

E. Listening Program for the Kindergarten and First Grade

1. Specific objective—to introduce one instrument from each family of the orchestra, depending on the children's interest and experience, like the following:

Percussion...............................bass drum
Woodwind..........................wood clarinet
Brass ....trumpet or cornet
String ....violin

2. Have the children tell about hearing or seeing a band or orchestra. Ask them if they can name any instruments. Do they know anybody who plays an instrument? Suggest that perhaps they would like to know something more about some of the instruments in the band or orchestra.

a. Bass drum
If possible, bring a bass drum to show to the children and explain how it is played. If one is not available, show pictures of the instrument and play records illustrating its use in the band or orchestra.
Instruments of the Orchestra.............C MX-250
Yankee Doodle.....................V 20166
Dixie—Emmett ....V 20166

b. Wood clarinet
Instruments of the Orchestra.............C MX-250
Elfin Dance—Grieg ....V 20079
At the Brook—Boisdeffre ....V 20344
Wind Amongst the Trees—Briccialdi.........V 20344
Rusty in Orchestraville....................DC 115

c. Cornet or trumpet
Show the differences between the cornet and the clarinet.
Instruments of the Orchestra.............C MX-250
Light Cavalry Overture...................V 20079

Minuet .... V 20164
Tubby the Tuba .... D CU106
Andante and Rondo—Haydn .... C 70106D
　　　　(For Trumpet and Orchestra)

d. Violin
Explain the parts of the violin (bow, bridge, strings, and pegs).
Instruments of the Orchestra .... C MX-250
Humoresque—Dvorak .... V 20164
Rock-a-bye Baby .... V 20174

e. Kettle drum or tympani
Motivate with pictures and teach in a similar manner.
Instruments of the Orchestra .... C MX-250

f. Trombone
Review the trumpet as an introduction.
Instruments of the Orchestra .... C MX-250
The First Nowell .... V 20174

g. Cello
Compare with violin.
Instruments of the Orchestra .... C MX-250

h. Piccolo
Compare with the flute.
Instruments of the Orchestra .... C MX-250
Badinage—Herbert .... V 20164
Yankee Doodle .... V 20166
Pee Wee, the Piccolo .... V Y344

A Typical Listening Lesson for Kindergarten and First Grade
A Toy Unit
(Suggested for Grade I)

I. AIMS AND OBJECTIVES
　　A. To translate the child's experiences with toys into musical experiences.
　　B. To show the child how toys are not only to be played with, but to be enjoyed and experienced musically in a variety of ways.

II. PROCEDURE
　　A. Introduction
　　　　1. Pupils must be in a listening mood, preferably after they have had a relaxation period.

2. Have many pictures of toys and toy instruments placed about the room.

B. Activities
1. *The Toy Symphony*—Haydn—Victor Record........20215
   a. Tell briefly and simply the story of Haydn and how he decided to write this little symphony. Then play the record.
   b. Group discussion on toy instruments.
   c. Play the toy instruments in a rhythm band with suggested possibilities coming from the children.
2. *The Waltzing Doll*—Poldini—Victor Record 1981.
   a. Tell this story; then play the record.
   b. Engage in free rhythms pretending to be waltzing dolls.
3. Play: *March of the Little Lead Soldiers*—Pierne—Victor Record 19730.
4. Play: *Parade of the Wooden Soldiers* — Jessel — Record C-35719.
5. Play: *March of the Toys*—Herbert—V-12592.
6. Sing many toy songs, such as:
   My Tambourine—American Singer, Book I. p. 165.
   My Rhythm Sticks—p. 160.
   My Drum—Ibid. p. 160.
   The Dancing Doll—Ibid. p. 147.
   The Cymbals—Ibid. p. 161.
   See-Saw—Our Songs. p. 130.
   Little Black Cat—Ibid. p. 126.
   Five Little Drums—Listen and Sing. p. 56.
   The Toy Shop—Ibid. p. 86.
   The Rhythm Band—New Horizons. p. 123.
7. Creative Activities
   a. A poem may be created about toys.
   b. The poem may then be set to music.

C. Correlation With Other Subjects
1. Reading Activities.
   a. Read many stories about toys.
   b. Make a booklet with drawings of such things as a drum, a trumpet, etc. Then write short sentences about each drawing.

2. Language Activities

a. Poetry appreciation from *Two Hundred Best Poems for Boys and Girls*—Marjorie Barrows.
   What the Toys Are Thinking—p. 134.
   Toys—p. 39.
   Raggedy Doll—p. 44.
   The Long Ago Doll—p. 51.

b. Dramatizations
   Little Boy Blue.
   The Toy Mender—Round About, Book II.   p. 15.

3. Physical Education

a. Interpreting a tin soldier march, doll dance, jumping jack.
b. Mimetic play on the marching toy band, jumping rope, bouncing balls, a train, flying a kite, etc.
c. Rhythm band activities.
d. Dramatizations.

4. Art

a. Make free hand drawings of all instruments.
b. Draw pictures of animated toys, decorative instruments, Raggedy Ann, and toy soldiers.

5. Outcomes

By listening, performing, and creating, the little child will be given a rich educational experience, the specific avenue of approach being toys.

Assignments

1. Present a listening lesson to the class, using an original idea, such as a toy farm.
2. In the listening lesson, mention integrative and correlative possibilities.
3. Continue to gather materials for your scrapbook.

III. RHYTHMIC RESPONSE

Every normal child has native rhythmic responses. Some children need a great deal of encouragement and help and it is the responsibility of the teacher to assist each child to respond to a wide variety of rhythmic activities.

A. Objectives *Know*

1. To develop the ability to interpret the mood, the meaning, and the motion of the music with large, bodily motions.
2. To develop the ability to sing simple songs rhythmically.
3. To develop the ability to interpret rhythm through dramatizations, singing games, and mimetic play. *→ imitate*
4. To develop the ability to respond to rhythm through the playing of rhythm instruments.

B. Procedures

1. Fundamental Rhythms

It is very important that this phase of rhythms be very well established, for an ability to respond accurately to them will facilitate the rhythmic approach to reading readiness, which will come later, and the introduction of folk dancing and singing games. To be able to execute all of the fundamental rhythms well will allow greater freedom and spontaneity.

   a. Walking 4/4 or 2/4. This will include marching in several ways, such as: military, toys, fairies, animals, etc.
      1. Encourage swinging the arms and putting as much of the entire body into motion as possible.
      2. Lift up feet, bend knees, and move with a "spring" in the step.

   b. Running 4/4, 2/4, or 6/8 meter.
      1. Move on tiptoes; keep movement light.
      2. Include activities such as snow falling, raindrops falling, trains moving fast, etc.

   c. Skipping 6/8 meter.
      1. Small fast skip on tiptoe with arms swinging.
      2. Large, fast skip where each step has a small leap in it with much bodily motion. Do this with complete abandonment.

   d. Hopping 4/4, 2/4, or 6/8 meter.
      1. Imitate a frog, a polliwog, or a rabbit.
      2. Avoid heavy movement, but keep a great deal of motion in the hop. Sometimes a suggestion like the following will bring the desired result:
      "Pretend you are a frog hopping from one lily pad to another."

    e. Jumping 4/4, 2/4, or 6/8 meter.
      1. Jumping rope.
      2. Animals jumping.

    f Galloping 6/8 time.
      1. Horses.
      2. Ponies

    g. Swinging 3/4 meter.
      1. Pushing someone in a swing.
      2. With arms give the swing motion in a smooth, sweeping way.

    h. Swaying 3/4 meter.
      1. Trees being swayed by the wind.
      2. Flowers blowing in the breeze, using the whole body with child's face being the flower, arms and fingers the leaves, the body being the stem. Keep the movements smooth.

2. Free Rhythm Play*
    a. The circus
      1. Circus train comes into town. 4/4 meter.
      2. Circus tent is erected: pounding in stakes. 3/4 time.
      3. The circus parade. 4/4 meter. Band plays (horns drums, cymbals, etc.).
        Animals.
        Clowns.
      4. The performance
        Trapeze swinging. 3/4 meter.
        Tight rope walking. Slow 4/4 meter.
        Waltzing horses and elephants. 3/4 meter.
        Monkeys running in the ring. 6/8 meter.
        Bare-back riding (gallop). 6/8 meter.
      5. The circus is over: "Let's run home!"

    b. Transportation
      1. Train 4/4. Start with a slow shuffle and gradually increase the speed. Have an engine and caboose. When each child can do his train motions independently, join each train into one large train with the engineer giving the starting signal, etc.

* Suitable piano music and/or phonograph recordings may be used for dramatizations and free rhythm play.

2. Airplane 6/8 or 4/4: Smooth, fast, soft running steps with arms extended, dipping as the plane soars through the sky.

3. Boat 3/4, 6/8: Row boat or canoe. Have the children sit on the floor as if they were in a boat, rowing or paddling the canoe in time to the music.

c. Seasons

1. Spring

The Flowers Awaken

a. Seeds asleep in the ground: children relaxed lying on floor.

b. Sun shines on seeds: one or two children pretend to be the sun swaying over the seeds.

c. Rain falls on seeds: several children run among seeds.

d. Breezes blow: one or two children are the breezes that blow the seeds.

e. Seeds grow: seeds slowly awaken with each chord.

f. They grow until they are fully grown.

g. Birds fly among the flowers.

h. Sun shines.

i. Breezes blow and sway flowers.

Spring Activities

Jumping rope, playing ball, planting the garden.

2. Summer

a. Swimming, 3/4 meter.

b. Going on a picnic; hiking, gathering flowers.

c. Raindrops falling.

d. Playing games: hopscotch, leap frog, etc.

3. Autumn

a. Raking leaves, 3/4.

b. Birds flying south, 6/8, 4/4, 2/4.

c. Jack Frost coming to put flowers asleep.

d. Winds blowing.

4. Winter

a. Snowflakes falling, 4/4, 2/4, or 6/8 meter.

b. Snow-balling, 3/4 meter.

c. Snow-shoe walking, 3/4 meter.

d. Ice skating, 3/4 meter.

e. Icicles hanging from the roof, melting slowly.

    d. Farm
        1. Playing farm yard animals: ducks, geese, horses, kittens, dogs, roosters.
        2. Pitching hay, 3/4 meter.
        3. Driving the tractor, 4/4 meter.
        4. Going to market, 4/4 meter.

3. **Mimetic Play:** this is an activity using various movements occurring in everyday life.
    a. Climbing a ladder, slow 2/4 meter.
    b. Planting a garden, 3/4 meter.
    c. Going to the store for Mother, 2/4 or 4/4 meter.
    d. Riding a tricycle, 6/8 meter.
    e. Jumping rope, 3/4 meter.

4. **Dramatizations**
    a. Peter and the Wolf
        1. Peter's friends: the bird, the duck, the cat.
        2. The approach of the wolf: slow 2/4 meter.
        3. Flight of the bird: 6/8 meter.
        4. Peter climbing the tree: 2/4 meter.
        5. Peter throwing the lasso: 3/4 meter.
        6. Hunters' approach: 4/4, 2/4 meter.
        7. Triumphal marching to the zoo: Peter, the wolf, cat, bird, Grandfather, and hunters.

    b. Snow White
        1. Page taking Snow White to the woods: 4/4 meter.
        2. Snow White running about the woods: 6/8 meter.
        3. Birds leading her to the cottage of the Seven Dwarfs: 6/8 meter.
        4. Snow White cleaning and dusting the cottage of the Dwarfs: 3/4 meter.
        5. Return of the Dwarfs: 4/4 meter.
        6. Dwarfs climbing stairs and finding Snow White: 2/4 meter.
        7. Dwarfs digging in the mines: 3/4 meter.
        8. Prince galloping to find Snow White: 6/8 meter.

    c. Of a Tailor and a Bear
        1. Tailor pressing and sewing: 3/4 meter.
        2. Bear entering the door: 2/4 meter.

Miss Harriet Nordholm, Elementary Music Supervisor, Austin, Minn.,

And a First Grade Class Engaged In Finger-Play.

First Grade Class, Austin, Minn., Elementary Schools, Engaged in Creative Rhythm.

3. Tailor tuning and playing his violin: 3/4 meter.

4. Bear dancing: 3/4 meter.

5. Bear walking down the street: 2/4 meter.

5. **Singing Games.** Divide the class. Have one group sing while the other group carries on the activity. Select only short, simple games with few actions.

Two Blackbirds—Listen and Sing................p. 90
Dance, Thumbin, Dance—American Singer, Bk. I..p. 99
Ten Little Indians—Ibid.........................p. 94
London Bridge—New Music Horizons, Bk. I......p. 4
Little Jack Horner—Ibid.........................p. 18
The Farmer in the Dell—Ibid....................p. 28
The Mulberry Bush—Ibid.........................p. 38
Jack Be Nimble—Listen and Sing................p. 20
Round the Pear Tree—Ibid.......................p. 12
Jim Along Josie—American Singer, Bk. I........p. 152

a. Suggestions

1. Encourage the movements to be as spontaneous as possible.

2. Respect the child's imagination. His idea of a flying bird may not agree with that of the teacher.

3. Do not insist upon graceful movements; let the child respond as he wishes.

4. Help to overcome feelings of self-consciousness and shyness.

5. Allow the child to set his own rhythm, the teacher then following that rhythm on the piano or tom-tom.

6. Use the piano if at all possible. It is most desirable for the teacher to adjust her rhythm to that of the children.

7. Occasionally the teacher using a triangle for a rhythm-setter, encourages soft, light responses.

b. Equipment

1. Miscellaneous supplies

a. A well-tuned piano.

b. A tom-tom.

c. A triangle.

d. A good phonograph; an ample record library.

2. Books containing rhythmic materials and good piano music.
   a. Annis, Elsie and Matthews, Janet. *Rhythmic Activities*. Ginn and Company, Chicago, 1944.
   b. Beattie, J. W., and others. *American Singer, Book I*. American Book Company, Chicago, 1946.
   c. Glenn, Mabelle, and others. *Play a Tune*. Ginn and Company, Chicago, 1936.
   d. Hughes, Dorothy. *Rhythmic Games and Dances*. American Book Company, Chicago, 1942.
   e. Waterman, Elizabeth. *Book of Rhythms*. A. J. Barnes Company, New York, 1936.

3. Phonograph records

Run, Run, Run—Concone	V 20162
Jumping—Gurlitt	V 20162
Waltzes Nos. 1, 2, and 9—Brahms	V 20162
Theme for Skipping	V 20526
Flying Birds	V 20526
High Stepping Horses	V 20526
Galloping	V 20526
Skaters Waltz—Waldteufel	V 21938
Air de Ballet—Gretry	C 71330
Papillons (Butterflies)—Schumann	V-E 73
Fairies and Clowns	V 19882
Valse Serenade—Poldini	V 22767
The Bee—Schubert	V 20614
Knight of the Hobby Horse	V 22162
Skipping—Phrasing	V 22765
Stars and Stripes Forever—Sousa	V 20132
Pop Goes the Weasel	V 20151
Marching	V 22764
Skipping, Running	V 22767
Soldier's March—Schumann	V 22168

Assignments

1. Be able to play on the piano the following selections for each of the fundamental rhythms:

   Walk—*Washington's March*. p. 90. Rhythmic Games and Dances. Hughes.

Walk—*Priest's March.* p. 90. Rhythmic Games and Dances. Hughes.

Run—*Country Dance.* p. 117. Rhythmic Games and Dances. Hughes.

Run—*Bagatelle.* p. 96. Rhythmic Games and Dances. Hughes.

Gallop—*The Wild Horseman.* p. 111. Rhythmic Games and Dances. Hughes.

Gallop—*Hunting Song.* p. 110. Rhythmic Games and Dances. Hughes.

Skip—*Pop Goes the Weasel.* p. 151. Rhythmic Games and Dances. Hughes.

Skip—*Rondo Theme.* p. 88. Rhythmic Games and Dances. Hughes.

Swing and Sway—*Landler.* p. 94. Rhythmic Games and Dances. Hughes.

Swing and Sway—*Cradle Song.* p. 93. Rhythmic Games and Dances. Hughes.

Jump, Hop, Leap—*Ecossaise.* p. 132. Rhythmic Games and Dances. Hughes.

Jump, Hop, Leap—*Ecossaise.* p. 119. Rhythmic Games and Dances. Hughes.

2. Show the class how rhythm may be set by a tom-tom or a triangle.

3. Have a member of the class teach a demonstration lesson.

Bibliography

Beattie, J. W., et al, *American Singer, Book I.* American Book Company, Chicago, 1946.

Hubbard, George, *Music in the Elementary School.* American Book Company, Chicago, 1934.

Krone, Beatrice P., *Music in the New School.* Kjos Publishing Company, Chicago, 1941.

McConathy, Osborne, L., et al, *The Music Hour in the Kindergarten and First Grade.* Silver, Burdett Co., Chicago, 1938.

Music Education in the Elementary School. California State Department of Education, Los Angeles, 1939.

Nohavec, Hazel, *Normal Music Methods.* University Publishing Company, Lincoln, 1926.

Perkins, Clella, *How to Teach Music to Children.* Hall McCreary Company, Chicago, 1936.

Wright, Frances, *Elementary Music Education.* Carl Fischer Co., New York, 1941.

IV. CREATIVE EXPERIENCES

Creative experiences enter into every lesson, if in no other way, through re-creating a known song. Little children are creating when they can sing a song beautifully. As has already been mentioned, they can create a dramatic action to a song or provide a rhythmic response to piano or phonograph music. They may also create their own musical instruments. Making up songs should be a regular part of the music program.

Little children are very free in making up their own songs. They often hum their own tunes at play or work. The method for guiding a class in creating a song will be explained under three headings.

A. Background

1. The children should previously know songs of marked rhythm and melodic patterns.
2. The teacher may sing all but the last word of each line or an unfamiliar song. The children supply the last word and note.
3. The teacher may sing questions while the children sing answers with original melodies.
4. The teacher may sing one line of a song unfamiliar to the children; the children make up a second line; the teacher sings the third line; and the children make up the last line.
5. The child may sing a thought instead of speaking it.
6. He may take a word (his name, for example) and sing it instead of saying it.

B. Introducing Creative Writing For The First Time

1. After beginning the class with familiar songs, the teacher might say, "Shall we make up a song today?"
2. The children might want to make up a tune for their favorite nursery rhyme.
3. The poem which is to be used (preferably one which has been written by the class) should be short and rhythmical.
4. It should be said over and over until the children feel the rhythm of it.
5. Then the teacher might say, "Instead of saying the first line of the poem to me, who will sing it?"
6. Or, "Instead of saying the poem, let's sing it."

7. Write the tunes as they come, line by line, or, for the entire poem.

8. The child usually needs very little stimulus after the first pleasant experience of making up a song.

C. The teacher of the kindergarten and first grade children must wait for the appropriate time for original song writing. As she observes the children at play time, she will often catch bits of melody that the children are making up. Sometimes when stories are being read the children might be inspired to make up a song about some incident. Teachers of small children should seize every opportunity to encourage creating songs and should copy them down and place them in a permanent file.

Parents should be encouraged to copy down original songs created by children at play in the home and send them to the teacher.

D. Reading References On Creative Experience
1. Coleman, Satis N. *Creative Music for Children.* Putnam and Songs, New York, 1936. pp. 173-177.
2. Gehrkens, Karl W. *Music in the Grade Schools.* C. C. Birchard Co., Boston, 1938. pp. 85-89.
3. Norton, Alma C. *Teaching School Music.* University of Southern California Pub., Los Angeles, 1932. pp. 73-76.

E. A Typical Creative Lesson
The following creative activity was carried on in a kindergarten:

It was a snowy day. The flakes that came down were large and soft. The teacher sang:

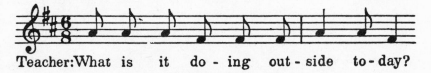

Teacher: What is it do-ing out-side to-day?

A five year old sang back to her:

Child: The snow is fall-ing down.

Then questions like these were asked:

Teacher: "Where do the snowflakes come from?"

Child: "They come from the sky."

Teacher: "Who will sing us a tune about falling snowflakes?"

This was the result:

Snow

The   snow   is   fall - ing   down   to   me,

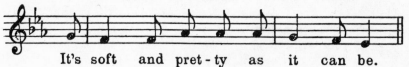

It's soft   and pret - ty   as   it   can be.

Assignments

1. Write an original two-phrase song.
2. Write an original four-phrase song.

Chapter IV
MUSIC IN THE SECOND GRADE
Reading Readiness

Before music reading is presented, it is well to keep in mind that all of the activities begun and carried on in kindergarten and first grade will be continued and enlarged upon. The song repertory will be extended and enriched by singing many songs relating to the interests and experiences of the child. The majority of the children should now be able to sing many songs artistically, in tune, rhythmically correct, and with good tone quality.

All of the areas of music education should continue to receive careful consideration: singing, listening, responding to rhythm, and creating. The program should be varied to meet the needs and the moods of the child.

A music period of at least twenty minutes each day should emphasize enjoyment, beauty, and fun. This will include the singing of many songs, listening to good music on the phonograph or piano, participating in rhythmic activities with emphasis on large, bodily movements, and creating songs, dances, and orchestrations for rhythm band.

The pursuit of techniques and the further development of capacities through the reading of music should be carried on in such a way that they will aid the child in gaining enjoyable music experiences.

There has been a tendency on the part of some music educators to insist that this reading be begun at certain grade levels, whether the class has been ready for it or not. Fortunately, of late, most music educators now agree that the reading of music should not be begun until the children have a readiness for it. This is termed "reading readiness" for music.

Perhaps some of the characteristics listed below will guide the teacher in determining whether or not her group has music reading-readiness.

1. Can the children sing many simple songs in tune and in an artistic way?

2. Are the children capable of giving accurate rhythmic responses, particularly to fundamental rhythms—walking, running, skipping, swaying, etc.

3. Have most of the out-of-tune singers from kindergarten and first grade improved to the extent that they can imitate motives or phrases accurately?

4. Can the children read the words on the printed page with ease and facility?

5. Do they know number combinations well enough to locate pages in their books?

If most of the children in the room can do the above, the teacher may proceed with the presentation of notation. Naturally, there will be some children who do not have reading-readiness, but the entire group should not be held back because of these few. The teacher must not expect everyone to develop musically at the same rate of speed; she should encourage individual development.

In the approach from rote singing to music reading there is a transition from the ear to the eye. This transition should follow through these types of songs: rote, rote-note, and note.

Having sung many rote songs and built up a strong aural perception of melody and rhythm, the child is now ready to begin the transfer of his attentions to the printed page and to develop a readiness for the independent reading which will soon follow.

It is generally agreed by teachers that the most satisfactory approach to music reading is through singing the notes on the printed page using the syllables do, re, mi, fa, so, la, ti, and do. To be able to read music accurately through the use of syllables is not an end in itself, but a means to an end.

Every teacher should be prepared to tell her students the history of syllables if they should ask about them. Guido of Arezzo, a Benedictine monk, planned a method of teaching the reading of music, improved the system of writing notes, and established a six tone scale. He noticed that a hymn which his choir sang went up one degree with each of the first six lines, so he used the first syllable of the first word in each line to name the tones of the scale.

Ut queant laxis	Famuli tuorum
Resonare fibris	Solve polluti
Mira gestorum	Labii reatum Sancte Joannes

The Italians changed the ut to do, and ti was added later.

The above hymn translated means: That thy servants may be able to sing thy deeds of wonder with pleasant voices, remove O holy John, the guilt of our sin-polluted lips.

It is called the "Hymn to St. John, the Baptist."[1]

Assignments

1. Have members of the class report on the origin of notes.
2. Have the class write papers on:
   a. The contributions of Lowell Mason to school music.
   b. Singing schools.
   c. Early American Hymnology.
   d. Origin of folk music in America.
   e. Development of church choirs.
   f. Symphony orchestras of the United States.
   g. Opera development in the United States.
3. Compile a list of folk songs from the state in which you live.
4. Make a list of American song writers.[2]

I. GENERAL TEACHING PROCEDURES FOR SINGING

A. The Rote Song

1. Characteristics of a good rote song.
   a. It should have a text which is interesting to the child.
   b. It should express his everyday interests and activities.
   c. The song should be within the child's level of ability.
   d. The melody should be appropriate to the text and within the range of the treble staff.
2. Teaching the rote song without books. (Refer to the whole song method and the phrase method, Chapter III.)
3. Teaching the rote song with books in the hands of the pupils.
   a. Show the children how to hold the book properly using both hands; have them sit erectly with both feet on the floor.

[1]Pratt and others, Grove's Dictionary of Music and Musicians, American Supplement. The MacMillan Co., New York, 1920.

[2]See the book Our New Music, by John Tasker Howard. Published by Crowell Publishing Company, New York; also, Composers in America, by Claire Reis. Published by The Macmillan Company, Chicago.

b. Show children how to open new books.

c. Encourage the children to examine their books.

d. Arouse interest in the song by calling attention to the title, content, source, pictures if any, and dynamics.

e. Teach the song by the whole method, if possible.

1. The teacher plays the song on the piano while the children "play" it in their books by placing their fingers on the note each time the teacher plays it on the piano.

2. Sing the entire song artistically while the children watch the words and music.

3. The teacher sings the entire song with the children by word or by a neutral syllable such as "loo."

4. Sing it several times, if necessary, but withdraw as soon as the children can carry on alone.

5. Repeat difficult phrases correcting any mistakes that occur.

B. Preparation for Music-Reading

1. Reading-readiness, with a strong element of the fun idea, may be begun by introducing the syllable as a second stanza.

   a. "Twinkle, twinkle little star"
      do do   so so   la la   so, etc.

   b. "Three blind mice"
      mi   re   do. etc.

   c. "Row, row, row your boat"
      do   do   do   re   mi, etc.

2. Bird calls: *so, do.* (up)

3. Echo effects: *do, la.* (down)

4. Good-bye: *so, do.* (down)

C. The Song for Musical Analysis

1. Purpose

   a. To introduce new problems.

   b. To serve as a foundation for the beginning of music-reading.

2. **Characteristics**
   a. It should be short.
   b. It should contain only quarter, half, dotted half and whole notes.
   c. It should be based on the tonic chord or the diatonic scale.
   d. It should be one which has been previously learned by rote.

3. **Procedure: The Motive Approach**

   The plan of beginning to read music through using a tonal pattern is accepted by many teachers and supervisors as being an effective, interesting and successful method.

   Use the song: "Hel-lo" (the motive to be learned is *so-mi.*) Teach the song by rote.

   When the song is well learned, inform the children that they are going to try something new.

   Find the motive *so-mi;* place it on the blackboard. Have children find the motive in the song.

Hello

Hel-lo, Hel-lo, I'm on the tel-e-phone, Hel-

so   mi

lo, Hel-'lo, Please an-swer if you're home.

Hel - lo, Hel - lo

   a. Teacher tells the children the syllable names of the notes in the motive.

   b. Teacher sings the syllables to the children.

   c. When the pupils have found the *so-mi* motive in their songs, the pupils sing it by syllables.

   d. Sing the entire song with "*loo*" except for the motive which should be sung by syllables.

   e. Sing the entire song with words.

   f. Teaching helps.

     1. Have the children cut out notes from black construction paper; have them build the *so-mi* pattern on a staff in the back of the book or on cardboard staves.

     2. Board work may be done by having a child go to a staff placed on the blackboard and writing the *so-mi* pattern.

   g. When the *so-mi* pattern is thoroughly learned, the next logical pattern to introduce is *mi-do;* the procedure for its introduction, practice, and mastery is the same as that for *so-mi*—through the rote songs learned by the children.

   h. When these two patterns have been learned both aurally and by sight, they may be combined into the *so-mi-do* pattern which forms the tonic chord.

   i. The tonal pattern of the scale may then be introduced in its ascending and descending forms.

   j. The only theoretical information the child needs is a brief explanation of the staff: It has five lines and four spaces which are counted upward from the bottom.

   k. Present rhythm to the children in the following way: While the teacher may direct and guide some of the movements and responses of the children, they should not be dictated to or made to follow exactly what the teacher may have in mind. One response to the exclusion of all others need not necessarily be the right one.

     Instead of approaching rhythm responses through a mathematical analysis, it might better be presented

Note: During kindergarten and first grade, the child will have mastered the fundamental rhythms; he will have had many experiences in dramatizations and mimetic play, and he will have participated in rhythm bands.

through feeling, which is an inherent response in each
child's activities.

1. Walking notes (quarter notes)

   a. Have children march (walk).

   b. Have them clap the time.

   c. Lines representing walking may be placed on the
   board thus: ─   ─   ─   ──   ·─   ─

2. Running notes (eighth notes)

   a. Have the pupils run in time.

   b. Have them clap running rhythm.

   c. Place lines representing running steps on the
   board: ─   ─   ─   ─   ─   ─   ─   ─

   d. Walking and running may be compared by
   chanting the movement, clapping the time and
   stepping the note valuations on the following
   rhythmic patterns:

   walk, walk, run, run, run, run

   run, run, run, run, walk, walk

   walk, run, run, walk, run, run

   walk, run, run, run, run, walk

   e. Slow notes: the foot motions on slow notes are
   given below.

      1. Half note: *step* with left foot, bend right knee
      and vice versa.

      2. Dotted half note: *step* with left foot, bring
      right foot out to the *side*, bring right foot
      back to left foot, and vice versa.

      3. Whole note: *step* with left foot, bring right
      foot *front*, bring right foot out to the *side*,

bring right foot *back* to meet left foot, and vice versa.

4. Dotted quarter note: *step* with left foot, *bend* right knee and vice versa.*

   f. Rhythmic exercises.

1. Chant, clap, step all rhythmic movements found in songs.

2. Have the class work out combinations to be done.

3. While the class chants the words to a song, have one child go to the board to draw the proper lines, as for instance:

"Ding dong bell, Pussy's in the well—"

   g. Find other songs from the basic series using the tonal pattern approach for the beginning of music reading.

1. American Singer, *Happy Builders,* p. 19, *so-mi* motive.

2. Tuning Up, *Bright Carpets,* p. 37, *so-mi* motive.

Assignments

1. How will a teacher know if her class has reading-readiness?
2. What is a satisfactory approach to music reading?
3. What is the history of syllables?
4. When should books be put into the hands of the children?
5. What is the song for musical analysis?
6. Explain thoroughly the motive approach to reading music.
7. How are rhythm symbols presented to the children?
8. Find songs in several basic song books where the tonal patterns *so-mi, mi-do, so-mi-do,* and other forms of the tonic triad are found, and use these songs for the beginning of music reading.
9. It is suggested that members of the teacher training classes teach

* These movements can be done by the rhythmically alert class. In cases where any difficulty might be noticed, the movement can simply be to hold or bend the knee for the required amount of time. It is possible to gain the greatest accuracy, however, using the above suggested movements.

these music reading procedures, step by step, to other members of the class.

10. Select several songs and write the foot movements for them.
11. Be able to step the rhythm patterns on any song on the second grade level.
12. Observe second grade music class.

II. LISTENING ACTIVITIES

Appreciation is not a special phase of the music program. It is an integral part of every lesson and must be woven into every music activity.

A. General Objectives

1. To establish the habit of active listening.
2. To help children find enjoyment in music as something heard as well as something played and sung.
3. To develop a sense of correlation with other subjects.
4. To encourage an emotional and intellectual response to various moods.

B. Specific Objectives (units) for use by teachers

1. To develop the ability to interpret a story of compositions.

Peter and the Wolf.............................V-DM 566
Through the Looking Glass....................C 350
Carnival of the Animals......................V-MO 785
Hansel and Gretel........................Musicraft RRc
The Toy Symphony...........................V 20215
Golliwog's Cake Walk..........................V-E-78
Songs of the Zoo............................V-Y 337

2. To establish a feeling of mood.

Wild Horsemen—Schumann ....V 20153
Lullaby—Brahms ....V 24271
Flight of the Bumble Bee—Rimsky-Korsakov.......V 1645
Rockabye Parade—de Leath....................V-Y 16
Papillon—Schumann ....V E-73
A Dream—Bartlett ....V 4367

3. To develop orchestral instrument recognition

Rusty in Orchestraville......................DC 115

March of the Little Lead Soldiers—Pierne........V 19730
(drum)

Nocturne—Tschaikowsky—violin ....V 20614

The Swan—Saint-Saens—cello ....V-MO 785

Poem for Flute and Orchestra—Griffes—flute....V 11-8349

Pee Wee the Piccolo..........................V-Y 344

The Rendesvous—Aletter.....................C 418M

4. To study the various types of marches

Stars and Stripes Forever—Sousa...............V 35805

Funeral March of a Marionette—Gounod........C 7374

March of the Toys—Herbert...................V 12592

March of the Caucasian Chief—Ippolitov.......V 1335

Parade of the Wooden Soldiers—Jessel...........C 35719

March of the Little Lead Soldiers—Pierne.......V 19730

5. To show the relationship of our flowers, animals, and birds to music.

To a Wild Rose—MacDowell.................C 4279M

To a Water Lily—MacDowell..................C 4279M

Narcissus—Nevin ....C 414

Canaries ....V 25-0001

Carnival of the Animals—Saint-Saëns.........V-MO 785

Butterflies—Lavalee VE-73

Papillon—Schumann V-E-73

Entrance of the Little Fauns—Pierne............V 4319

6. To study toys and music

Waltzing Doll—Poldini ....V 20161

Serenade for the Doll—Debussy ....V 7147

Dance of Reed Pipes from Nutcracker Suite—
Tschaikowsky ....V-DM 1020

Toy Symphony—Haydn ....V 20215

Babes in Toyland—Herbert....................V 12592

7. To show the relationship of music and the weather

The Storm from William Tell Overture........V-DM 605

Spring Song—Mendelssohn ....V 20195

Rustle of Spring—Sinding ....V 18153

C. Procedures

An example of a typical listening lesson on instrumental recognition is given below. This same general plan could be worked out for a listening lesson of any type. This type of lesson should only be done if the children manifest an interest in instrumental music.

A Typical Listening Lesson for Grade II

Recognition of the Common Orchestral Instruments

I. AIMS AND OBJECTIVES

To develop an appreciation of good music through listening to the various instruments.

To acquaint the child with orchestral instruments, so that he will recognize them by sight and sound.

To develop discrimination and recognition of instru-ments as heard in a composition.

To stimulate a desire on the part of the child to play an instrument.

II. PROCEDURES

A. Introduction

1. Approach the problem through music, not through me-chanics.

2. Use only good music to demonstrate.

B. Activities

1. *Rusty in Orchestraville*—Capitol BC-35

   a. Use this album as an introduction to the study of various instruments.

   b. Play the entire album.

   c. Then play the album again and as each instrument is heard, stop and discuss it. Have an older child bring in his instrument to demonstrate. The following plan may be followed, using the instruments in the order in which they appear.

   1. *Vera, the Violin*

      a. Discuss the violin. Have the class become familiar with the bow, strings, and bridge.

    b. Have pictures of the violin, or better still, the violin itself.

    c. Play these records illustrating the violin:

        Instruments of the Orchestra........C-MX250

        Humoresque—Dvorak ....V 45096

2. The 'Cello and Bass Viol

    a. Discuss the parts of the 'cello and double bass.

    b. Play records of the violin, 'cello, and bass so that the class may hear the differences.

    c. Identify these instruments with the "string family."

    d. Play these 'cello records:

        Instruments of the Orchestra..........C-MX250

        The Swan—Saint-Saëns MO-785

3. *Tommy, the Trumpet*

    a. Identify this with the "brass family."

    b. Explain that the trumpet is played by blowing into the mouth piece.

    c. Explain the mouthpiece, the keys, the bell.

    d. Listen to these records:

        Instruments of the Orchestra........C-MX250

        Light Cavalry Overture—Suppe........V 20079

4. *Tony, the Trombone*

    a. Compare the trumpet and trombone: the trumpet has keys; the trombone a slide. They are both members of the brass family.

    b. Call attention to the differences in the quality of the tone and the pitch.

    c. Play this record:

        Instruments of the Orchestra........C-MX250

5. *Clarence, the Clarinet*

    a. Identify this with the "woodwind family".

    b. Demonstrate how the tone is produced with a single reed.

    c. Play these records:

Note: With each instrument studied, have an adult or an older student demonstrate the instrument.

Instruments of the Orchestra........C-MX250

Tarantella—Mendelssohn ....V 20079

6. *Bobo, the Oboe*
   a. This is identified with the woodwind family.
   b. Demonstrate how the tone is produced with a double reed.
   c. Play the record:

   Instruments of the Orchestra........C-MX250

7. The Flute
   a. Explain that this is a member of the woodwind family, but that it has no reed.
   b. It is one of the oldest instruments.
   c. Play these records:

   Instruments of the Orchestra........C-MX250
   Poem for Flute and Orchestra........V 11-8349

8. The Piccolo
   a. The piccolo is the flute's "little brother."
   b. Compare the flute and the piccolo as to size and pitch.
   c. Play these records:

   Instruments of the Orchestra........C-MX250
   Yankee Doodle ....V 20166
   Pee-Wee, the Piccolo

9. The Bassoon
   a. This is the bass of the oboe family (of the woodwinds).
   b. Compare the oboe and bassoon as to size and pitch.
   c. Play these records:

   Instruments of the Orchestra........C-MX250

10. *Sammy, the Saxophone*
    a. This is a member of the woodwind family (single reed).
    b. Compare it with the clarinet.

11. Drums
    a. Identify with the "percussion family."

    b. Name the varieties of drums:

      Snare Drum: Discuss the parts of the snare drum (head, snares, sticks); it is often used for marching.

      Kettle Drum: (tympani): Demonstrate the difference between the snare and kettle drums as to size, sticks, kinds of beat.

      Bass Drum: Show the difference in this and the other two drums as to size, shape, tone quality, and rhythm.

    c. Play records:

      Instruments of the Orchestra........C-MX250

  12. Bells, Chimes, Xylophones

    a. Make a comparison of these three members of the percussion family through pictures, demonstrations, etc.

    b. Play record:

      Instruments of the Orchestra........C-MX250

  13. *Peter, the Piano*

    a. Explain that this usually is classified in the percussion family.

    b. Trace a brief history of the piano through discussion and demonstrations.

    c. Play the record:

      Shepherd's Hey—Grainger............V 20802

 2. Singing many songs about instruments such as:

  Playing in the Band—New Music Horizons, Bk. II. p. 8
  The Rhythm Band—New Music Horizons, Bk. II.. p. 123
  My Fiddle—Our Songs.........................p. 116
  The Triangle—Our Songs.....................p. 111
  We Sing as We March—Our Songs.............p. 110
  My Fiddle—Tuning Up........................p. 121
  The Flute and the Drum—Tuning Up.........p. 145
  The Village Band—American Singer.........p. 178
  The Marching Soldiers—American Singer.......p. 43

 3. Participating in rhythmic activities

  a. The rhythm band.

b. Free play (dramatization) on Rusty's trip to Orchestraville.

4. Participating in creative activities
   a. Original poetry and songs about instruments.
   b. The setting up of original orchestrations for rhythm band.

C. Correlation With Other Subjects

1. Reading activities
   a. Read many stories about instruments — (Kinscella Reader No. 2).
   b. Make booklets with pictures of instruments with short sentences of explanation for each.

2. Language activities
   a. Read poems about bands, orchestras, and instruments.
   b. Dramatize the painting, "The Spirit of '76."

3. Art
   a. Make a mural of Rusty's trip to Orchestraville.
   b. Make free hand drawings of instruments.

D. Materials

Let's Explore Music—Cline—Ginn & Co.

Kinscella *Readers*

Music Appreciation for Children—RCA Manuacturing Co.

Illustrations for each lesson presented.

Related song materials.

Geiringer—*History of Musical Instruments*.

E. Outcomes

1. Do the children enjoy hearing many types of music?
2. Are their listening habits good?

History of Instruments

Assignments

1. Each member of the class should present an original listening lesson to the other members of the class.
2. Write the lesson plan for the above assignment.

3. Present as many instruments as possible.

4. Continue gathering scrap-book materials.

III. RHYTHM RESPONSES

Children are so rhythmic that they automatically and spontaneously react to music when they hear it. The guiding and directing by the teacher of these reactions from her students is an important means of fostering appreciation.

A. Objectives

1. To develop the ability to respond to music of different types and moods with strong emphasis still being placed on large, bodily movements.

2. To have perfected the fundamental rhythms, so that these concepts can later be applied in reading-readiness.

3. To develop the ability to sing all songs rhythmically.

4. To develop a strong feeling for phrase and accent.

5. To perfect performance on rhythm instruments.

6. To develop the ability to interpret rhythms through dramatization, singing games, mimetic play, and folk dances.

B. Procedures

1. Perfect and further develop the fundamental rhythms.

    a. Devices

        1. Have the children do rhythmic patterns by clapping, using the walk, skip, gallop, or any other rhythm; transfer this clap to motion while part of the class chants, with the remainder interpreting the rhythm.

2. Make up verbal chants like one of the following:

"O, Mary come and skip with me,"

Chant it, clap it, skip it.

      or

"Robin, hop! hop! hop!
Never stop! stop! stop!"

Chant it, clap it, hop.

3. Take a child's name, like "Helen Louise"—chant, clap, and step.

b. Work out combinations of fundamental rhythms. This is an excellent plan to follow both for increasing knowledge of fundamental rhythms and also for introducing folk dancing. Some excellent examples of these are:

Walk, walk, walk, walk, slide, slide slide, slide.

Walk, walk, walk, walk, skip, skip, skip, skip.

Run, run, run, run, walk, walk, slide, slide.

c. Games using fundamental rhythms

1. Work out a round rhythmically, as:

Three blind mice, three blind mice — — — walk

See how they run, see how they run — — — — — run

They all ran after the farmer's wife — — — — — skip

She cut off their tails with a carving knife — — jump

Did you ever see such a sight in your life — — slide

As three blind mice? — — — — — — — — — — — walk

2. Leap frog: Form lines with players squatted down. The "leaper" moves in time to the music.

3. Circle games: Divide the class into four groups—(a) the walkers (b) runners (c) skippers (d) hoppers. All are in a single circle. When the music being played is of the type represented by one of these groups, that group proceeds into the center of the circle, doing its particular rhythm. When the rhythm changes, the next group performs, etc.

d. Additional relaxation exercises.

1. Candle melting: Stand on tiptoe with arms representing the flame. Slowly, to music, melt to the floor.

2. Icicles melting: Same as above.

e. Ball bouncing.

1. Bounce on the accent. When the accent changes, change the bounce.

2. Half of a group bounce on accents, the other half on unaccented beats.

3. Bounce balls in partner combinations using two, four, six, or more people in one group.

4. Work out pictures: one person bounces ball; the other partner simultaneously throws his into the air.

f. Feeling the accent.

1. Have the children sit on the floor, clap on the floor for the accent and in the air for unaccented beats.

2. Children stand, walk, and show the accent with a strong step and bodily dip.

3. Clap the hands on the accents.

4. When playing the piano or tom-tom, change the accent often.

5. Units of activity extended (Consult Chapter III).

6. Dramatizations (Consult Chapter III, p. 86).

7. Singing games. Divide the class. Have one group sing while the other group carries on the activity. Select short simple games with few actions like the following:

All Around the Kiǎchen—New Music Horizons, Bk. II . . . . . . p. 10
Go In and Out the Window—New Music Horizons, Bk. II . . p. 27
Did You Ever See a Lassie—New Music Horizons, Bk. II . . p. 54
John Brown Had a Little Indian—
      New Music Horizons, Bk. II . . . . p. 64
All Around the Maypole—American Singer, Bk. II . . . . p. 164
Skip to My Lou—American Singer, Bk. II . . . . p. 166
Go Tell Aunt Rhoday—American Singer, Book II . . . . p. 170
Bouncing Ball—Tuning Up . . . . p. 58
The Dancing Lesson—Tuning Up . . . . p. 122
Jack-in-the-Box—Tuning Up . . . . p. 66
I'm Learning to Dance—Our Songs . . . . p. 107
Hippity-Hop—Our Songs . . . . p. 112
Swinging—Our Songs . . . . p. 14

8. If there is some child with an aptitude for directing, pick out some simple songs and teach him a few rudiments of conducting, and let him lead the class occasionally.

9. Jumping rope.

10. Dalcroze Eurhythmics. This is a rather complex system of rhythmic response evolved by Jacques Dalcroze, a S w i s s, where music is interpreted through large bodily movements. As a rhythmic approach to reading-readiness, these movements are invaluable. If interested in developing this type of rhythmic activity, consult Dalcroze's book.

Assignments

1. Teach an original simple folk dance using a combination of fundamental rhythms.

2. Work out several ball bouncing sequences.

C. Equipment (refer to Chapter III).

IV. CREATIVE ACTIVITIES

The ability to create will manifest itself in many ways at this level, and every type of creativity must be given encouragement. It will be found that the child's ability to recreate a song artistically and beautifully will come naturally; his dramatic actions will be much more imaginative; his rhythmic responses will be greatly improved over those made in kindergarten and first grade. He will be able to construct instruments more skillfully, and he will show definite tendencies toward making up his tunes.

All of these endeavors are a worthy part of the music education program and should be carefully included in the regular music lesson.

A. Procedures

1. Creative song writing (refer to Chapter III)

a. Teacher may sing a question such as: "What did you see on your way to school?" This was done in a second grade and the results were as follows:

Teacher:

What did you see on your way to school?

Pupil:

I saw a dog!

b. The teacher should write her part of the song and the pupil's answer on the blackboard. Have the class sing the entire song.

The teacher then suggested that they might write a song about the dog David saw coming to school. It was written on the blackboard and this was the result:

The Dog

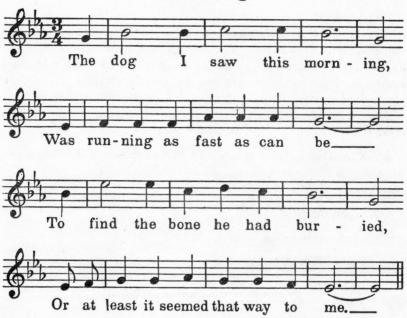

The dog I saw this morn - ing,

Was run - ning as fast as can be____

To find the bone he had bur - ied,

Or at least it seemed that way to me.____

Know (handwritten margin note)

c. Setting a poem to music

There may be a poem of which the children are especially fond. This will lend itself well to a song.

1. Read the poem until the words are "swinging." Teachers voice should inflect while reading.

Put on board under staff (handwritten margin note)

2. Children may tap or beat pulse while the teacher reads the poem.

3. If possible, draw out a tune for the entire song. If it will not come this way, approach it line by line.

4. Phrase the song with arm motions.

5. Through their feeling for accent, question the class as to how it swings: in twos, threes, or fours.

6. Keep all original songs in a note-book for future reference.

7. Occasionally an original song may be placed upon tagboard and displayed.

8. Encourage the children to make illustrations of their song.

9. The children should be encouraged to make up tunes, outside school. The writing of original poetry for creative purposes should be done. A song which is entirely their own, words and music, is of much satisfaction to children.

d. Using a well-known story as the medium for creative expression.

1. Choose a story like *The Three Bears* or *Little Black Sambo* and write poetry and music.

2. Work out the dramatizations, dances and actions of all kinds for such stories.

e. After several songs have been created, they may be woven into a story to make up a simple operetta. Dances and action may be worked out, simple costumes and stage sets may be designed and made, making the entire project completely creative.

f. Constructing instruments

For the construction of instruments, refer to Chapter III, p. 69.

Assignments

1. Write an original song.
2. Adapt a story such as *The Three Bears* into a simple operetta.

BIBLIOGRAPHY

Hughes, Dorothy, *Rhythmic Games and Dances*. American Book Company, Chicago: 1942.

Mursell, James and Glenn, Mabelle, *Psychology of School Music Teaching*. Silver, Burdett Company, Chicago: 1938.

Perkins, Clella, *How to Teach Music to Children*.   Hall, McCreary Company, Chicago: 1936.

Pratt et al, *Groves Dictionary of Music and Musicians*. American Supplement, MacMillan Company, New York: 1920.

Chapter V

MUSIC IN THE THIRD GRADE

Introduction

The four areas of music education will continue to receive consideration. Much rote singing for joy and recreation will be done; an elementary skill in music reading will be developed; listening lessons with emphasis on attentive listening will be given; coordination in rhythmic response will be noticed, and creative musical expression will continue to be developed.

As the pupils become more independent singers, the teacher will be giving less help. At this level, it will be noticed that there are fewer out-of-tune singers. For the few who are found to be still tonally deficient, it might be well to work individually with them outside of regular school hours.

I. GENERAL TEACHING PROCEDURES

A. The Rote Song

1. The Importance of Rote Singing—
The rote song should continue to play an important part in the child's musical development. Many songs with a variety of texts should be sung as artistically as possible.

2. Types of Rote Songs—
   a. Songs of everyday life and familiar things centered around the children's interests.

   b. Songs of nature and of the seasons.

   c. Songs of special days.

   d. Singing games and dances.

   e. Patriotic songs.

   f. Songs for recreational or assembly singing.

   g. Pet songs.

3. How to Teach a Rote Song—
For teaching a rote song (with or without books in the hands of the children) consult chapter III, p. 55. Use the

whole method for teaching whenever possible as explained in chapter III, pages 3 and 4.

4. Additional Suggestions for Teaching the Rote Song:

a. The teacher should strive to sing with a light, clear voice.

b. The song should be taught in the key in which it was written. - *can usually depend on*

c. Insist that the children sing at all times using light, high voices.

Very Omp. d. Always rely on the pitch pipe; do not guess at the pitch.

e. Sing the song in the mood and tempo in which the song was intended to be sung. *Don't be afraid to use own ideas.*

f. Enunciate clearly; explain unfamiliar words.

g. When the song is well learned, an accompaniment which is played softly and artistically may be added. *— not too softly.*

5. How to Phrase a Rote Song—

not so good a. Have a child start walking in one direction on the first note of the song. *— No Good*

b. When the phrase changes, he turns and walks in the opposite direction from which he began.

c. Several children might go to the blackboard and draw the phrases (arcs) of the song.

Good Method d. The other children in the room may phrase with their arms.

B. The Song for Musical Analysis

1. Objectives—

a. To acquaint the child with musical notation.

b. To give the child a working music vocabulary.

c. To acquaint the child with the mechanics of music reading.

2. Suggested Teaching Procedure—

a. Studying skips

My Hungry Dog

Hear my hun-gry dog-gy beg for food,

I will give him some if he is good.

1. Teach the song by rote.

2. Place on the board this skip:

fa   re   fa   re

3. Have the children sing the skip using words, and "loo."

4. Have the children build this tonal pattern on cardboard staves using black cut-out notes.

Note: **Many text books** have staves in the back of the book. Cut out black notes from construction paper which will fit into the space on the staff. If cardboard staves are to be made, they should be four inches, measuring from the first line to the fifth line. Make the lines heavy. Notes should be cut out which will fit one space of the staff.

5. Children sing this skip by syllables from their books.

6. Have children point out measures that are alike.

7. Sing the entire song with "loo" except for the motive which is sung by syllables.

8. Sing the entire song with words.

b. Doing individual work

1. Individual work, either by one pupil or by several children in a small group should be stressed more and more in the third and succeeding grades. The children are at an age when individual recitation is a natural activity.

2. As the analysis song is being studied, individual work may be done on skips or the scale. Do this through the use of songs, blackboard, staves, and cut-out notes, or the scale ladder.

Draw on the blackboard a scale ladder like the following illustration. Then by using this scale ladder, give exercises employing the following skips and melodic fragments: *do-mi, do-so, do-mi-so, mi-so, fa-re, la-fa, do-la, re-so, re-ti, so-do, re-fa, do-re-mi-re, do-so-la-so, re-mi-do, do-re-mi-fa-so-la-ti-do,* and *do-ti-la-so-fa-mi-re-do.* It may be necessary to review materials from the second grade before proceeding to third grade work.

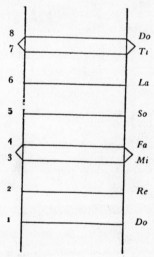

The teacher points to various syllables on the scale ladder and the children sing them.

C. The Reading Song

1. Objectives—

    a. To give an elementary degree of skill in translating music notation into musical conceptions.

    b. To develop independent reading with little or no help from the teacher.

    c. To give the child additional experience in reading the more complicated rhythmic and tonal patterns from the printed page.

2. Suggested Teaching Procedures—

    a. Have the group sing several rote songs from the book in the same key as the reading song.

Signs of Autumn*
Jean Hoover

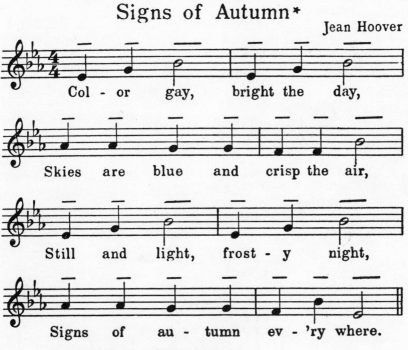

Col - or gay, bright the day,

Skies are blue and crisp the air,

Still and light, frost - y night,

Signs of au - tumn ev - 'ry where.

    b. Have the children locate *do*.

    c. Rhythm may be established in several ways:

        1. Read the words of the song in correct meter, as in

* Beattie, J. W., American Singer Series, Book III. American Book Co., Chicago, 1944.

poetry scansion; establish a feeling for its "swinging" in twos, threes, or fours.

2. Chant the rhythm of the notes.

    a. Above the notes are lines which are visual representations of the duration of tones.

    b. With the aid of these lines, the child is able to chant the rhythm by saying: "walk, walk, walk, bend, walk, walk, walk, bend" for the first phrase, continuing to chant the rhythm of the entire song in this way.

Note: Refer to Chap. IV, pp. 99-100 for the method of stepping time.

    c. When rests occur, say the word "rest."

        1. When stepping the rhythm and rests occur, walk on the notes; then, with the opposite foot off the floor, indicate the rests with movements of the foot.

        2. As an added means of feeling rests, this plan might be followed:

        Clap on one, indicating the rests with a definite sideward motion of the hands on each beat. Thus:

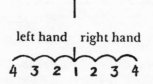

3. Phrase the song. (Refer to previous chapters for additional suggestions for phrasing.)

a. Each time the phrase changes, small groups may walk in a different direction.

b. Use hands in a circular motion while seated at desks, having the hands come down at the end of each phrase.

c. On the song *Signs of Autumn,* the following phrase markings may be drawn by the children either at the board or at their seats:

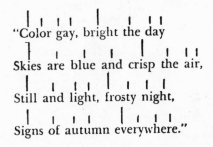

"Color gay, bright the day
Skies are blue and crisp the air,
Still and light, frosty night,
Signs of autumn everywhere."

"Color gay, bright the day

Skies are blue and crisp the air,

Still and light, frosty night,

Signs of autumn everywhere."

d. Sound *do* on the pitch pipe; have the class find and sing the beginning pitch through the tonic triad skips or the diatonic scale.

e. Sing the song by syllables in rhythm.

   1. The teacher should keep the rhythm flowing and not stop the class if an error is made; the teacher may occasionally sing the syllables with the children at the place where there is difficulty.

2. If difficulty in rhythm is encountered, the error should be isolated by writing the rhythmic pattern on the board and chanting, clapping or stepping the pattern.

3. Tonal patterns giving difficulty should be isolated from the printed page and built upon the staff at the back of the children's books.

   a. The teacher sings the tonal pattern to be built. She sings the syllable. for the first note of the pattern. The other notes she sings with "loo."

do   loo   loo

   b. The children should repeat the pattern, singing all the syllables in the pattern. Example:

do   mi   so

   This step is very important, for it not only trains the ear, but the eye as well.

   c. Children build the pattern on the staff.

   d. Their work is then checked by the teacher or a dependable pupil.

   e. Sing the song with the neutral syllable "loo."

   f. Sing the song with words artistically and with expression.

   g. Frequently while reading songs, individual work should be done to point out good work or the necessity for remedial work.

3. Teaching Aids

a. Emphasize smooth singing with no break in the phrase.

b. Establish correct breathing habits through good posture.

c. Emphasize good tone quality with a light, pleasing tone.

d. Work for clear enunciation and interpretation.

4. Additional Suggestions—

a. The lesson plan:

At the beginning there should be several songs sung for *— old songs which they know & like,* enjoyment; the close of the lesson should end happily. At all times the aim should be toward appreciation and enjoyment. The lesson should be of at least twenty minutes duration each day.

The first five minutes should be spent singing interesting rote songs. A ten minute learning period may be devoted to any one of the following activities: *close with rote song*

1. Reading new materials.

2. Teaching new rote or recreational songs.

3. Listening to one another sing, to the phonograph, or to the piano.

4. Participating in rhythm activities.

5. Doing creative work.

Occasionally the five minute pleasure period may consist of individual work so that the child may have an opportunity to express himself.

b. Primary chorus:

As a culmination of much pleasurable classroom work there may be organized a primary chorus consisting of all the children from grades one through three. This affords an opportunity for group activity and for performing songs with recreational appeal.

Having groups of children perform for one another has great value and appeal.

Some songs which might be used in the primary chorus or for recreational or community singing are:

America the Beautiful—American Singer, Bk. III . . . . p. 198

The Rye Waltz—American Singer, Bk. III . . . . p. 186

Old Folks at Home—American Singer, Bk. III . . . . p. 112

Sleep and Rest—New Music Horizons . . . . p. 156

Sweet and Low—New Music Horizons . . . . p. 139

Pop Goes the Weasel—New Music Horizons . . . . p. 108

On Parade—Merry Music . . . . p. 96

I'm a Duck—Merry Music . . . . p. 52

Robin in the Rain—Merry Music . . . . p. 49

The Telephone Call—Rhythms and Rimes . . . . p. 164

Oopsy Daisy Oh!—Rhythms and Rimes . . . . p. 120

Chinese Evening Song—Rhythms and Rimes . . . . p. 90

Our First Songs to Sing With Descant—Krone—Kjos.

Assignments

1. Members of the class should be able to teach several rote songs from all available third grade music books.

2. List the ways in which a rote song may be phrased. Be able to do an example of each.

3. What new tonal patterns should be presented in the third grade?

4. Each member of the class should make a cardboard staff and set of six black cut-out notes.

5. How may individual work be carried on?

6. What is the difference between the song for musical analysis and the reading song?

7. Write the foot motions and be able to step them.

8. How is the problem of rests handled in the reading song?

9. Write the entire procedure for teaching a reading song; be able to teach a song using these various steps.

10. Mention several aids for the teaching of a reading song.

11. Write out a lesson plan for the teaching of a third grade singing lesson.

12. Make a list of songs from the books of the basic series using skips and scales within the same song.

13. Make a list of songs using the motive *fa-re-fa* or *fa-re-fa-re*.

14. How do various authors approach music reading? Write a short paper on this.

15. Observe a third grade singing class.

II. LEARNING THROUGH LISTENING

Music appreciation will continue to be developed through all phases of music education.

A. Objectives

1. To develop the habit of quiet, intelligent listening.

2. To gain genuine appreciation through participating in all music activities.

3. To develop a sense of correlation and integration with other subjects.

B. Some Units for Third Grade Listening

1. To Gain Knowledge of Indian Music

Chant of the Eagle Dance—Hopi ......Victor Album F. 89
Winnebago Love Song
Love With Tears—Cheyenne
Pueblo Lullaby
Omaha Ceremonial
The Sunrise Call—Zuni
Dance Song—Omaha
Shuffling Feet—Sioux

From an Indian Lodge—MacDowell. .Victor Album E-89
Love Song—MacDowell
Shawnee Indian Hunting Dance
    —Skilton
War Dance—Cheyenne
By the Waters of Minnetonka—Lieurance .... V 21972

Note: For a model listening lesson on Indians, see page 127.

2. To Study the Music of Our Country

Patriotic Songs of America .... Victor Album E-91
The Star Spangled Banner—Key-Smith
America the Beautiful—Bates-Ward
America—Smith-Carey
Columbia, the Gem of the Ocean—Becket
Hail Columbia—Hopkinson-Phile
Battle Hymn of the Republic—Howe
Dixie—Emmet

Pledge to the Flag—Malotte .... V 4535

3. To Develop Ability to Interpret the Story of Compositions—

Nutcracker Suite—Tschaikowsky .... in V-DM 1020
Peer Gynt Suite—Grieg .... V-DM 1100
Through the Looking Glass—Taylor .... C-MM 350
Hansel and Gretel—Humperdinck .... Musicraft RR3

4. To Develop Discrimination in Mood—

Air de Ballet—Jadassohn .... in V-E-72
Old Folks at Home—Foster—Richard Crooks.... V 1825
Juba Dance—Dett .... V 21750
Baby's Boat—Gaynor .... V 24534
Lullaby—Mozart .... V 22160

5. To Develop a Knowledge of the Names and Music of Some of the Great Composers—

Beethoven: *Minuet in G* . . . . .V 20164
Bach: *Minuet* . . . . .V 20079
Schubert: *Marche Militaire* . . . . .V 22766
Haydn: *The Toy Symphony* . . . . .V 20215
Brahms: *Waltz, Opus 39* . . . . .V 20079

6. To Increase Powers of Instrument Recognition—

Rusty in Orchestraville . . . . .Capital BC-35
Instruments of the Orchestra . . . . .C-MX 250
Cello: *First Movement of*
  Unfinished Symphony—Schubert . . . . .V-DM 1039
Double Bass: *The Elephant*
  from *Carnival of the Animals*—Saint-Saëns . . V-MO 785
Oboe: *Country Dance* from
  Symphony No. 6 in F Major—Beethoven . . . . .V-DM 417

These records, plus many others, should be played and
studied so that at the end of the third grade the children
recognize the common instruments by sight and sound.

7. To Show How Music May Paint a Picture—

a. *The Hurdy Gurdy Man*—Debussy . . . . .V 21945
b. *The Swan*—Saint-Saëns . . . . .in V-MO 785
c. *Country Gardens*—Grainger . . . . .V 20802

Note: For stories described by music on phonograph records, see Appendix.

An example of a typical listening lesson on Indian music
is given below. This same general plan could be worked
out for a listening lesson of any type.

A Typical Listening Lesson for Grade III

Indian Music

I. AIMS AND OBJECTIVES

A. To give an appreciation of the Indian background through
his contributions to music.

B. To appreciate Indian tribal music and learn how it came to
be written.

II. PROCEDURE

A. Arouse the interest of the children in Indian music by placing about the room many pictures of Indians engaged in a variety of activities.

B. Explain the different types of Indian music to the children.

1. **Music That is Sung—**
   a. Lullabies
   b. Work songs
   c. Spinning songs
   d. Songs for fasting, praying, and for every important act of life

2. **Music That is Played—**
   a. Signals
   b. The call to battle
   c. The love song
   d. Dances and accompaniment to singing
   e. Instruments used are drums, rattles, flutes and whistles

C. Music Activities

1. **Sing Many Indian Songs**
   a. *Indian Lullaby*—Rhythms and Rimes, p. 76.
   b. *Indians*
   c. *Indian Lullaby*—New Music Horizons, Book III, p. 8.
   d. *Sunrise Song*—Our Songs—p. 77.
   e. Hy-Ya-Ho—p. 78.
   f. *Smoking the Peace Pipe*—p. 79.
   g. *Indian Cradle Song*—American Singer, Book III, p. 79

   There are other fine Indian songs, dances, and stories beginning on page 35 in *American Singer*, Book II.

2. **Listen to Records—**
   a. Tell the story of *By the Waters of Minnetonka*—Lieurance—V 21972; play the record.

b. Play these records, plus others listed on page 126 of this chapter.

1. *Winnebago Love Song*................in V-E-89
2. *Pueblo Lullaby* ....in V-E-89
3. *From the Land of the Sky Blue Water*....V 1115

3. Engage in Rhythmic Activities

a. Doing many varieties of Indian dances.

b. Creating Indian dances for "The Eagle Dance" and the "Snake Dance."

c. Carrying out the Indian rhythms as suggested on pages 38, 39, 40, 41 of the *American Singer*, Book II.

d. Each child playing the Indian instrument he has made during the activities period (see below) in time to Indian music with original suggestions for orchestrations.

4. Participate in Creative Experiences—

a. Use a subject such as a hunter, a papoose, an Indian warrior.

b. Write a poem and set it to music, or write the words and music simultaneously.

5. Correlate With Other Subjects—

a. Read stories from:
   Wigwam Stories—M. C. Judd.
   How the Indians Lived—Dearborn
   Indian stories from any other source.

b. Matching, filling blanks, and multiple choice seatwork tests can be used following each topic of study, such as people, homes, food, customs, etc.

c. Nature study
   Make collections of nuts, twigs, bark, acorns, etc.

d. Art and crafts

   1. Making necklaces by stringing and painting macaroni.
   2. Making Indian head gear with feathers.
   3. Weaving baskets.
   4. Making papoose dolls.
   5. Carving miniature totem poles.

6. Making a frieze or mural depicting different phases of Indian life.

7. Making illustrations of language stories.

8. Making instruments such as drums, rattles, whistles, etc. For directions see Chapter III.

9. Constructing a tepee.

D. Books

1. **Books for the Teacher—**
   Burch. *A Child's Book of Famous Composers.* Barnes Pub. Co., New York.

   Coleman, Satis N. *The Drum Book.* John Day Publishing Company.

   Faukner, Anne. *What We Hear in Music.* Victor Co., Camden.

2. **For the Third Grade Reading Shelf—**
   Fun with Flutes. University of Chicago Press, Chicago, Ill.

   Jerry and Janet on the Farm from Growing Up with Music. Kjos Publishing Co.

   Come, Let Us Make a Garden. Ibid.

   Songs of Travel and Transportation. Ibid.

   Kinscella Readers, "*The Man and the Drum*". University Publishing Co., Lincoln, Neb.

Assignments

1. Write out plans for a third grade listening lesson.

2. Present your listening lesson to the class.

3. What radio programs of interest to third grade children are available?

4. Continue to add materials to your scrapbook.

5. The class may attend a rehearsal or a program of a band or an orchestra.

III. RHYTHM RESPONSES

Emphasis should still be on large, bodily movements in response to rhythmic activities.

A. Objectives

1. To continue to develop the ability to perform all of the fundamental rhythms accurately.
2. To develop a strong feeling for phrase and accent.
3. To grow in ability to create simple dance forms.

B. Procedure

In the newer series of books are found numerous singing games and folk dances for children of this age. In most cases directions are given; those which do not have directions can, with pupil-teacher planning, easily be worked out into attractive little dances.

In all activities, free play and spontaneity of action should be emphasized.

1. Rhythmic Activities (folk dances)—

World of Music Series, Ginn and Company
> Use the book *Rhythmic Activities*—Annis and Matthews.
> Follow suggestions as given on pages 29-42.

New Music Horizons, Book III. Silver Burdett.

Voulez-vous Danser? .... p. 107
Pop! Goes the Weasel .... p. 108
Merry Merry May Day .... p. 110

Merry Music. C. C. Birchard Co.
> In the Section entitled *Moving to Music* from pages 83-92 are found attractive action songs.

American Singer, Book III. American Book Company.

Heel and Toe .... p. 44
Waltz Song .... p. 56
Shoo Fly .... p. 64
Way Down in Paw-Paw Patch .... p. 66
Rye Waltz .... p. 136
Broom Dance .... p. 162

Some folk dances suitable for third grade
> *Peas Porridge Hot*

Carrousel
Jolly Is the Miller
Indian Dances
Hansel and Gretel Dance
Ten Little Indians

2. **Jumping Rope and Bouncing Ball—**
3. **Conducting—**

Have the children conduct with a small baton or ruler following the plan for 3/4, 4/4, and 2/4, directing as outlined in Chapter II.

4. **Marching in the Band—**
5. **Dramatizations—**

Encourage creative rhythmic responses whenever possible. When a listening lesson has been presented, it is well to follow it with rhythmic dramatizations. Consult Chapter III, page 86 for suggestions for equipment and books.

Assignments

1. Teach a folk dance suitable for the third grade.
2. Mention several listening lessons which could be followed by creative dramatizations.
3. Members of the class should perform the folk dances listed and should be able to sing the accompanying songs.

IV. CREATIVE ACTIVITIES

Each child possesses some creativity. He should be given many opportunities to express himself either through song writing, through creative dancing, or through making instruments.

A. Objectives

1. To give the children the opportunity to develop their musical imagination through creative activities such as writing songs and operettas, construction of instruments, folk dances, and rhythmic responses.
2. To increase the musicianship of the children through the notating of their melodies.

B. Procedures

1. **Create a Song**   (refer to Chapter III, pages 90 and 91). The child should be encouraged to sing about his experiences.

   a. Have the children read the poem (either an original one or one already written) in unison to get the full meaning and rhythm of the words.

   b. The tonic chord may be played on the piano to give the children a feeling for tonality and "home tone."

   Note: A record on bugle calls may be used to develop the feeling of the tonic triad.

   c. Have as many children as possible make up a melody for the first phrase.

   d. Allow the class to decide which melody they wish to use.

   e. With the pupils participating as much as possible, write the first phrase.

   f. Phrase, clap, and tap to discover what the meter signature is.

   g. Sing the first phrase again, then let the children make up a melody for the second phrase and select the best one.

   h. Continue in the same way until the entire song has been written.

   i. Make a copy of the song for future reference.

   j. Encourage the children to illustrate the song by drawing pictures of it.

   k. Whenever possible, encourage working for more than one phrase at a time.   It may not be possible to get the entire song, but perhaps two or three phrases will come at one time.

2. **Create New Words to a Known Tune.**

3. **Create an Operetta.**

   a. Decide on an appropriate text.

   b. Ask for many suggestions for story possibilities.

c. Copy down all of the ideas that come.

d. Have the class decide which ideas they wish to use; weave these into a story.

e. Adapt parts of the story into poetry.

f. Set the poetry to music following suggestions given in previous chapters.

g. Urge the children to be on the alert for dramatization or action possibilities; allow them to create dances.

h. Design simple stage sets and costuming.

i. In presenting the operetta, rotate parts so that many children will have the opportunity to play the "leads."

Assignments

1. Individual class members should write an original song.

2. The entire class should collaborate in writing a song.

3. Each member of the class should write an original operetta (words and music) about your town, county, or state.

(Those who do not have sufficient background may use songs from the basic series or other sources.)

V. PLAYING INSTRUMENTS

A. Objectives

1. To give the child his first experience with melodic instruments.

2. To create enthusiam for playing band and orchestra instruments.

3. To aid the child in learning to read music.

4. To provide a happy group activity.

B. Suggestions

1. Use melody instruments such as tonettes, flutophones, song flutes, harmonicas, etc.

2. There will be found listed in the Music Educators Journal names of many reliable music dealers from whom instruments and instruction books may be purchased.

C. Teaching Procedures

1. The Tonette and Harmonica

a. Select all of the instruments in the same key.

b. Have each child use only his own instrument.

c. Use the correct names of notes and theory terms.

d. Stress the value of reading music when playing the tonette and harmonica.

e. Use the same procedure as in singing: syllables, clapping the meter, etc.

Note: Plans for teaching the tonette will not be further developed since instruction books give thorough directions.

2. Class Piano

a. Each child should have his own books and keyboard.

b. As one child plays the selection at the piano, another child stands by awaiting his turn while the other children play the piece on their keyboards. Selections in good singing range may be sung with words or syllables.

c. Give each child his turn at the piano.

d. Some children will progress more rapidly than other members of the class. Use them as assistants.

e. Sing and play.

f. As individual differences are observed, divide the class into several groups to permit the better students to progress more rapidly.

g. The following books are recommended for class piano:

Note: Plans for teaching class piano will not be further developed since instruction books give thorough directions.

Blake, Dorothy Gaynor. *Keyboard Secrets,* Willis Music Co., Cincinnati, Ohio.

Daniels and Leavitt. *World of Music Piano Course,* Ginn and Co., Chicago, Ill.

Gilman, *Picture Tunes,* Singing Approach to Piano, Paul A. Schmitt Music Co., Minneapolis, Minn.

Oxford, *Course of Piano Instruction,* Carl Fischer, Inc., New York.

John Thompson's *Modern Graded Course*, Boston Music
Co., Boston, Mass.

Williams and Turner, *Singing and Playing*, Boston
Music Co., Boston, Mass.

Burrows and Ahearn, *Young America at the Piano*, C. C.
Birchard and Co., Boston, Mass.

Assignments

1. Learn to play several melody instruments well enough so you
can teach children to play on them.

2. Make and tune a xylophone using the following directions.

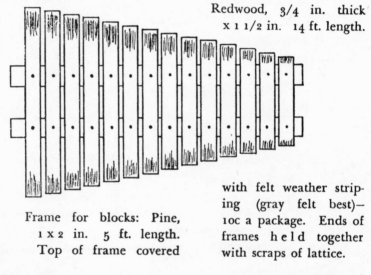

Redwood, 3/4 in. thick
x 1 1/2 in. 14 ft. length.

Frame for blocks: Pine,
1 x 2 in. 5 ft. length.
Top of frame covered

with felt weather strip-
ing (gray felt best)—
10c a package. Ends of
frames held together
with scraps of lattice.

a. Cut the first bar 17 in. long. Gradually decrease the size so the
smallest one will be approximately 9 in.

b. Tune to the piano in the key of C. To tune, cut very gradually with the coping saw. Sanding the ends is usually sufficient to slightly alter the tone.

c. Bore holes in bars as illustrated.

d. Use a 1¾ finishing nail to hold bars in place.

e. The bars are nailed (not too tightly) to the frame.

f. The mallets may be obtained from any music supply house or they may be made from dowel-rod for handles with Fuller balls for strikers.

Tools

Coping saw   Sandpaper

Hammer   Plane

Brace (drill)

Constructing instruments (refer to Chapter III, pages 67-68). If instruments other than the simpler ones are to be constructed consult the Coleman book *Creative Music for Children* and *Guide to the American Singer, Book III,* and *Cancioncitas,* by McLaughlin & Stanchfield—Paul A. Schmitt Music Co.

Following the suggestions for creative music in the basic texts, this list of books may be of assistance:

Merry Music. C. C. Birchard Company. Refer to page 114. For verses which might be set to music, see pages 13, 38, 42, 45, 48, 72, 105, 109, 153.

American Singer, Book III. American Book Company. See pages 26, 61, 94, 148, 188.

New Music Horizons, Book III. See pages 12, 68, 29, 52, 71.

BIBLIOGRAPHY

Beattie, J. W., et al, *Guide to American Singer, Book III,* American Book Co., Chicago, 1944.

Gerhkens, Karl, *Music in Grade Schools,* C. C. Birchard Co., Boston, 1938.

Hubbard, George E. *Music Teaching in the Elementary Grades.* American Book Co., Chicago, 1934.

Chapter VI

MUSIC IN THE FOURTH GRADE

Introduction

All of the experiences from the third grade will be enlarged upon and further developed.

In order to continue the child's musical development, the daily music period should be for no less than twenty-five minutes.

I. GENERAL TEACHING PROCEDURES

A. The Rote Song

There should still be much rote singing for pleasure and recreation. For methods of teaching the rote song with books in the hands of the children, consult Chapter IV. Occasionally the teacher will wish to teach rote songs without books. For teaching plans, consult Chapter III.

B. The Reading Song

For methods of teaching the unison reading song, consult Chapter IV. Whenever possible, attempt to sing the song at sight with words.

Continue doing much individual work by:

1. Building tonal patterns on cardboard staves and singing them with syllables.

2. Reading phrases or entire songs with syllables and words.

3. Continuing to help those whose tones are faulty.

C. New Rhythmic and Tonal Problems to be Studied in the Fourth Grade.

1. The dotted quarter note followed by the eighth note.

   a. Have the class sing *America,* observing that the words " 'tis of thee" are uneven.

   b. As the class claps the rhythm they observe that the word "of" is sung quickly just before "thee."

   c. Explain that the *dot* after the note increases the value of the note by one-half the original value.

[handwritten marginalia: Longer notes dotted. How we got it? ↓ erase ½ note turning into a dot. D. It effects any note]

138

d. Show how to count the new rhythmic pattern.

1   2   &   3

e. Let them scan the words of other songs containing the new rhythmic problem.

Note: For other plans of teaching rhythm consult previous chapters.

f. Teach a reading song containing the dotted quarter note followed by the eighth note. Example:

A Merry Song

1. Scan the words of the song to secure correct rhythm.
2. Teach each phrase with words, "loo" and syllables.
3. Have them read the entire song with syllables.
4. If difficulties in rhythm still exist, have them scan the words of the song.

5. Let them sing the song again with syllables.

6. Now let them sing the song with "loo" and then words.

2. Teaching Songs Having Chromatically Altered Tones.

a. The ascending chromatic scale.

Note: It will be assumed that the teacher knows the chromatic scale. Refer to Chapter I, p. 12.

1. Teach several rote songs containing chromatically altered tones; call attention to the tones that are altered.

2. Have the class sing the C Major scale with syllables while watching the piano keyboard or the cardboard keyboard. They will observe that the scale uses only the white notes on the piano.

3. Explain that from one key to the next is a half step. A whole step will be two half steps. Have the class discover and name the whole and half steps on keyboards.

4. They will discover that the *major scale* is made up of the following steps: 1 1 ½ 1 1 1 ½;

5. Play and sing the chromatic scale:

Note: Piano fingering for the right hand is as follows:

do,	di,	re,	ri,	mi,	fa,	fi,	so,	si,	la,	li,	ti,	do
1	3	1	3	1	2	3	1	3	1	3	4	5
do,	ti,	te,	la,	le,	so,	se,	fa,	mi,	me,	re,	ra,	do
5	4	3	1	3	1	3	2	1	3	1	3	1

6. Place on the blackboard the motive containing the chromatically altered tone:

so   fi   so

7. Have the class sing the motive.

8. Compare *so-fa-so* and *so-fi-so.*

9. Let the children read a new song having a sharp chromatic. Example:

Dandelions*

Wilson

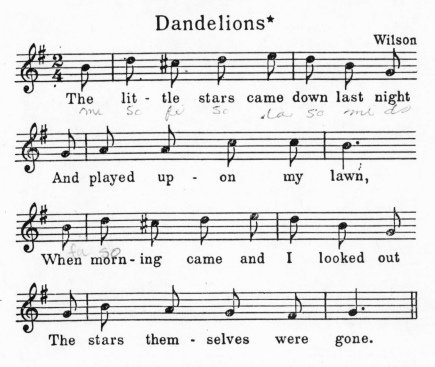

The lit - tle stars came down last night

And played up - on my lawn,

When morn - ing came and I looked out

The stars them - selves were gone.

a. Let the children assist with writing the chromatic scale, starting on *G* on the blackboard; write the syllable names under the notes. Example:

do di re ri mi fa fi so si la li ti do

b. From the above scale, let them find the syllable name for the chromatically altered note (*fi*) in the song.

c. Teacher sings new tonal pattern (*so fi so*); then children sing the same tonal pattern.

* Beattie, John W., et al. American Singer, Book IV. American Book Company, Chicago, 1945. p. 170.

   d. Now let them sing the entire song with syllables; teacher gives help only when necessary. If difficulties in rhythm occur, scan the words.
   e. Sing the song with "loo."
   f. Sing the song with words.
10. Songs from other basic texts having chromatically altered tones are as follows: (Ascending scale)

   Armitage, Theresa et al. We Sing, *Little Owl* (*ri*)
   Beattie, J. W. et al. *American Singer* (*fi*)
   McConathy, Osbourne et al. *New Music Horizons*
   Book IV... (*fi*)
   Glenn, Mabelle et al. Songs of Many Lands,
   Spring Messengers .... (*fi*)
 b. The descending chromatic scale.
      1. Select a song having a chromatically altered tone—descending scale. Example:

Sliding

Slid   ing   down   the   hill

On   my   nice   new   sled_____

Some - times   I   do   slide

Till   it's   time   for   bed._____

      2. Place the chromatic scale—descending—on the

blackboard, starting on C; add syllables under the notes.

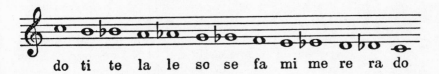

do ti te la le so se fa mi me re ra do

3. If the song to be read is in a key other than C, have the children build the descending chromatic scale in that key on the blackboard.

4. In the song above, the children will discover that *la* is lowered a half step and becomes *le*.

5. The teacher now sings with syllables the phrases containing the altered tones and the children imitate.

6. Now let the children sing the entire song with syllables in correct time. If difficulties in rhythm occur, let them scan the words.

7. Have them sing the song with *"loo,"* and then words.

c. Songs from other basic texts for teaching the descending chromatic scale:

Armitage, Theresa et al. *We Sing.* C. C. Birchard and Co., 1940.

Glenn, Mabelle et al. Songs of Many Lands, *Just Suppose.* Ginn and Co., Boston: 1943.

3. **Teaching the Minor Mode**

a. Have the children sing several rote songs in the minor mode to establish the mood of minor songs.

b. Have them discuss the difference between the moods of major and minor songs, as for example:

Major	Minor
Joy	Loneliness
Restfulness	Darkness
Brightness	Mystery
Peace	Tenderness

c. Teacher sings minor or major scale with "loo." The class repeats with *so-fa* syllables naming the scale (major or minor).

d. After the teacher has given the pupils certain characteristics of the minor mode (for example: songs that begin on *mi* or *la* usually end on *la*) the pupils should be able to determine by observation before singing a song whether or not it is a minor song.

e. To introduce the normal *minor* scale,

   1. Use the following song:

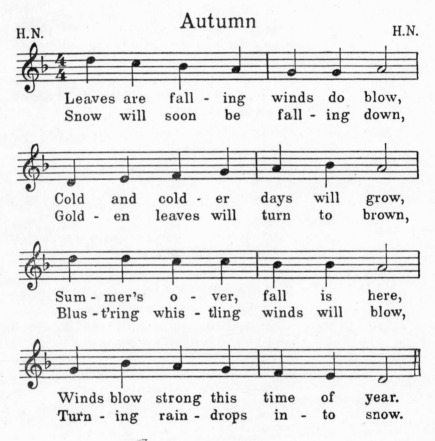

Autumn

2. Notice that this song begins and ends on *la*.

3. Write on the blackboard the F major scale; have the class sing this scale with syllables.

4. Erase *ti* and *do* at the top of the scale, then add notes for *la* and *ti* at the beginning of the scale. The minor scale will look as follows:

Key of *d* minor (normal minor)

la   ti   do   re   mi   fa   so   la

5. After giving the pitch for *do* (F), have the class sing down to *la*.

6. Then starting on *la*, have them sing the normal minor scale with syllables.

7. Explain that songs written in the minor scale usually begin and end on *la*.

8. The rhythm for the song may be studied by chanting the words in correct meter, stepping the notes while reading the words, or by clapping each note while counting the beats.

9. After the children have found the starting tone, let them sing the song in correct rhythm with syllables.

10. Now, let them sing it with "*loo,*" then words. If difficulties are encountered, work on individual phrases or assist by singing with the children.

4. **Two-part Singing**

Two part singing should not be attempted unless the group sings one-part well. One-part reading must precede two part music reading.

a. Preparation for two-part reading.

1. Children will enjoy singing rounds in two parts. The room should be divided so some leaders are on each side. The following rounds are suitable:
Row Your Boat—American Singer, Book IV.
May Bells—American Singer, Book IV.
To Market—American Singer, Book IV.

Lovely Evening—We Sing.
Alleluia—We Sing.
Clocks—We Sing.
The Night Sky—New Music Horizons, Book IV.
Fruit—New Music Horizons, Book IV.
The Hillside—Songs of Many Lands.
The Ball of the Seasons—Songs of Many Lands.

2. Descants may be used as an approach to part singing.
   The following descants are suitable:
   All Through the Night—American Singer, Book IV.
   Wise Ben Franklin—American Singer, Book IV.
   Silent Night—American Singer, Book IV.
   Echo—New Music Horizons, Book IV.
   Brothers Row—We Sing.
   Fair is the Summer—We Sing.
   Tunes With Descants—We Sing.
   Our First Songs to Sing with Descants, by The
        Krones, Beatrice and Max. Kjos Pub. Co.,
        Chicago, 1941.

Singing in thirds

3. Half of the class may sing the scale up and down
   with syllables; the other half will begin when the
   first side has reached *mi*.

4. Two-part exercises may be written on the blackboard
   for the children to sing.

b. Teaching procedures for two-part reading song.

   1. If possible, select a song that has equal note values
      for both upper and lower part, as in *Village Talk*,
      from Songs of Many Lands.

   2. Have one side of the room sing the upper part—
      the other side, the lower part. Change parts in
      different songs, not on the same song.

   3. Refer to the parts as upper and lower rather than
      soprano and alto.

   4. Sound *do* and let each group find its beginning tone.

   5. Sing both parts at the same time with syllables. If
      and when difficulty is encountered, the parts may be
      sung separately.

Partner songs important also!

6. If rhythmic difficulties arise, chant the words, step the notes while reading the words, or clap the notes while counting the beats.

7. Sing the song with "loo."

8. Sing the song with words with good enunciation and interpretation.

D. Results Expected of the Singing Program

Each fourth grade child should know approximately fifty songs from memory. He should be able to sing in tune with good quality of tone, proper phrasing, correct pronunciation, and clear articulation.

Assignments

1. Using all of the available fourth grade song books, list two songs from each of the following divisions: (a) The dotted quarter followed by the eighth note, (b) The chromatically altered tones, (c) Songs in normal minor, (d) Two-part songs.

2. Choose one song from each of the above divisions and be able to teach them.

3. Divide the class into "duets." Have each two people learn a number of two-part songs outside of school.

II. THE LISTENING PROGRAM

In music teaching the first concern is not only with the music, but with its influence on the child. It is with this in mind that the correlation of music with other curriculum subjects becomes important; for, if music is to play an important part in the life of the child, it should be woven into the various activities of the child's daily experience. Music can contribute to different subjects in the school.

Example: Pioneer Music

A. Aims and Objectives

1. To develop an understanding of and an appreciation for the music that afforded so much enjoyment and relaxation for our early settlers.

2. To give each child a deep insight into pioneer life through singing, dancing, playing, listening, and creating.

3. To correlate all of these music activities with other subjects in the curriculum.

B. Procedure

1. Interest the pupils in frontier and pioneer music by telling a short story about it:

   "When our great grandparents went to a corn husking, the party would always end with dancing and singing to the tunes of *The Arkansas Traveler, Captain Jinks,* or some other rollicking tune. Their fun was a real trouble chaser in the hard life of the early settlers. Many of these songs were folk tunes made by hundreds of untrained singers and fiddlers while young America was growing up to more scholarly music. Over and over this fun music, even today, takes its place in the music literature of America."[1]

2. Prepare the class for listening to *The Arkansas Traveler* by showing the picture of *The Arkansas Traveler* by Edward Washburn, and telling the story.

3. Activities

   a. Have the class sing the song, *The Arkansas Traveler,* and listen to the phonograph record V 20638.

   b. Play Victor Record 21751 A and B to enjoy the following frontier songs:

Away for Rio	*Sweet Kitty Clover*
Blow the Man Down	*Bendemeer's Stream*
Sourwood Mountain	*Frog Went a Courtin'*
Billy Boy	*Spanish Guitar*
Begone Dull Care	

   c. Play Victor Record No. 22991 of the *Quadrille* and *Virginia Reel,* No. 20447

   d. Sing some of the following songs:

   A Frog Went a Courtin'—American Singer, Book IV. p. 12.

   Shake That Little Foot—American Singer, Book IV. p. 14.

   Old Brass Wagon—American Singer, Book IV. p. 66.

   Oh! Susanna—We Sing. p. 5.

   She'll Be Comin' 'Round the Mountain—We Sing. p. 162.

---

[1] Buchanan, Fannie R. Stories of American Music. Follet Publishing Company, New York, 1937.

Paw-paw Patch—New Music Horizons, Book IV. p. 2.

Polly Wolly Doodle—New Music Horizons, Book IV.
p. 8.

e. Creative activities

1. Original poems written in language class about
   pioneers might be set to music.
2. Write an operetta. Several pioneer songs might be
   written which could be woven into an operetta.

3. Correlation with other subjects
   a. Physical education
      1. Learn the dances for:
         Old Brass Wagon—American Singer, Book
         IV. p. 66.
         The Caller's Song—American Singer, Book
         IV. p. 67.
         Virginia Reel—Rhythms and Dances—La
         Salle. p. 88.
         Captain Jinks—Rhythms and Dances—La
         Salle—p. 49. Plus songs and dances from
         the other basic texts.
      2. Pioneer games (many of these are the same
         that our children play today).

         Hide and Seek
         Drop the Handkerchief
         London Bridge

   b. Reading
      1. Stories of pioneers from all available readers.
      2. Stories of outstanding pioneers: Abraham
         Lincoln, Daniel Boone, Kit Carson.
      3. Study of pioneers: *Singing Wheels* is an
         excellent text.
      4. Locate settings for stories; trace routes of the
         pony express, and routes taken by early settlers
         going west.

c. Language

1. Original stories about pioneers—homes, food, work, schools, fun, etc.
2. Original poems.
3. Stories of soap making, dipped and molded candles, etc.
4. Book reviews about pioneers.
5. Dramatizations of stories of pioneer activities.

d. Spelling: Learning to spell words peculiar to frontier life.

e. Art

1. Making a pioneer frieze or mural.
2. Constructing Conestoga covered wagons.

Note: Conestoga wagons were constructed in Conestoga, Penn.

3. Clay molding of oxen, pioneer tools, etc.
4. Soap carving of pioneer furniture, animals, buildings, etc.

Note: The outcomes will be: greater enjoyment of pioneer and frontier music, and greater appreciation of pioneer people through an integrated study of their music.

5. Other topics that might be developed into units of study.

a. Great musicians and their compositions
Bach—*Air for G String*.........V 7103
Beethoven—*Minuet in G*....C 71411-D
Brahms—*Hungarian Dance No. 5*.V 4321
Grieg—*Peer Gynt Suite*......V-DM 1100
Haydn—*Toy Symphony*.........V 20215
Schubert—*Ave Maria*........V-DM 1020

b. Voice classification
Soprano: Helen Traubel, *Oh! Hall of Song* from *Tannhauser*—Wagner.V 17268
Contralto: Marian Anderson, *Dere's No Hiding Place*...................V 2032
Tenor: James Melton, *I'll Take You Home Again Kathleen*—
Westendorf ....V 18219

Baritone: Lawrence Tibbett, *Toreador Song* from Carmen ....V 8124

Bass: Paul Robeson, *Ol' Man River* from *Show Boat* ....V 25376

c. Dance forms

Minuet: *Minuet*—Gluck ....V 20440

Gavotte: *Amaryllis*—Ghys..........V 20169

Gavotte—Handel ....in V-E-74

Mazurka: *La Czarine*—Ganne......V 20430

Polka: *Thunder and Lighting* —Strauss ....V 4319

Waltz: *Blue Danube Waltz*—Strauss..V 15425

Skater's Waltz—Waldteufel ......V 21938

d. Design in music (ABA Binary) — (ABC Ternary).

1. As a background for listening to design in music, sing such songs as:

Drink to Me Only With Thine Eyes—Binary.
Silent Night—Ternary.
Dixie—Binary.
Lullaby—Brahms—Binary.

Note: The Binary form is composed of two distinct sections, usually of 8 measures each. The first part, phrase A, is repeated and followed by phrase B which is an entirely different melody.

Example: *Drink to Me Only With Thine Eyes*

A. Drink to me only with thine eyes
And I will pledge with mine.

A. Or leave a kiss within the cup and
I'll not ask for wine.

B. The thirst that from the soul doth rise
Doth ask a drink divine

A. But might I of Jove's nectar sip,
I would not change for thine.

The ternary form consists of three distinct sections.

Example: *Silent Night*

A. Silent Night! Holy Night!
   All is calm, All is bright,
B. Round yon virgin mother and Child!
   Holy Infant so tender and mild,
C. Sleep in Heavenly Peace!
   Sleep in Heavenly Peace!

2. Play the following records
   Minuet—Mozart ....V 20440
   Farandole from L'Arlesienne Suite—Bizet......CX-69
   Dance of the Mirlitons from Nutcracker Suite—
      Tschaikowsky V-DM-1020
   Minuet in G—Beethoven.................C 71411-D

e. Theme recognition (how many times does the theme appear
   in selection?)
   Andante from Surprise Symphony (No. 94)—
      Haydn ....V-DM 1155
   Amaryllis—Ghys ....V 20169
   Country Gardens—Grainger ....V 20802
   Spinning Song—Mendelssohn ....V 20195

f. Contrasting moods in music
   William Tell Overture—Rossini ....V-DM 605
   March of the Caucasian Chief—Ippolitov-Ivanov..V 1335
   The Wild Horseman—Schumann ....V 20153

g. Music in the minor mode
   Pathos: *Ase's Death* from Peer Gynt Suite—
      Grieg ....V-DM 1100
   Happy minor: *Moment Musical*—Schubert ......V-M 684
   Rhythmic minor: *Hungarian Dance No. 5*—Brahms.V 4321

h. Instrumental recognition
   String family
      Unfinished Symphony (No. 8)—Schubert...VDM 1039
      Fifth Symphony—Beethoven ....V-DM 640
   Woodwind family
      Morning from Peer Gynt Suite—Grieg....V-DM 1100

Brass family

Magic Fire Music—Wagner ....V 15800

Don Quixote—Strauss ....V-DM 720

Percussion family

Nutcracker Suite—Tschaikowsky ....V-DM 1020

Semper Fidelis—Sousa ....V 18-0053

Instruments not members of a family

Harp: *The Swan*—Saint-Saëns.................C 418

Organ: *Arioso*—Bach ....V 11-8236

Piano: *Polonaise in A Flat Major*—Chopin. .V 11-9065

Assignments

1. Find two songs each in binary and ternary forms, indicating each section by the proper letter name.

2. Be able to describe each of the following dance forms: minuet, gavotte, mazurka, polka, and waltz.

3. Continue collecting scrapbook materials.

III. RHYTHMIC ACTIVITIES

In the primary grades, rhythmic experiences consisted of fundamental forms of locomotion (walking, running, skipping, sliding, jumping, hopping, etc.) and much free play and dramatization. In the fourth grade these experiences become directly related to skills utilized in music reading: meter, phrasing, keeping time, and to the development of more complex folk dances.

A. Folk Dances

In the newer music text books are found folk dance materials with the directions carefully given. Any of the following are excellent:

The Weggis Dance— (Swiss). We Sing. p. 102.

Jibi-De, Jibi-Da— (French). We Sing. p. 104.

Cshebogar— (Hungarian). We Sing. p. 106.

Varsovienne— (Unknown). We Sing. p. 108.

A Nick and a Nock— (Swedish). American Singer, Book IV. p. 46.

Old Brass Wagon— (American). American Singer, Book IV. p. 66.

Caller's Song— (American). American Singer, Book IV,   p: 67.

Oh! Susanna— (American).   American Singer, Book IV.   p. 68.

Folk Dance— (Czech).   New Music Horizons, Book IV.   p. 16.

Waltzing— (American).   New Music Horizons, Book IV.   p. 16.

Polka— (French).   New Music Horizons, Book IV.   p. 97.

Wooden Shoe Waltz— (Dutch) New Music Horizons, Book IV. p. 166.

The Sailor— (English).   Rhythmic Activities for Songs of Many Lands.   p. 44.

Harvest Dance— (Polish).   New Music Horizons, p. 47.

Laughing Lisa— (French Canadian).   New Music Horizons. p. 49.

Turkey in the Straw— (American).   New Music Horizons. p. 51.

B. **Singing Games**
There is a tendency to use fewer singing games at this grade level, but whenever they occur in the books, the group may be divided in half, having one group sing while the other group does the action.

C. **Dalcroze Eurythmics**   (Chapter IV, page 111), presents a further development of this activity.

Assignments

1. Learn the fourth grade dances mentioned in any available fourth grade book.   Teach these dances to other members of the class.

2. Be able to step out the rhythm found in fourth grade song books. (Especially emphasize the dotted quarter followed by the eighth note.)

IV. CREATIVE ACTIVITIES

For a child to have gained the satisfaction which results from having created or helped to create, is to him a beautiful and infinitely worthwhile experience.

All of the creative experiences begun in primary grades should be carried on and further developed at this level.   The children should now be given the opportunity to notate their melodies.   They should know they are creating through interpretation—by having them determine the way in which a song should be sung; adding original stanzas to familiar songs; setting an original or a familiar poem to music; re-creating a lovely song and devising original dance patterns to instrumental music.

When a class has sufficient interest, it will be entirely possible for fourth grade children to write an operetta. In an integrated program, a very fine original operetta may be planned, written and performed as a culmination of their study of pioneers.

This would include, besides the actual melody writing, planning the staging, making up dances, fashioning costumes, etc.

To stimulate creativity, the authors of our basic texts included materials as follows:

New Music Horizons, Book IV.

a. Adding original stanzas 35, 115
b. Creative rhythmic activities 16, 86, 87
c. Creative instrumentation 79, 164
d. Inventing songs 116, 71, 117
American Singer, Book IV.
    Pages 59, 71, 109, 111, 123
We Sing
    Pages 121, 122

For a method of creating original songs, refer to Chapter V, page 133.

The following original two-part round was written by a group of fourth grade children:

The Bluebird
(A Two-part Round)

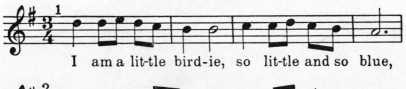

I am a lit-tle bird-ie, so lit-tle and so blue,

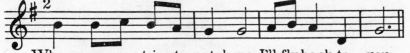

When some one tries to catch me, I'll fly back to you.

Assignment

1. As a class activity, write a two-part song.

2. As a class activity, write a one-part song with descant.

BIBLIOGRAPHY

Buchanan, Fannie R. *Stories of American Music.* Follett Publishing Company, New York, 1937.

Gehrkens, Karl. *Music in the Grade School.* C. C. Birchard Company, Boston, 1938.

Jones-Barnard. *Introduction to Musical Knowledge.* Schmitt Music Co., Minneapolis, 1935.

Music Education in the Elementary School. California State Department of Education, 1939.

Chapter VII

MUSIC IN THE FIFTH GRADE

In the fifth grade, the teacher should aim to continue the development of beautiful singing. It is recommended that simple unison songs be sung with words at sight for enjoyment and recreation, with two-part singing being continually developed. There should be increased coordination of eye, ear, and voice, and greater familiarity with chromatic progressions and new minor tonalities. At least twenty-five minutes per day should be devoted to music.

I. SINGING

When the problems of the fourth grade have been mastered, the following may be presented:

Intervals with emphasis on the skip approach—*do, so, ti, la, so, ti, la,* etc., and also chromatic intervals.

The dotted eighth note followed by the sixteenth.

6/8 meter with two beats to the measure.

Harmonic minor scale.

More difficult two-part music.

A. Teaching Procedures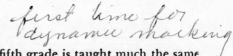
   1. The Rote Song

   first time for dynamic marking

   a. The rote song in the fifth grade is taught much the same as in the fourth grade, with emphasis placed upon interpretation of the dynamic markings.

   b. Those songs appropriate for seasons, holidays, historical and geographical subjects.

   c. A plan for teaching the rote song:
      1. The children sing the song with the teacher the first time, except when it is difficult. In this case, the teacher sings the song for the children.
      2. After the class and the teacher discuss such things as the rise and fall of melody and dynamic markings, the teacher sings it again.
      3. The next time through, the children sing with the teacher.
      4. The class tries singing the song alone.
      5. If difficulties arise, the teacher isolates the problem

by singing the difficult phrase or motive for the children.

6. The class then sings the phrase or motive alone.

7. They sing the entire song, paying attention to expression marks and interpretation.

d. The importance of securing good tone.

1. The teacher should sing artistically, with good tone quality because children will imitate her tone and manner of singing.

2. Do not allow the children to sing too loudly, as their voices are apt to break.

2. The Harmonic Minor

a. Approach the teaching of the harmonic minor through the singing of rote songs. Call attention to the mood of the songs.

b. Place the song to be studied on the blackboard.

Clouds

Oh where   do   the   white clouds go,

When   they   go   sail - ing   by,

And   will   they   come   back   a - gain,

Float - ing   'cross   the   sky.

c. Have the students place the scale of F major on the blackboard. Have them sing it with syllables.

d. Have the children change the scale to the relative normal minor. Let them sing it with syllables.

e. Explain that the harmonic minor is the same as the normal minor except that the seventh tone is raised one-half step. The syllable *so* now becomes *si*.

f. Play it on the piano; now let them sing it with syllables.

g. Let the pupils discover the syllable name for the chromatically altered tone in the song. Teach them the phrase containing the chromatically altered tone by rote; syllables, "loo" and words.

h. Now let them sing the entire song by syllables, "loo" and words. Interpret the song through the dynamic markings.

3. New Problems in Rhythm

a. Before a new rhythmic problem is to be taught, several rote songs should be learned in which the problem occurs. Call attention to, and if necessary, explain the rhythmic pattern.

b. Place-the phrase containing the new problem to be taught on the blackboard.

c. Scan the words to secure the proper rhythmic feeling.

d. Teach the phrase by rote with syllables, "loo" and words.

e. Read the song from the book with syllables; if difficulties arise, isolate the problem with the teacher giving assistance.

f. The following rhythmic figures are taught in the fifth grade:
  1. Dotted eighth followed by a sixteenth. Examples of this problem may be found in the following books from the basic series:
  Robin Hood and Little John—Blending
    Voices .... p. 152
  Daniel Boone—Our Land of Song .... p. 94
  The Stars—American Singer, Book V ...... p. 191

2. Sixteenth note followed by a dotted eighth.

3. Compound Time (6/8).

Note: Attention should be called to the fact that the principal accents in
6/8 time fall on one and four. The children should feel, also, that
as the tempo is increased, the measure will receive two beats instead
of six. Reading or scanning the words will help the children feel
the rhythm.

4. **Teaching Chromatics**
As new chromatic problems appear, follow the suggestions
for teaching as given in the previous chapter.

5. **The Study of Theory**
a. If the instrumental program is begun in the fifth grade,
the children may learn the letter names of the lines and
spaces if they have not previously learned them. The
following plan may be used:

1. Write the letter names of the lines on the staff—
e, g, b, d, f. Now write in the letter names for the
spaces—*f, a, c, e.*

2. Have the children write notes on the staff as they
are named by the teacher.

3. Using a familiar song from the book, have the children name the notes as they appear in the melody.

b. Teaching the major scale may be done as follows:

1. Starting on C, have the children sing the scale with
letters; now let them play the scale on their piano
keyboards as they sing the scale with the letter names.

Note: Teach them the correct fingering—
right hand—1 (thumb) 2, 3, 1, 2, 3, 4, 5.

2. Show them that between e and f, and b and c there
are no black keys; therefore these steps are half steps.

When there is a black key between two white ones, the distance is a whole step.

3. Let them discover how many whole steps and half steps there are in the major scale. They will find the following steps—1 1 1/2 1 1 1 1/2.

4. Now let them start on G and play the major scale. They will discover that the seventh tone has to be raised one-half step to make the proper arrangement of steps in the scale. They will learn the purpose of the black keys on the piano since they will need to play F♯ in order to play the scale correctly.

5. Have them write the scales of C and G, and write the syllables under the notes.

6. Let them play the scale starting on F. They will discover the fourth tone too high. Explain that to lower a tone one-half step, the next key down, either black or white, must be played. They will then discover B♭. Have the children write the scale in the key of F placing a flat in front of the note B.

6. The Reading Song

The unison reading song is taught the same as in the previous chapter. The same is true of teaching the two-part song. It is not advisable to teach two-part music reading at all in this grade unless the children can read one-part fluently. Rote singing should have an important part in the singing program.

Assignments

1. Observe a fifth grade music class, noticing especially the class enthusiasm and participation.

2. Have several members of the class practice in teaching rote songs to the other members of the class.

3. Make a list of seasonal songs, songs for holidays, historical and geographical songs, and songs about great characters in history that are appropriate for the permanent repertory of the fifth grade children.

4. Teach songs in the harmonic minor to other members of the class, discussing strong and weak points.

5. Make a list of several songs in the harmonic minor, from the basic series.

6. Make a list of several songs from the basic series that contain new rhythmic problems.

7. Teach the class the problems of rhythm.

II. LISTENING EXPERIENCES

Every music lesson should be a listening lesson. Realizing that children have a real urge for expressing themselves musically, each lesson presented should satisfy that desire.

Children at this level are now becoming more intelligent listeners. They are recognizing phrasing and phrase design, simple song forms, music of the masters, and music that tells a story. Their abilities to recognize solo instruments and families of the orchestra have been increased. They are becoming acquainted with typical voice qualities, and are gaining the ability to follow two or more voices as they sing in harmony.

There should be possibilities for correlation with other subject areas, including music of the Negro, music of occupational groups in our country, music of various regions in our country, and music suggesting historical episodes in world development. In addition, there should be correlation with poetry, drama, science, painting, and the dance.

The following typical listening lesson on Negro music may serve as a model for other types of lessons:

A. Negro Music in America
  1. Aims and Objectives
    a. To give an understanding of the Negro in his contributions to music.
    b. To create a feeling of friendliness between the black and white races.
    c. To appreciate many negro spirituals and know how they came to be written.
  2. Procedure
    a. Arouse the interest of the pupil in negro music by showing pictures of the Negro engaged in a variety of activities.
    b. Explain different types of negro music, such as:
      1. Work songs of the Negroes of the deep south.

2. Spirituals.

    a. Negroes of the South were deeply religious as
    illustrated by the following songs:

    Nobody Knows the Trouble I've Seen
    Deep River
    Were You There

    b. Negroes who spent many years on the same
    plantation were usually happy and sang songs
    like:

    Good News
    Every Time I Feel the Spirit
    Climbin' Up the Mountain

Many negroes have a great deal of musical talent, with
an accurate sense of melody and rhythm. It has often
been difficult to put down on paper true negro music,
because of the curious melodic and rhythmic patterns
of his songs.

The negro works better if he sings at his labor; in fact,
employers often hired song leaders to speed up and cheer
up the work. For instance, when they were picking
cotton, they sang constantly as they went down the rows.
Groups would sing one song together, or each would
sing a stanza alone as fancy suggested. One of the favor-
ites was this: one of the fastest groups in the cotton
patch had for its leader an old man. He seemed so
engrossed with his singing that he never seemed to tire.
He would sing the first stanza of this song:

    "Wouldn't drive so hard, but I needs de arns,
    Wouldn't drive so hard, but I needs de arns

As he sang, the others added their contributions with
the following composite result:

    Snatchin' and crammin' it in my sack,
    Gotta have cotton if it breaks my back
    Wouldn't drive so hard, but I needs de arns
    Wouldn't drive so hard, but I needs de arns."[1]

The true negro "shout" took place on Sunday nights or
on praise nights. When the regular meeting was over,
the benches were pushed back and young and old alike

[1]Gellert, Lawrence. Negro Songs of Protest. American Music League, 1936.

began first to walk and shuffle around, one after another in a ring. Songs were sung, hands were clapped, feet shuffled and all was very energetic. It was said that these shouts could be heard a half mile from the praise-house.

3. Activities

a. Sing many negro spirituals and songs of Stephen Foster, such as:

Old Folks at Home—Songs of Stephen Foster. p. 43.

Carry Me Back to Old Virginny—America Sings. p. 22.

Swing Low Sweet Chariot—America Sings. p. 119.

The Camptown Races—Songs of Stephen Foster. p. 88.

Ring, Ring de Banjo—Songs of Stephen Foster. p. 35.

Nelly Bly—American Singer, Book V. p. 55.

The Glendy Burk—American Singer, Book V. p. 53.

Steal Away—New Music Horizons, Book V. p. 90.

¡Where O Where Is Old Elijah?—Our Land of Song. p. 20.

Climbing Up Zion's Hill—Our Land of Song. p. 120

b. Play the following records:

Were You There? . . . . V 1966

Every Time I Feel the Spirit . . . . V 2032

Swing Low Sweet Chariot . . . . V 2168

Steal Away . . . . V 2211

Deep River . . . . V 2032

c. Study the lives of famous negro music personalities, such as:

James Bland
Marian Anderson
Paul Robeson
Dorothy Maynor
Katherine Dunham
Nathaniel Dett

Roland Hayes
Ella Belle Davis

d. Creative activities

1. Set original poems written in language class to music.

2. Write an operetta following suggestions found in previous chapters.

e. Rhythmic experiences

1. Free rhythms on negro songs about picking cotton and pushing barges using such songs as *Camptown Races* and *Ring, Ring de Banjo* for accompaniment.

2. Clapping and shuffling to rhythms of songs such as *Oh! Susanna* and *Climbin' Up the Mountain*.

f. Correlation with other subjects

1. Physical education: Learning negro dances—the jig, and simple tap dances. Consult *Physical Education in Elementary Grades*, Nielson, Van Hagen.

2. Reading

   a. Stories of lives of negroes from all available readers and library books.

   b. Stories of outstanding negroes: George Washington Carver, Booker T. Washington, James Weldon Johnson, Jesse Owens, Dr. Charles Drew, Brigadier General Benjamin O. Davis and others.

3. Social studies

   a. Use the study of the negro in connection with the study of the Southern states and in historical period of early colonization. Consult *The Growth of the American People and Nation* by Kelty.

   b. Locate on the map the settings of negro stories.

4. Language

   a. Original stories about negroes; their homes, work and play.

   b. Original poems, plays, radio scripts, and round table discussions.

5. Art

   a. Make a mural or a frieze on a phase of negro life.

   b. Draw pictures of negro activities.

   c. Make puppets; use them in an original puppet show.

4. Outcomes

   a. Greater enjoyment of negro music.

   b. Greater appreciation of negroes through an integrated study of their music.

B. Other Listening Lessons

1. Dance Forms

Minuet: *Minuet*—Boccherini.................... V 7256

Gavotte: *Gavotte* from Mignon—Thomas......... V 1361

   Gavotte from Manon—Massenet........... V 11-8259

Mazurka: *Mazurka in C♯ Minor*—Chopin........ V 1327

Polka: *Polka and Fugue* from Schwanda—

   Weinberger .... V 12-0019

   The Bartered Bride—Smetana................ V 8694

Ballet: *Dance of the Hours* from La Gioconda

   Ponchielli .... V 11833

   The Swan Lake—Tschaikowsky.......... V-DM 1028

Waltz: *Estudiantina Waltz*—Waldteufel.......... V 35798

   Invitation to the Dance—Weber............. V 15192

2. Marches

Coronation March from The Prophet—

   Meyerbeer .... V 7104

War March of the Priests from Athalia—

   Mendelssohn .... V 7104

Funeral March—Beethoven.................... V 24795

Wedding March from Midsummer Night's

   Dream—Mendelssohn .... V 20036

3. **Overtures**
   William Tell—Rossini.....................V-DM 605
   Egmont Overture—Beethoven..................V 7291
   Die Meistersinger Overture—Wagner...........VDM-731
   Tannhauser Overture—Wagner................VDM-530

4. **Orchestral Instruments**
   In the fifth grade the various families or choirs of the orchestra are combined to make the symphony orchestra. Emphasis should still be given to each of the four families before studying the full orchestra.

   Bring out the fact that the band is an out-growth of the orchestra, and that it is used for concerts, for parades and for coronations and inaugurations.

   Play the following records to emphasize instrumental combinations and orchestral effects:

   The Music Box—Liadow (Woodwinds)...........V 19923
   Morning from Peer Gynt Suite—Grieg (flute,
      oboe, piano).............................V 19926
   Adagio and Rondo—Mozart.................V 11-9570
   Andante and Rondo from Concerto for
      Trumpet—Haydn ....C 70106D
   Pizzicato Polka—Strauss (Strings pizzicato)
   Intermezzo from Cavalleria Rusticana—Mascagni
      (all instruments) .... V 4303
   El Capitan—Sousa (Band)................... V 35805

5. **Voice Classification** (review materials from previous chapter).

   Soprano: *Jewel Song* from Faust—Gounod
      sung by Eleanor Steber.................V 11-9838
      One Fine Day from Madame Butterfly
      sung by Bidu Sayo......................V 71320
   Contralto: *My Native Land* from Aida—Verdi
      sung by Rose Bampton....................V-8994
      Virgin's Slumber Song—Reger
      sung by Kirsten Thorberg.................V 2133
   Tenor: *Hear De Lambs A'Cryin'*—Spiritual
      sung by Roland Hayes....................C 69812
      Little Karen—Danish Folk Song
      sung by Lauritz Melchior................C-MX 233

Baritone: *Water Boy*—Robinson
sung by Norman Cordon................V 10-1114
Home on the Range—Cowboy song
sung by John Charles Thomas...............V 1525
Bass: *Temple Scene* from Aida—Verdi
sung by Ezio Pinza.....................V 9111
Waltzing Matilda—Cowan
sung by Peter Dawson...................V 10-1025

6. **Mood**
Sadness: *Ase's Death* from Peer Gynt Suite—
Grieg .... V-DM 1100
Calmness: *To a Water Lily*—MacDowell ...... C 4279M
Humor: *Golliwog's Cake Walk*—Debussy........inV-E-78
Imagery: *Marionettes*—Glazounoff .... V 20914
Religion: *Deep River*—Burleigh................V 2032

7. **Descriptive or Program Music**
Reflections on the Water—Debussy.............V 6633
Papillon—Grieg .... V 18153
Pavanne for a Dead Princess—Ravel..........V-E-81
Ride of the Valkyries from The Valkyrie—
Wagner .... C 11987D
Flight of the Bumblebee—Rimsky-Korsakov......V 7193
Firebird Suite—Stravinsky....................V-DM 933

8. **Music of America**
Pledge to the Flag—Malotte..................V 4535
Patriotic Songs.............................V-E-91
Juba Dance—Dett............................V 21750
On the Trail from Grand Canyon Suite—
Grofe .... C 7390M
Old Folks at Home—Foster...................V 22083

Assignments

1. Continue to add materials to scrapbooks.

2. Work out a listening lesson keeping in mind correlative and integrative possibilities.

3. Have each member of the class present a listening lesson to other members of the class.

Note: Combine the singing of many American songs with the playing of recordings of various American songs and pieces.

III. RHYTHMIC ACTIVITIES

At this level, rhythm responses have become more accurate and meaningful; muscular coordination is good and all of the concepts developed in the lower grades can now be utilized in the various dance forms suggested in the music text books.

Listed below are the activities recommended for fifth grade children:

Shoot the Buffalo (American) American Singer, Book V. p. 63.

Swing on the Corner (American) American Singer, Book V. p. 64.

Weevily Wheat (American) American Singer, Book V. p. 67.

Old Dan Tucker (American) American Singer, Book V. p. 68.

Rhythmic Activities for Blending Voices—pp. 55-70 in the book Rhythmic Activities—Annis, Mathews.

Morris Dance (English) Our Land of Song. p. 53.

Rigadoon (English) Our Land of Song. p. 37.

Sweetheart Out A-Hunting (American) Our Land of Song. p. 126.

Four in a Boat (American) Our Land of Song. p. 128.

The Wishing Well—Waltz. (Czech). New Music Horizons, Book V. p. 88.

Old Zip Coon (American) New Music Horizons, Book V. p. 128.

Ballad of Cousin Mike — Schottische. New Music Horizons, Book V. p. 109.

Start the Music — Polka. (Czech). New Music Horizons, Book V. p. 147.

It is very necessary to motivate physical expression within the range of natural interests of the fifth grade boys and girls. The games and dances must be suitable for their development level so that their performance will be one of spontaneous enjoyment.

The following rhythmic activities should be carried out in the fifth grade. Of those listed, folk dances are the most widely used.

1. Fundamental forms of locomotion as a basis for folk dancing.
2. Dance steps to be used in folk dances and singing games: march. waltz, polka, gavotte, mazurka, schottische.
3. Dramatizations of songs.
4. Creative dances.

Assignments

1. List songs from the basic series which have possibilities for dramatizations.

2. Make up a dance using fundamental rhythms as the basis for the dance.

3. Learn several singing games on the fifth grade level, having half the class sing while the remainder of the class does the actions.

IV. CREATIVE ACTIVITIES

At the fifth grade level, it is possible for the children to do some fine creative work. Because of a wealth of past experiences in all phases of music education, each child will have an adequate background for the various creative activities.

It is well for the teacher to keep in mind that the approach to practically all of the music activities should be in a creative spirit. This should include creative interpretation, creative rhythmic activities, adding original stanzas, and creative listening.

An important fact for the teacher to keep in mind when the class is engaged in any creative activity is that she must not make too many suggestions lest the children become discouraged and feel that the work is not their own, but that of the teacher.

The development of the children through creative music is a serious but most joyous undertaking.

    A. Song Writing

        1. The poem to be set to music should contain these characteristics:

            a. It should be thoroughly familiar and well liked by the children.

            b. It should be simple but rhythmical.

        2. Methods of setting poetry to music have been dealt with rather completely in previous chapters. The following additional suggestions should give a clear picture and make writing an activity to be entered into with a feeling of confidence by the teacher:

            a. The poem having either been written or chosen by the class is written on the blackboard under the staff.

b. Discuss the story and the meaning of the words, suggesting that the tune match the words.

c. Scan the poem; clap it; step it.

d. Establish the tonality by singing or playing the tonic chord on E, E♭, or D.

e. Call for volunteers for a melody for the first phrase.

f. If there are second or third melodies offered for any line, put them on the board also, and allow the children to vote on their choice.

g. Sing or play the first phrase several times until the second phrase comes.

h. Do this with each phrase until the song is completed.

i. Have the children notate as much as possible, deciding upon the meter and key signatures.

j. Occasionally write a second part (alto) or a descant to the melody.

k. Keep the worthwhile original songs in a notebook.

l. Have the class write an operetta, following previous suggestions.

B. **Other Creative Activities**

1. **Rhythms and Dances.** When a song suggests actions, make up a simple dance or rhythmic action.

2. **Instrumental Music.** Encourage writing melodies for the piano or some other instrument. Small groups of children might compose duets, trios, or quartets.

3. **Instrument Construction.** Instruments such as xylophones, psaltries, pitchforks, 'cellos, and cigar box violins may be made and bottles filled with water at different levels might be experimented with to attain pleasing effects.

4. **Dramatizations and Pantomimes:** the various song books offer many possibilities for this activity. This is a splendid way of developing a high degree of enthusiasm for music.

Assignment

1. As a class activity make up a two-part song, words and music.

2. As a class activity, write a descant to a familiar melody.

3. Have each member of the class write a simple operetta or pageant.

Chapter VIII

MUSIC IN THE SIXTH GRADE

The ideal to be kept ever in mind in the sixth grade is that the pupils should know many beautiful songs, and should learn them quickly and accurately.

The following aims should be carefully considered and carried out:

1. To continue the development of the voice through the singing of many fine songs.

2. To develop three-part singing.

3. To further acquaint the children with songs using chromatic scales and minor tonalities.

4. To develop the ability to sing well at sight, unison, and two-part songs with words, and an elementary degree of skill to sing three-part songs at sight.

5. To develop an increasing coördination of eye, ear and voice.

6. To continue to develop the ability to create and notate songs.

7. To develop acquaintance with, and an appreciation of the opera and oratorio, and to continue the study of instruments and instrumental combinations.

8. To continue studying the theory of music.

9. To develop the skill to master the various problems (rhythmic and otherwise) common to this grade.

I. GENERAL TEACHING PROCEDURES

A. The Rote Song

1. **The Importance of Rote Singing**

   There should continue to be a great deal of rote singing for recreation and enjoyment. For suggestions for teaching the rote song, consult previous chapters.

2. **The Art Song**

   a. The art song is taught as a rote song.

b. The accompaniment, which is a part of the art song, should always be used when singing the song.

c. The composers of art songs are known, while the composers of folk songs are usually unknown.

d. Types of art songs

   1. Those written in folk-song style. Examples:
     Who Is Sylvia—Schubert
     Calm as the Night—Bohm

   2. The art-ballad song tells a story. Examples:
     The Erl-King—Schubert
     The Two Grenadiers—Schumann
     (These songs are to be listened to, not sung by sixth grade children.)

   3. The art song, where the accompaniment follows the mood of the words throughout the song, without repetition of the melody. Examples:
     The Lotus Flower—Schumann (for listening)
     Dedication—Franz (for singing)

e. Books containing art songs
   Keep on Singing, Clarke
   Art Songs for School and Studio, Volume I, Glen
   The Art Music Reader, Volumes I, II, Ripley and Schneider
   55 Art Songs, Spaeth-Thompson

B. The Reading Song

1. The Unison Reading Song

The unison reading song is taught in the same way as has been outlined previously. Whenever possible, sing the song first by words. If difficulties arise use syllables. Then, when singing by words again, observe the dynamic markings.

2. The Two-part Song

The two-part reading song is taught in the same way as was outlined for fourth grade. Again, sing the song with words if possible, omitting syllable singing. Emphasize artistic interpretation.

3. Three-part Singing

a. Testing voices

1. Test voices frequently so that changing voices may be discovered and placed in the proper section.

2. Listen for quality as well as range.

   a. Have the pupils sing the octaves by syllables, as in the following test:

   b. A girl's soprano voice will be thin and transparent; a boy's soprano voice has a brilliant quality.

   c. Alternate the parts of songs unless the voices have definitely changed; parts should not be alternated on the same song, but each time a new song is learned, change parts.

   d. If a child has a wide range, but has a voice of a heavy quality, he should be placed on lower parts.

b. Seating arrangements for three-part singing

   1. Place the second sopranos in the middle of the room so that they can sing either soprano or alto when two-part songs are being sung.

Alto	Soprano II	Soprano I

   (The dotted line indicates how the group may be divided for two-part singing.)

   2. If there are six rows in the room, the following plan is especially good for doing trio work:

Sop I	Sop II	Alto	Sop I	Sop II	Alto

   3. A similar plan may be followed using this arrangement:

Alto	Sop II	Sop I	Alto	Sop II	Sop I

(A heterogeneous plan of seating, as discussed in previous chapters, might well be followed when doing three-part work, the advantage being that it removes any feeling of ability consciousness.)

c. Suggestions

   1. Establish good two-part singing before three-part work is begun.

   2. The chorale type of singing with simple rhythmic patterns and common chord progressions is best for beginning three-part music.

d. Teaching procedure

   1. Simple rounds may be sung in three parts.

   2. Choose an easy three-part reading song, such as *Winter* by Wolverton, in Book IV of American Singer or *Papaya Tree,* a Filipino folk song in Tunes and Harmonies.

   3. Scan the words of the song in correct meter.

Note: At this level, rhythm has been so well established that except in difficult songs where there are numerous rhythmic problems, it may no longer be necessary to step out the rhythm. Occasionally it will be helpful to isolate the rhythm problem and work on it, as explained in previous chapters.

   4. After sounding *do* on the pitch pipe, have each section sing its beginning note while listening to the other parts.

   5. Sing the song by syllables.

     a. Have the class endeavor to sing the entire song without stopping, even if an error is made.

     b. The teacher, or teacher and class may conduct, as a means of establishing rhythm while the class sings.

     c. The teacher may occasionally sing the syllables with the children when there is difficulty.

     d. Try to keep all three parts moving simultaneously, but help individual parts if difficulties arise.

     e. Whenever possible, have the children read the words by sight, omitting the syllables.

6. Sing the song with "loo."
7. Sing the song with words.

e. Additional suggestions:
   1. Chord work, using the progressions as found below, may be given:

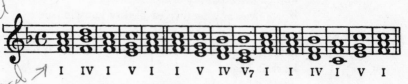

I IV I V I I V IV V₇ I I IV I V I

(handwritten: Introduction for 3 part chords suggested →)

a. Be sure each chord is being sung correctly before proceeding to the next chord.
b. Name the chords which the class is to sing: such as, "one," "four," "five."
c. Give the words for a well known song such as *Swanee River* and place the chord symbols directly under the proper word syllables.

2. When a song is learned, the teacher may conduct it, observing dynamic markings.

4. **New Rhythm Problems in Songs**

a. <u>The triplet</u>

1. Teach the triplet through the study of a rote song containing that figure.
Examples:
Holy, Holy—New Music Horizons, Book VI, p. 199.
The Terek—American Singer, Book VI, p. 135.
In the Alps—Tunes and Harmonies. p. 102.
Meander in Mexico—Music Everywhere. p. 68.
2. Scan the words of the song to get the feeling of three notes on one beat.
3. Teach reading songs containing this problem, following the procedure found in Chapter V.

(handwritten: 3 like notes getting the count of two notes. Use of the notes.)

b. Sixteenth note combinations

1. Teach this combination using a rote song.

Examples:

The Cuckoo—New Music Horizons, Book VI. p. 170.
The Cat and the Catboat—Music Everywhere. p. 52.
Smiling Spring—American Singer, Book VI.
Swing Low Sweet Chariot—Tunes and Harmonies p. 186.

2. Scan the words of the song to get the feeling of four notes to a beat.

3. Teach reading songs containing this figure following the procedure found in the previous chapter.

c. Syncopation

1. Have the class sing several rote songs containing syncopation.

2. Discuss and explain syncopation. (Refer to Chapter I on theory, for the explanation of syncopation.)
Reveille—American Singer, Book VI. p. 20.
If I Could Fly—Music Everywhere. p. 204.
Go Down Moses—Tunes and Harmonies. p. 181.
All 'Round the Mountain—New Music Horizons, Book VI, p. 206.

3. Scan the words rhythmically.

4. Drill the class on the syncopated figure until they can sing it by words, "loo," and syllables.

5. Teach a reading song containing syncopation following the plan in Chapter VII, page 159.

5. The Melodic Minor Mode

a. There are many beautiful songs written in the melodic minor mode. The following, from the basic series for the sixth grade should be learned as rote songs.
Sea Mist—Music Everywhere. p. 59.
Down to the Sea—Tunes and Harmonies. p. 163.
The Shepherd Boy—American Singer, Book VI, p. 51.

b. An example of a song written in the *melodic* minor mode is as follows:

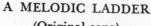
A MELODIC LADDER
(Original song)

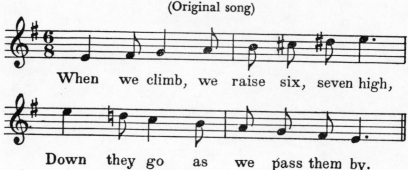

When   we climb,   we   raise   six,   seven high,

Down   they go   as   we   pass them by.

c. From the song above, place the phrase containing the raised sixth and seventh tones on the blackboard.

d. Now place the normal minor scale in the same key on the blackboard.

e. Have the class sing the normal minor scale with syllables, giving them the pitch for *do,* and having them sing down to *la* before singing the scale.

f. Change the scale to the harmonic minor; have the class sing it with syllables.

g. Raise the sixth tone also; after the class has found the correct syllable name for the tone, have them sing the scale with syllables, imitating the teacher or piano.

h. Have the children write the three types of minor scale syllables in this way:

Note: There are songs written that have the raised sixth and seventh in the descending scale. There is a trend in some schools to call this the melodic minor while the scale that uses the normal minor in the descending scale is called the mixed minor. The above terminology is acceptable if the teacher wishes to use it.

Note: Explain to the class that the lower tetrachords for the three kinds of minor are the same; the upper tetrachords differ; sing each upper tetrachord and make comparisons.

Normal	Harmonic	Melodic
la	la	la la
so	si	si so
fa	fa	fi fa
mi	mi	mi mi
re	re	re re
do	do	do do
ti	ti	ti ti
la	la	la la

i. It will now be necessary to teach them that the descending scale for the melodic minor is the normal minor. Have them sing the ascending and descending scales for the melodic minor.

j. When a new song in the melodic minor is to be read by the children, place the phrase containing the altered notes on the blackboard. Have them sing it with words, "loo" and syllables.

k. Let them read the song in correct meter. Work out difficult sections as suggested in previous chapters.

6. Basic Fundamentals

In continuing the study of music fundamentals, a number of basic facts should be established. (Refer to Chapter I.)

a. Basic essentials are to be taught as they occur in the songs.

1. Rule for finding *do*.

2. Major key signatures are as follows (teach only those keys found in songs): C, G, D, A, E, B, F♯, C♯, F, B♭, E♭, A♭, D♭, G♭, C♭.

3. Minor key signatures are as follows (teach only those keys found in songs): a, e, b, f♯, c♯, g♯, d♯, a♯, d, g, c, f, b♭, e♭, a♭.

4. Meter signatures.

a. The upper number indicates the number of beats in one measure; the lower number indicates the kind of a note that receives one beat.

b. The common meter signatures are: 4/4 (C) ¢, 3/4, 6/8, 2/4.

        c. Other meter signatures should be taught as they occur in songs: 3/8, 6/8, 9/8, 12/8, 2/2, 4/2, 6/4.

  b. Modulation

    Modulation is taught through the analysis of rote and reading songs. As the following songs are sung, the class will discover the melodic progression from one key to another. It will be observed that at the end, the songs return to their original key.

      1. New Music Horizons, Book VI.
         Holy, Holy—p. 199.
         Charlie Is My Darling—p. 183.

      2. The American Singer, Book VI.
         On Wings of Song—p. 58.
         Come Ye Thankful People—p. 92.

      3. Tunes and Harmonies.
         When Twilight Gathers—p. 50.
         The Pioneers—p. 166.

      4. Music Everywhere
         Now Thank We All Our God—p. 176.
         Frog Went A-Courting"—p. 107.

C. The Intermediate Grades Chorus

    There are many advantages in organizing a chorus including children from grades four, five, and six. If a child manifests an interest in this type of activity, he should be encouraged to join the chorus. By singing with such a group he will learn to:

    1. Sing under direction, following the baton of the leader.

    2. Sing with piano accompaniment.

    3. Sing more difficult music than is possible to master in a regular music class.

    4. Develop good singing habits. It will give him an elementary knowledge of correct breathing and phrasing, good enunciation, and the correct use of his singing voice.

    This activity is carried on outside of the regular music period. There may be one forty minute or two thirty minute periods per week devoted to chorus practice.

Such a group as this can lead in assembly sings, present programs for the school, and in cases where there are several elementary grade buildings in a town, the choruses from each building may culminate the year's activities by presenting a song festival.

Materials may be chosen from many sources. The regular music text books contain many songs suitable for a chorus.

In the following supplementary books will be found excellent materials:

> *Festival Program Book.* S.S.A. Kjos Publishing Company, Chicago, Illinois.
>
> *Great Songs of Faith.* Krones. S.S.A. Kjos Publishing Company, Chicago, Illinois.
>
> *A Cappella, A Collection of Songs.* S.S.A. Wick Publishing Company, Minneapolis, Minnesota.
>
> *Choral Program Series I, II.* Wilson. Silver, Burdett Publishing Company, Chicago, Illinois.
>
> *From Descants to Trios,* Krones. Kjos Publishing Company, Chicago, Illinois.

Assignments

1. Make a list of ten songs from the basic series containing one or more of the following problems: normal, harmonic, and melodic minors, syncopation, the triplet figure, and sixteenth note combinations.

2. Be able to teach songs containing the above problems, to members of the class.

3. List ten each of typical folk songs, art-songs, and ballads.

II. THE LISTENING PROGRAM

Listening experiences should not be isolated to a single period of the day, or confined to a certain day in each week, but should rather be a part of many school activities.

Sixth grade children are mature enough to study the opera, the

Note: In the Appendix will be found information about the folk music of the several countries studied in the sixth grade.

oratorio, and the art song, and to listen to instrumental and vocal
ensembles. They will become familiar with additional composers and
the music they have written.

Careful consideration should be given to correlation of music with
other subject matter areas.

A. **Folk Music and Nationalism.** Play the records and sing songs
typical of that country, do appropriate folk dances, and make
a mural depicting life in that country.

1. **Great Britain**
   Drink to Me Only With Thine Eyes .... V 10-1218
   Pomp and Circumstance .... V 6648
   Irish Washerwoman .... V 22131
   Comin' Through the Rye .... V 2055

2. **Scandinavia**
   Norwegian Dance—Grieg .... V 22171
   Swedish Wedding March—Soderman .... V 20805
   Peer Gynt Suite—Grieg .... V-DM 1100
   Finlandia—Sibelius .... V 7412
   Piano Concerto in A Minor—Grieg .... V-DM 900

3. **Russia**
   Symphony No. 5 in E Minor—Tschaikowsky .. V-DM 1857
   Song of the Volga Boatman .... C 4276
   Prelude in C♯ Minor—Rachmaninoff .... V 11922
   The Firebird Suite—Stravinsky .... V-DM 933
   Symphony No. 1—Shostakovitch .... V-DM 192

4. **Spain**
   Habanera from Carmen—Bizet .... V 14419
   Toreador's Song from Carmen—Bizet .... V 8124

5. **Germany**
   Air for G String—Bach .... V 7103
   Piano Concerto No. 5 (Emperor)—Beethoven V-DM 989
   Hallelujah Chorus from The Messiah—Handel .. V 11825
   Ave Maria—Schubert .... V 11-9836
   Festival March from Tannhauser—Wagner ...... V 7386

6. **America**
   Rhapsody in Blue—Gershwin .... C-MX 251

Sixth Grade Chorus, Austin, Minn., Elementary Schools.

Boys' Quartet from 7th and 8th Grades, Austin, Minn.

On the Trail from The Grand Canyon Suite—
Grofe .... C 7390M
Juba Dance—Dett............................V 21750
Through the Looking Glass—Taylor.........C-MM 350
Ol' Man River from The Showboat—Kern......V 25376

B. The Opera (in telling the stories of operas, the teacher should relate only those portions that will be interesting and suitable to sixth grade children).

Die Meistersinger—Wagner
Prize Song.....................................V 7105
Act III....................................VDM-538
Madame Butterfly—Puccini
One Fine Day..................................V 6790
Acts I and II..............................VDM-700
Aida—Verdi
Heavenly Aida..............................V 7770
Temple Scene...............................V 8111
The Mikado—Gilbert and Sullivan
Little Maids from School....................V 36148
A Wandering Minstrel........................V 36148
H.M.S. Pinafore—Gilbert and Sullivan
Gems from Pinafore.........................V-P 120
Pinafore (complete)........................VDC-13

C. The Oratorio
The Messiah—Handel
Behold the Lamb of God......................V 11824
Pastoral Symphony...........................V 7316
He Shall Feed His Flock.....................V 18324
Hallelujah Chorus...........................V 11825
Elijah—Mendelssohn
O Rest in the Lord..........................V 18325
If With All Your Hearts.....................V 12609
The Creation—Haydn
The Heavens Are Telling.....................V 11960
Achieved Is the Glorious Work...............V 11960
Christmas Oratorio—Bach
Shepherd's Christmas Music..... ....V 7142

D. Instrumental Study

Andante Cantabile, (string quartet)................V 66$_3$4

Intermezzo from Midsummer Night's Dream—
   (woodwind trio).............................V 4312

Instrumental combinations: violin, 'cello, harp,
   oboe, flute, piano, piccolo, bassoon, piano........V 19926

Sonata for Flute, Harp and Viola, No. 2—Debussy..V-DM 873

E. Vocal Ensembles

A Mighty Fortress is our God—Luther
   Hymns of all Churches album..............V-P 162

A Cappella Choir
   Beautiful Savior—Christiansen...................V 15644

Accompanied ensemble
   Sextette from *Lucia di Lammermoor*
   Donizetti—(soprano, contralto, tenor,
   baritone, bass)...........................V 10000

Act I—*Madame Butterfly*—Puccini (soprano, mezzo-
   soprano, tenor, baritone, bass)............V-DM 700

Assignments

1. Continue to collect scrapbook materials of artists, performers, composers, etc.
2. Have the class listen to the Metropolitan Opera broadcasts and give reports on the operas.
3. Have each member of the class choose the music of one country for a listening lesson project. Teach the lesson to other members of the class and explain how it may be correlated with the other subjects in the curriculum.
4. Attend band and orchestra concerts and give your impressions to the class.
5. To become more familiar with opera and oratorio, listen to excerpts from those that are well-known.
6. Make a brief study of the origin of the opera and the oratorio.

III. RHYTHM RESPONSES

Having had many rich and happy experiences in the various rhythmic activities in previous grades, sixth grade boys and girls should now have excellent muscular coördination. They have responded to a variety of rhythms with large bodily movements, having thus built up a splendid background for the folk dancing in which they will now be participating.

The basic music texts have carefully considered the rhythm program as related to singing. Many songs have dance directions given for them. It would be a worth while activity, on those songs which do not have written directions but which would lend themselves to a dance, to have the class create an appropriate dance routine.

The following list of folk dances will be of help in planning rhythmic activities:

New Music Horizons, Book VI
> *The Irish Washerwoman*—p. 44.
> *Captain Jinks*—p. 88.
> *Weevily Wheat*—p. 125.

Music Everywhere
> *Lead Through That Sugar and Tea*—p. 105.
> *Old Brass Wagon*—p. 105.
> *The Waltz of the Broom*—p. 142.

The American Singer, Book VI
> *Thunderdrums*—p. 102.
> *Come to the Land*—p. 126.
> *Ring the Banjo*—p. 44.

Tunes and Harmonies

Refer to *Rhythmic Activities for the World of Music*, pp. 71-86 for suggestions of folk dances relating to materials in Tunes and Harmonies.

The following dances may be done in the sixth grade (refer to *Rhythms and Dances for the Elementary School*—LaSalle, for directions):

The Kerry Dance

Tinker's Dance

Sicilian Circle

Virginia Reel

Polka

Schottische

Waltz

Assignments

1. Learn the folk dances typical of the sixth grade. Be able to teach any one of them to the other members of the class.
2. Find songs from the basic textbooks which will lend themselves to dance routines. Make up several dances and present them to other members of the class.

IV. CREATIVE ACTIVITIES

The approach to practically all music activities should be in the creative spirit. These activities will afford self-expression and the development of the individual initiative of the pupils.

These creative activities have been given thorough consideration in previous chapters. It is suggested that ways and means of engaging in the following creative experiences be read in the foregoing chapters.

A. Creating a Melody

Two and three-part songs, rounds, and songs with descants should be written by children on this level. For procedures refer to previous chapters.

It should be remembered that the attributes of a good melody are these:

1. The entire phrase, rather than separate notes, should be thought of when writing a melody.
2. There should be variety in the rhythmic pattern.
3. The melody should rise and fall.
4. There should be a marked feeling for tonality or home tone.

If these various qualifications are brought to the attention of the children, their creative efforts may be more satisfactory.

B. Creative Interpretation

As children grow in experience, they gain greater powers to interpret songs artistically.

C. Creative Rhythmic Activities

This has been rather carefully considered in previous chapters. Reference may be made to the possibilities for carrying out creative rhythms.

The following three-part song with descant, the words and music of which are original, was written by a sixth grade

and performed by an elementary chorus for a Christmas pro
gram.

Christmas Song

1. A long time a-go   On glad Christ-mas Day
2. The an - gels came And sang of their King!

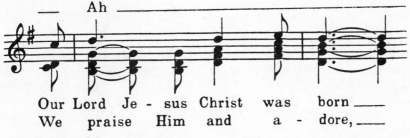

Our Lord Je - sus Christ   was   born____
We   praise   Him   and   a - dore, ____

A   Star shone bright o'er the place where He   lay
The wise-men came and   to Him gifts did bring

That first   glad Christ - mas   night.____
We   love   Him   ev - er   more. ____

Assignments

1. As a class activity, make up a three-part song with words and music.

2. Refer to Melodic Dictation from Chapter II. Review this study to acquire the necessary skills for taking down tunes given by the children.

3. As a class activity, write an original round. (Analyze several rounds and note that heavy accents fall on the *do-mis.*)

4. As a class activity, write an original descant to a familiar melody.

BIBLIOGRAPHY

Mursell, James and Glenn, Mabelle, *The Psychology of School Music Teaching.* Silver, Burdett Co., Chicago, 1938.

Shaw, Lloyd, *Cowboy Dances.* The Caxton Printers, Caldwell, Idaho, 1947.

Ford, Mr. and Mrs. Henry, *Good Morning.* Dearborn, Michigan, 1943.

Metropolitan Opera Guild, *Opera News.* Metropolitan Opera Guild, New York, 1944.

Chapter IX

MUSIC IN THE SEVENTH AND EIGHTH GRADES

The music activities carried on in grades seven and eight should maintain high standards of quality, usefulness, and suitability. The good teacher must be ever alert to the adapting of methods to the needs of the individual child.

There should be at least a twenty-five minute daily music period. By continuing to listen, to perform, and to create, development of the pupils in the following ways will be noted:

Greater use of the singing voice through much singing of art and folk songs.

Continued development in the ability to sing parts independently.

Greater enjoyment in listening to much fine music.

Marked improvement in the creating of songs, operettas, and dances.

Greater interest in learning to perform on musical instruments.

I. GENERAL TEACHING PROCEDURES

A. The Rote Song

1. The Importance of Rote Singing.

At this level, there should continue to be a great deal of rote singing done for recreation and enjoyment. If possible, the rote singing should be done with piano accompaniment, with emphasis placed on artistic interpretation.

2. Types of Rote Song Materials.

The song material selected should be suitable and stimulating to the interests and needs of the group.

American folk songs, songs from other countries, patriotic songs, religious songs, and songs for holidays and seasons should be sung.

B. New Teaching Problems

The problems which were presented and developed in the previous grades will continue to receive consideration as they occur in songs. Theory material which has been presented should be reviewed.

1. The Presentation of the Bass Clef

If there are boys in the seventh grade with changed voices. S.A.B. music should be used and the bass clef taught. Draw the great staff on the board, explaining the names of the lines and spaces in the bass clef. Have the children learn the letter names of the bass clef. (See Chapter I on theory.)

2. Testing Voices

Voices should be tested at frequent intervals throughout the year. The girl's voice does not usually change as noticeably as that of the boy, but the change is present nevertheless. Listen for both quality and range.

a. First soprano

1. The quality of the voice is high, clear, and flute-like.

2. If the compass extends easily to G above the treble staff, the voice should be classified as first soprano.

First Soprano Range

b. Second soprano

1. The second soprano has much the same quality as that of the first soprano.

2. If the range does not extend above E (fourth space), the voice should be classified as second soprano.

Second Soprano Range

c. Alto

1. The quality should be rich and full.

2. The range should be from A (below the staff) up to third space C with lower notes possessing deep warm qualities.

Alto Range

3. If four-part (SSAA) treble music is sung, the lower or second alto part is assigned to those who sing the low tones easily.

d. Alto-tenor (boy)

1. Boys whose voices are showing definite evidences of change should be classified as alto-tenors.

2. They should sing alto in three-part songs except for occasional notes above their range, which should be omitted. Their range is:

Alto Tenor

e. Changed voices: baritone and bass

1. Whenever there are a sufficient number of changed or changing voices, use three and four-part music: soprano, alto, baritone, or soprano, alto, alto-tenor, baritone.

2. Give the boys with changed or changing .voices much encouragement; in three-part songs they may sing the second soprano or alto part an octave lower. Their range is:

Bass

3. Seating Arrangements for Various Groups:

Soprano 2	Soprano 1	Alto

Alto	Soprano	Baritone

Tenor	Soprano	Alto	Baritone

Some teachers prefer seating according to ability; however, if this is done, great care must be used so that the child with few abilities does not feel chagrined or embarassed.

C. The Reading Song

1. The words of the song may be scanned whenever necessary to establish the rhythm.
2. Sing all parts simultaneously, reading the song at sight with words; if difficulties are encountered, the song may be sung by syllables.
3. If difficulty is still encountered, the phrases giving difficulty may be isolated, with the teacher assisting by singing or playing the piano.
4. Review and study theory, such as key signatures, scales, meter signatures, kinds of notes and corresponding rests, as they occur in song material.
5. Establish these good singing habits: good intonation, correct breathing and phrasing, clear tone, and good enunciation.

D. Suggestions for Singing Experiences

1. Song Repertory.
   a. Unison songs of all kinds with piano accompaniment should be included in these grades.
   b. Sing the folk songs of all nations, in unison or parts.
   c. Sing many art songs.
   d. Hymn tunes, both familiar and unfamiliar, should be sung.
   e. Include patriotic songs and songs for holidays and special occasions.
2. Selection of Materials.
   a. Choose songs that appeal to boys and girls of this age level.

    b. Use as much variety as possible.

    c. Correlate and integrate as much as possible, to enhance units of work in social studies, literature, art, etc.

3. Organizing a Chorus.

    a. Purpose

      1. To give the better singers additional experiences in choral singing.

      2. To perform more difficult and varied music than is possible during the regular class.

      3. To perform for assemblies and programs of various kinds.

    b. Materials (octavo)

    The teacher must be careful to sing only music of good quality. The following suggestions may be helpful:

      1. By sending to a music store for on-approval music, the teacher can select suitable and current octavo music.

      2. Visit the nearest music store that carries a stock of octavo music and play through the selections to decide on their suitability.

      3. Attend as many choral clinics as possible.

      4. Ask the nearest music dealer for lists of standard and new octavo music for junior high school.

      5. Ask successful junior high school choral directors for copies of programs and for suggestions.

      6. Much suitable material may be found in the following basic texts:

      Dykema, Peter, et al. *Sing Out.* C. C. Birchard Company, Boston, 1944.

      McConathy, Osborne. *New Music Horizons, Book VII.* Silver, Burdett Company, Chicago, 1947.

      Beattie, J. W., et al. *American Singer, Book VII.* American Book Company, Chicago. In preparation.

      Wilson, Harry R. *Choral Program Series.* Silver, Burdett Company, Chicago, 1946.

Wheeler and Siegmeister. *Singing Down the Road.* Ginn and Company, Chicago, 1947.

McConathy, Osborne, et al. *Music of Many Lands and People.* Silver, Burdett Company, Chicago, 1932.

McConathy, Osborne, et al. *Music Highways and Byways.* Silver, Burdett Company, Chicago, 1936.

Assignments

1. Each member of the class should have experience conducting one or more of the following: SA, SSA, SAB, and SATB choruses, while the class serves as a laboratory chorus.
2. Make a list of six octavo choruses for each type of chorus listed above.
3. Visit a junior high school chorus rehearsal and report to the class.
4. Learn six art songs that would be suitable for teaching junior high school students.
5. Write a paper correlating music with at least one academic subject in junior high school.
6. As a class, sing through several unison, two, three, and four-part songs, as found in one or more of the basic series recommended for junior high school.
7. Test twelve voices in the college class to determine what voice parts they sing.

LISTENING EXPERIENCES

There should be much listening to good music so that the musical masterpieces of the world may be appreciated and understood.

A. Suggested General Procedures
   1. Tell something of interest about the composer and music. (See Appendix for suggestions.)
   2. Occasionally before listening to a recording, sing or play a characteristic theme from the composition.

3. While the record is being played, refrain from comment. When the record has been played, encourage comments from the children.

4. Keep the listening period short.

5. Correlate with social studies whenever possible.

B. Specific Listening Lessons Which May Be Studied

1. **Fundamental Forms**
   a. The binary form
      The binary form is founded on two principal themes, or divided into two distinct or contrasted sections (A-B). Examples:

      Dixie - Emmett.......................... V 21950

      Lullaby - Brahms......................... V 1756

   b. The ternary form
      The ternary form of movement is founded on two principal themes with the first theme repeated after the second theme (A-B-A). Examples:

      *Believe Me If All Those Endearing
      Young Charms*....................... V 10-1247

      All Through the Night................. V 1558

2. **Dance Forms**
   Most musical dance forms which were based on court and and peasant folk dances, have their origin in the classic suite, which originated in the later middle ages. At first the suites had four principal movements or divisions: allemande, courante, sarabande, and gigue. The bourree, gavotte, minuet, musette, loure, passepied, and pavanne forms were introduced at will.

   a. Allemande
      1. The allemande is of German origin.
      2. It is in 4/4 time, of moderate rapidity.
      3. It begins with one short note at the end of the bar.
      4. There is usually a highly figurative melody with a comparatively simple accompaniment.
      5. Unless preceded by a prelude, it is the first movement in the suite.
      6. Characteristics of the allemande:

a. Uniform and regular motion of the upper part.

b. Avoidance of strongly marked rhythms.

c. Absence of accents on the weak parts of the bar.

d. Simple meter.

e. Consists of two parts, each of which is repeated: these two parts are usually 8, 12, or 16 bars in length, occasionally 10 bars in length.

f. An example of the *Allemande* is the French Suite in E Major—Bach. V 14384.

b. Bourree

1. The bourree is of French origin.

2. It is written in 4/4 meter and the tempo is rapid.

3. It begins on the fourth beat of the bar.

4. Examples are:

Bach, *Bourree* from Suite No. 2 in B Minor. V 6915
Bach, *Bourree* from French Suite No. 6 in E Major .... V 14384

c. The courantes

1. The French courante

a. The name "courante" is derived from a French word meaning *to run*.

b. It is in 3/2 meter and is rather rapid.

c. It begins with a short note at the end of the bar; contains many dotted notes and is staccato in style.

d. There are two parts, each of which is repeated.

e. The last bar of each part is in 6/4 meter.

f. An example is the *Courante* from Suite in G—Bach. C-MM232

2. Italian courante

a. Consists chiefly of running passages played in rapid tempo.

b. Is usually in 3/8, but sometimes in 3/4 meter.

c. Examples:

Bach, *Courante* from Partita No. 5 .....V 14384
Bach, *Courante* from French Suite No. 6 .V 14384

d. Gavotte

1. The gavotte is an old French dance.

2. It is in 4/4 meter at a moderately quick tempo.

3. There are two parts, each of which is repeated.
4. The gavotte usually begins on the third beat.
5. Examples:
   Ghys, *Amaryllis*........................V 20169
   Thomas, *Gavotte* from Mignon..........V 20443
   Bach, *French Suite No. 6 in E Major* ......V 14384

e. Gigue
1. The gigue is an old Italian dance.
2. It may be written in 3/8, 6/8, 3/4, 6/4, or 12/8 meter.
3. It is lively in character.
4. The gigue is usually the concluding number in the suite.
5. The second part of the gigue may be built on an inversion of the first subject.
6. An example is the *Gigue* from the French Suite No. 6 in E Major, Bach. V 14384.

f. Loure
1. The loure is an old dance, slower than the gigue, and is usually in 6/4 meter. It is played in the style of old bagpipe airs.
2. The loure is legato in style.
3. It is found in pastoral, rustic, or mountaineer music.

g. Minuet
1. The minuet is believed to be of French origin.
2. It is in a rhythmic triple meter.
3. There are usually two eight-measure periods, each of which is repeated. There is a third part written in ABA form, similar in form to the first part, but contrasted in feeling. The B section is called "trio."
4. Haydn was the first composer to use the minuet in symphonic writings.
5. Examples:
   Mozart, *Minuet* from Eine Kleine Nacht
   Music ....V-DM 1163
   Bach, *Minuet* from French Suite No. 6 in
   E Major ....V 14384

h. Musette

1. The musette is a short piece imitating in style the type of music played on bagpipes.
2. It is soft and gentle with a drone bass.
3. An example of the musette is the Handel, *The Gods Go a-Regging* .... C 68881D

i. Passepied

1. The passepied originally was a sailor's dance.
2. It resembles a minuet but is much faster.
3. The passepied always begins on the last beat of the bar and is in 3/4 or 3/8 meter.
4. There are two, three or four parts of eight or sixteen bars each played with two or more repeats.
5. The first part is usually in a major key; the last part forms a trio and is in minor.
6. An example is the *Passepied* from Bergamasque C-70406D

j. Pavane

1. The pavane is a slow and solemn dance popular in the sixteenth and seventeenth centuries.
2. It is in *alla-breve* meter.
3. An example is the *Pavane* by Byrd-Stokowski .... V 1943

k. Sarabande

1. The sarabande is a stately dance of oriental origin.
2. It may be written in either a major or minor key in 3/2 or 3/4 meter.
3. It usually consists of two eight or twelve bar divisions. It begins on the down beat and ends on the second or third beat.
4. The sarabande precedes the gigue in the suite.
5. An example is the *Sarabande* from French Suite No. 6 in E Major—Bach. .... V 14384.

3. Overtures

    a. The prelude type of overture

        1. This overture is an instrumental prelude to an opera or oratorio.

        2. Its themes are based primarily on themes in the composition to follow.

        Beethoven, Ludwig, *Overture to Egmont*... V 7291

        Mozart, Wolfgang, *Overture to Marriage of Figaro* ....V 11242

        Wagner, Richard, *Overture to Tannhauser* C-MX123

    b. Complete or concert type of overture

        1. This type of overture is an orchestral piece intended for concert use. It sometimes may bear a specific title indicating the composer's intention to illustrate some poetical or legendary subject.

        2. Examples:

        Brahms, Johannes, *Academic Festival Overture* CX-200

        Tschaikowsky, Peter, *1812 Overture* .....V-DM 515

4. Preludes

    a. A prelude is a piece of music introductory or preparatory to a more extended movement or composition, or to a dramatic performance, church service, etc.

    b. The prelude has no distinctive form, but being of an independent character, is often adapted to what is to follow.

    c. Examples:

    Chopin, Frederic, *Prelude in D♭*.............. V 6847

    Wagner, Richard, *Prelude to Act III of Lohengrin* .... V 7386

5. Modern Orchestral Suites

    a. Types of suites

        1. A series of extracts from incidental music written for a drama, as for example:

Grieg, Edvard, *Peer Gynt Suite* ....V-DM 1100

2. A series of extracts from incidental music written for an opera or ballet, as for example:
Tschaikowsky, Peter, *The Nutcracker Suite* .... V-DM 1020

3. A series of narratives or descriptive pieces:
Grofe, Ferde, *Grand Canyon Suite* ....V-DM 1038
Moussorgsky, Modeste, *Pictures at an Exhibition* VDM-706

6. **The Sonata**
  a. The sonata is an instrumental composition in three or four movements contrasted in theme, tempo, and mood. It usually follows a definite form or plan.
  b. Most sonatas consist of three movements:
    1. The first movement, which is rather vigorous.
    2. The second movement, which is slow and lyric.
    3. The third movement which is rapid and lively.
  c. Outline of the sonata
    1. The first movement
      a. Part I - Exposition
        1. First subject in the tonic key, as for example: *Sonata in E Minor, Opus 57*—Beethoven.
        2. Intermediate group (episode) establishing the key of the dominant.
        3. Second group in the dominant key.
        4. Closing group or episode concluding at the first double bar in the dominant.

      b. Part II - Development
        1. Any thematic material from Part I may be used and combined with new materials if desired.
        2. At the conclusion it merges naturally into Part I.

      c. Part III - Recapitulation
        1. First subject as it originally appeared.
        2. Intermediate group in the tonic key.
        3. Closing group in the tonic—often prolonged by a coda.

2. The second movement

    a. Theme and variations—AA' A"A''' A''', etc.
    Example: Mozart, Wolfgang, *Sonata in A Major.*
    V 11593.

    b. Rondo: A B A C A D A E A F, etc.
    Example: Mozart, Wolfgang, *Rondo in A Minor.*
    V 15421.

    c. Composers may also use the three-part form or
    sonata form in the second movement.

3. The third movement

    a. First movement (sonata) form.

    b. Rondo form. Example: Beethoven—*Sonata in
    C Minor* — V 16250.

d. In the four-movement sonata, the third movement may become the fourth movement. A minuet and trio, or scherzo then becomes the third movement. Example: Mozart, Wolfgang, *Sonata No. 11 in A Major* — V 11593-11594.

7. The Symphony

a. The symphonic form

1. The first movement (allegro) is majestic and stately; it is written in the sonata form, as for example: Haydn, Joseph, *Surprise Symphony No. 94 in G Major.* V-DM1155.

2. The second movement (andante) is slow and deeply emotional. It may be written in one of the following forms:

    a. Theme and variations.
    Theme: Second movement, *Surprise Symphony.*

    b. Rondo form A B A C A D, etc.

    c. Song form: A B A, etc.

3. The third movement is in a light and happy mood. It is usually written in

    a. Minuet and Trio A B A form.

    b. Example: Third movement, *Surprise Symphony.*

    4. The fourth movement is rapid and majestic.
        a. Sonata form. Example: Fourth movement, *Surprise Symphony.*
        b. Theme and variation.
        c. Rondo.

b. Symphonies that seventh and eighth grade children can understand and enjoy:

Beethoven, Ludwig, *Symphony No. 5 in C Minor* VM-640

Dvorak, Anton, *Symphony No. 5 in E Minor* V-DM899

Mendelssohn, Felix, *Symphony No. 4 in A Major* VM-294

Schubert, Franz, *Symphony No. 8 in B Minor* .... VM 319

c. Good books for the reading shelf

Barber, G. E. *The Wagner Opera Stories.* Bloomington: Public Schools Publishing Company, 1916. $2.00.

Burch, Gladys. *A Child's Book of Famous Composers.* New York: A. S. Barnes and Company, 1939. $1.50.

Cummings, D. E. *Making an Orchestra.* New York: MacMillan Company, 1931. $1.75.

La Prade, Ernest. *Alice in Orchestraville.* New York: Doubleday, Doran Company, 1940. $1.00.

Wheeler, Opal and Deucher, Sybil. *Curtain Calls for Joseph Haydn and Sebastian Bach.*

Wheeler, Opal and Deucher, Sybil. *Mozart the Wonder Boy.* New York: E. P. Dutton Company, 1939. $2.00.

d. Books for the teacher

Erskine, John. *A Musical Companion.* New York: Alfred Knopf Publishing Company, 1935. $2.25.

Hamilton, Clarence G. *Music Appreciation.* New York: Oliver Ditson Company, 1920.

Ward, Arthur E. *Music Education for High Schools.* New York: American Book Company, 1941.

C. Bibliography

Bernstein, Martin. *An Introduction to Music.* New York: Prentice-Hall Incorporated, 1937.

Elson, Louis C. *Elson's Music Dictionary.* Oliver Ditson Company, Philadelphia: 1933.

Faulkner, Anne S. *What We Hear in Music.* Camden: R. C. A. Victor Company, 1931.

Spaeth, Sigmund. *The Art of Enjoying Music.* New York: Whittlesey House, 1933.

Wilm, Grace. *The Appreciation of Music.* MacMillan Company, New York: 1928.

Assignments

1. As a class activity, analyze a sonata by using miniature scores, and listening to a recording of it.

2. As a class activity, analyze a symphony. (Haydn's Surprise Symphony is recommended.)

3. Listen to one example of each of the dance forms as listed on the preceding pages. Explain how they differ as to form, rhythm, mood, and tempo.

4. Listen to the different types of overtures as listed in this chapter. Explain how they differ.

5. Listen to examples of the different types of suites.

III. CREATIVE ACTIVITIES

Those children possessing special creative talents should be given many opportunities for self-expression. With the abilities gained and the skills developed throughout the first six grades, the musical background will in many individuals, manifest itself through creative expression.

A. Objectives

1. To give the pupils many opportunities for creative expression.

2. To aid the child in developing skill at notating original music.

3. To teach the fundamentals of harmony, so that occasionally not only the melody, but the harmony as well may be written.

4. To encourage the class to create dances to certain songs.

B. Procedures

1. Use a well known story on the seventh and eighth grade level; arrange the story into poetry which may then be set to music; design and make scenery and costumes, and stage the production under the direction of the children themselves with guidance of the teacher.

2. Create songs while in certain social studies units.

3. The pupils' efforts should be praised so that they will be encouraged to go on.

Assignments

1. Have each member of the class write one song in each of the following arrangements: SA, SSA SAB, SATB.

2. Write a simple operetta or pageant choosing a subject which would be of interest to a seventh or eighth grade group of children.

3. Complete the collection of scrap book materials. File them systematically.

Bibliography

1. Beattie, J. W. and others, *Music in the Junior High School.* Silver Burdett, New York, 1938.

2. Earhart, Will, *The Meaning and Teaching of Music.* M. Witmark and Sons, New York, 1935.

1. Pitts, L. B., *Music Integration in the Junior High School.* Birchard, Boston, 1935.

4. Rorke, G. A., *Choral Teaching at the Junior High School Level.* Hall, McCreary, Chicago, 1947.

Chapter X
MUSIC IN THE RURAL SCHOOL

The need of music in the rural school is very great. Although modern transportation facilities, telephones, and the radio have done a great deal to overcome the isolation formerly felt in rural areas, in many localities the opportunities for coming into direct contact with music activities and for participating in them continue to be very limited. It is extremely important, therefore, that music education in the rural school occupies the important place to which it is entitled. Each rural child should have the happy privilege of experiencing music in all of its aspects—singing, listening, playing, participating in rhythmic experiences, and creating.

The problems of organization in the music program of the rural school are many. One of the most difficult of these problems arises from the varying number of grades in the room. Since four-, two-, and one-room schools have different administrative problems, each type will be discussed separately.

A. Music in the Four-Room School

The trend in rural education today is toward enlarging school facilities by reorganizing or consolidating school districts. The consolidated school with four rooms is frequently found. This setup means that the teacher in each room may organize the curriculum with the two grades in mind. For the teaching of music, however, this arrangement presents problems, since the teacher must be careful not to use merely the same material for the children who are in their second year in the room. On the other hand, the new children must not be neglected. At times, also, overlapping from other grades is necessary because of crowded conditions in other rooms. It is impossible, therefore, to develop a suggested plan for every situation; the teacher must use ingenuity in developing a program to fit her own particular needs.

1. The First- and Second-Grade Room
a. The music program

Note: This chapter was first written by the authors for A GUIDE FOR INSTRUCTION IN MUSIC, published by the Minnesota State Department of Education. It is used with the permission of Mr. Dean Schweichard, Commissioner of Education.

In this room emphasis should be placed upon the activities outlined in Chapters III and IV with special emphasis as follows:

1. The children should learn the use of their singing voices by singing an abundance of good, interesting rote songs.

2. Attention should be given to individual singing to develop independence and to give the teacher opportunity for remedial work with the out-of-tune singers.

    A child may sing an entire song or only a phrase or a line. Study plans are developed in Chapters III and IV.

3. The children should be given opportunities to enjoy rhythm games and the rhythm band even though most of the time should be spent in rote singing.

    In these two grades the teacher should not attempt to have the children learn to read music unless there is a definite readiness for it. Much preparation for music reading can be accomplished *incidentally*, however, by teaching rote songs with books in the hands of the pupils and by using reading-readiness aids as outlined in Chapter IV.

4. The listening program as outlined in Chapters III and IV should be followed.

5. The creative activities developed in Chapters III and IV should be carried out.

b. Suggested basic texts

Books for each level may be selected from those mentioned for the lower grades in the two- and one-room school or from the following:

Armitage, M. T. and others. *Our First Music.* Singing School Series. Birchard, 1941.

————. *Our Songs.* Singing School Series. Birchard, 1939.

Glenn, Mabelle and others. *Listen and Sing.* World of Music Series. Ginn, 1943.

————. *Tuning Up.* World of Music Series. Ginn
1943.

Beattie, J. W. and others. *American Singer,* Bks. 1
and 2. American Singer Series. American Bk.,
1944.

McConathy, Osbourne and others. *New Music Horizons,* Bks. 5 and 6. New Music Horizons Series,
Silver, Burdett, 1944.

Note: It is suggested that the first book used should be one for the
first grade, but for additional song materials the second-year
book should be chosen either from the same series or from
another series. It is advisable for the teacher to have available
for herself several books from which she may teach the pupils
other songs.

2. **The Third- and Fourth-Grade Room**

It is in this room that special emphasis can be given
to music reading. Methods for developing reading
readiness have been discussed in Chapter IV and should
be studied thoroughly. If the teacher should wish to
use the tonal pattern approach to music reading, it would
be helpful to begin with the *American Singer,* Book 2,
if it was not used in the first- and second-grade room.
Otherwise, the first book bought for the children should
be one for the third grade. If the group is talented, the
next book added should be a fourth-grade book. If the
group is not above average, it is better to add another
third-grade book since that will give the children much
new material with which to work. Music reading should
not be introduced unless the group sings well. Rhythm-
band and melody-band instruments used with emphasis
on reading from the score will assist with the music-
reading problem.

a. Suggested cycle of activities for the week.
Each section, (1)-(5), below indicates the work to be
given on any one day of the week.

1. Learning and singing songs of general interest—
patriotic, folk, religious and seasonal songs.

2. Reviewing new songs learned previously.
Continue to develop reading by the plans outlined
in Chapters IV and V. When the children read
well, the following material should be taught only

as it appears in the reading songs that are sung:
a. Major scale.
b. Normal minor scale.
c. Chromatic scale.
d. Two-part songs.
e. Tempo.

    1'. Time signatures—2/4, 3/4, 4/4.
    2'. Rhythmic patterns.
        a'. Quarter notes (step).
        b'. Half notes (step, bend).
        c'. Eighth notes (run).
        d'. Dotted half notes (step, bend, bend).
        e'. Whole notes (step, bend, bend, bend).
        f'. Dotted quarter followed by eighth note (step, bend, run).

3. Learning new rote songs with books in the hands of the pupils.

Continue the reading of the songs not completed on the previous day. It is better not to do much part singing unless the group is well advanced in rote singing and can read unison songs well. Correlate with other subject-matter areas whenever possible.

4. Studying the rhythm band only if the emphasis is on reading from the score or orchestrating the score by the children.

Later the children may learn to play melody instruments. Class piano may be introduced in alternate years. Plans for teaching are found in Chapter V.

5. Listening to the phonograph or radio.

As effective motivation, correlate the listening program with other subject-matter fields. For records to be purchased and books for background material see the Bibliography and Index.

b. Suggested basic texts.

If song books must be shared by the other grades in the building, books may be selected from those suggested for the one-room and two-room school. The

list of books below is recommended when music reading is to be developed and when a wealth of rote
songs on the third- and fourth-grade level is desired.

Armitage, M. T. and others. *Merry Music.* Singing
School Series. Birchard, 1939 (Third-grade book).
————. *We Sing.* Singing School Series. Birchard,
1940 (Fourth-grade book).

Beattie, J. W. and others. *American Singer,* Bks. 3
and 4. American Singer Series. American Bk., 1944
and 1945.

Glenn, Mabelle and others. *Rhythms and Rimes.*
World of Music Series. Ginn, 1943. (Third-grade
————. *Songs of Many Lands.* World of Music
Series. Ginn, 1943 (Fourth-grade book).

McConathy, Osbourne and others. *New Music Horizons,* Bks. 3 and 4. New Music Horizons Series. Silver, Burdett, 1944 and 1945.

Note: Good singers should have both a third-grade and a fourth-grade
book from which to sing. The second book added should be
another third-grade book if the pupils do not sing well. A list
of good community song books will be found in the section on
the one-room school in this chapter.

3. The Fifth- and Sixth-Grade Room

The core of the program is still rote singing with books
in the hands of the pupils; but in this room the teacher
may emphasize music reading Whether or not music reading should be taught depends upon the ability of the group;
it should by all means be delayed until the group is ready
for it. When part singing is introduced, it may be well to
do so through descants and rounds. For methods refer to
Chapter VI. As a continued aid to music reading, instruction in melody instruments and class piano may be given.

a. Suggested cycle of activities for the week.

Each section, (1)-(5), below indicates the work to be
given on any one day of the week.

1. Singing many recreational and community songs,
with a review of the rote songs previously learned.
Having the pupils engage often in singing for relaxation. For teaching suggestions see Chapters VII
and VIII.

2. Reading music
It is in this room that two-part singing should be developed and three-part singing begun. It is important also to let the pupils read songs in the minor keys—natural, harmonic, melodic, and mixed. Methods of teaching are found in Chapters VI, VII and VIII.

3. Learning new rote songs
Read the suggestions given in Chapters VII and VIII. Continue also to develop the note-reading problems previously begun.

4. Studying the melody band or class piano
It these have not been previously taught, use the plans outlined in Chapter V. Continue with rote singing and music reading if instruments are not being studied.

5. Listening to the phonograph or radio

b. Suggested basic texts
If the pupils are not advanced, the books listed for grade four should be used; if they sing well, one book from the fifth grade group may be chosen. When the pupils are well advanced, books from the sixth grade series should be used. The following basic textbooks are recommended:

Armitage, M. T. and others. *Our Land of Song.* Singing School Series. Birchard, 1942 (Fifth grade book.)

————. *Music Everywhere.* Singing School Series. Birchard, 1943 (Sixth-grade book.)

Beattie, J. W. and others. *American Singer,* Bks. 5 and 6. American Book Co., 1945.

Glenn, Mabelle and others. *Blending Voices.* World of Music Series. Ginn, 1943. (Fifth-grade book.)

————. *Tunes and Harmonies.* World of Music Series. Ginn, 1943 (Sixth-grade book).

McConathy, Osburne and others. *New Music Horizons,* Bks. 5 and 6. New Music Horizons Series. Silver 1946.

Note: Additional books for recreational singing are listed in the section of this chapter devoted to the one-room and two-room schools.

4. The Seventh- and Eighth-Grade Room

In this room there should be a continuation of emphasis on the community and recreational type of singing. There should be part singing also (two and three part). Continue to teach syllable reading and teach facts and skills not taught previously, such as the names of lines and spaces and key and time signatures. When the pupils can read a song by using words, syllable reading should be discontinued. As soon as the boys' voices have changed, the names of lines and spaces in the bass clef should be taught and the singing of simple three- and four-part songs begun.

a. Suggested cycle of activities for the week.

Each section, (1)-(5), below indicates the work to be given on any one day of the week.

1. Singing many community and recreational songs, with a review of rote songs previously learned.

2. Reading notes

   If the pupils read one part well, part songs should be sung. Study plans for two and three-part singing are listed in Chapters VI, VII, and VIII. The study of theory might now include scales and key signatures in major and minor keys. The names of the lines and spaces in the treble and bass clefs should be taught.

3. Learning new unison rote songs, with books in the hands of the pupils.

   The singing of many fine unison songs is still an important part of the program. When note-reading problems were not previously completed, a part of this period may be used for that purpose.

4. Continuing the study of class piano or melody instruments.

   If the children have had these experiences in previous grades, this period might be given over to music reading and enjoyable singing of new and old rote songs.

5. Listening to the phonograph and radio.

   Study the correlated program in Chapter IX for

suggested procedure to enrich the listening program.

b. Suggested basic texts and octavo songs.

Community song books may be selected from the books listed for the one-room rural school in this chapter.

A list of octavo songs which may be used for advanced groups is as follows:

Krone, Max and Krone, Beatrice *Hiking Sing.* SATB. Kjos music, 1937.

————. *Swiss Skiing Song.* SATB. Kjos Music, 1937.

Larson, Earl Roland, *Carrousel,* SATB, Paul A. Schmitt Music Co. 1947.

Mork, W. H., Krone, Max and Krone, Beatrice. *Abide With Me.* SAB. Belwin, Inc., 1945.

Schuetky, Fr. Joseph and Hornisch, Guy. *Send Forth Thy Spirit.* SAB. Pro-Art Pub., 1943.

Note: When additional octavo music is needed, write to the nearest music store for on-approval copies.

c. Additional suggestions for the music program.

1. Folk dances and other rhythmic experiences can be carried out satisfactorilly through the physical-education program.

2. Creative activities with the entire school participating should be promoted regularly. An operetta might be composed, in which the story could be created, songs composed, scenery built, folk dances created, dramatizations worked out, and plans for the staging selected and carried out by the pupils themselves.

3. In schools where electricity is available, audio-visual aids may give much additional teaching material for all school activities. Much material is available for the music program. The teacher should strive to correlate this material with all curricular experiences. It also may provide much program material for community functions.

B. Music in the Two-Room School

1. The Lower Group—Grades I through III or IV.

Note: The fourth grade should be with the upper grades if the pupils sing well.

a. The music program.

It is advisable to restrict music reading in the lower group since rote singing with books in the hands of the pupils should furnish the core of the music program. If the group sings well, however, a certain amount of reading readiness may be developed by using plans outlined in Chapter IV. There should be much emphasis on rhythmic games and listening to good music on the phonograph and radio. The program may be so arranged as to take advantage of the music-appreciation programs broadcast on all networks. Methods for presenting rote songs, rhythmic games and dances, and listening lessons and for developing reading readiness will be found in Chapters III, IV and V.

The daily program should be no less than twenty minutes in length. The order in which the various activities may be presented can be varied to meet the needs of the class; for instance, not one day exclusively should be designated as listening-lesson day. Rather, the listening lesson should be presented when it most adequately correlates with other experiences, regardless of the day or time of day.

b. Suggested basic texts.

Note: Any book listed in Chapters III, IV and V may be used for supplementary song material.

Beattie, J. W. and others. *American Singer,* combined grades. American Singer Series. American Bk., 1947.

Dykema, P. W. and others. *Happy Singing.* Singing School Series, Birchard, 1947.

Fullerton, C. A. *New Elementary Music,* a one-book Course. Follett, 1936.

Hood, M. V. and others. *On Wings of Song.* World of Music Series. Ginn, 1945.

—————. *Singing Days.* World of Music Series. Ginn, 1944.

McConathy, Osbourne and others. *New Music Horizons,* two-book course. New Music Horizons. Silver-Burdett.

2. **The Upper Group—Grades IV or V through VIII.**
   If through good teaching the children have acquired a love for singing and listening to good music in the lower grades, they will be prepared to develop additional musical skills in the upper grades. If the pupils in the fourth grade sing well, they should participate in the activities on the upper-grade level; if they are below average ability they will be a part of the lower-grade group. It must be kept in mind that rote singing with books in the hands of the pupils is still the core of the music program.

   a. Rote singing.

   The objective of all our music teaching is to encourage children to love music. There is no more enjoyable activity than unison singing of rote songs by the entire group. For the methods of presenting rote singing with and without books in the hands of the children, refer to chapter IV.

   b. Music reading

   1. Using the syllables.
      Since music reading offers unique problems in the rural school, the following plan might be used when introducing it into a school for the first time:
      a. Introduce music reading through the song for musical analysis, as outlined in Chapter IV.
      b. Teach the syllable names of the scale by rote.
      c. Teach the rules for finding *do* when there are sharps, flats, or no sharps and flats in the signature, as outlined in Chapter V.
      d. When the song to be taught has been selected, write the scale in the key of that song on the blackboard.
      e. After the children have found *do,* have them write the syllable names under the notes.
      f. Write the song on the blackboard and have the

pupils find the syllable names from the scale which has been placed on the blackboard.

g. Have the pupils chant the words or step the time as outlined in Chapter V.

h. Point out like and unlike phrases.

i. After giving the pupils the pitch for *do,* have them find the pitch for the starting tone.

j. Have the pupils sing all the notes with syllables in correct time.

If either a rhythm or pitch difficulty arises which the children cannot master, isolate the problem for them, singing it with syllables, words, or "loo." The pupils will learn the phrase containing the problem by imitating the teacher.

k. Have the pupils sing the song with "loo" and words.

l. Now let the pupils open their books and sing the song as printed; call attention to composer, dynamics, expression marks and other related material.

m. In like manner teach new reading songs from the books.

The tonal or rhythmic pattern to be taught should be isolated and the entire phrase containing the problem placed on the blackboard and learned by syllables, "loo," and words. Plans for teaching new reading songs are found in Chapter V.

2. The tonal-pattern approach

It is possible to use the tonal-pattern approach to reading in these upper grades if the plan is carefully developed. As a guide the teacher should study *The American Singer, Book 2.* The plan may be used with any text if the steps listed below are followed.

a. Let the pupils, with books in their hands, chant or step the time as outlined in Chapter V.

b. Let the children learn the song as a rote song; give help only when necessary.

    c. Place the interval skips on the blackboard, teaching the children to sing them by syllables, "loo," and words.

    d. Now let the pupils sing the song with "loo," but, when they sing the problem to be studied, have them sing the correct syllables. Gradually they will develop independence in reading more and more difficult skips.

    e. Now let the children sing the song with words.

    f. Discuss composer, tempo markings, dynamics, and related material.

3. New rhythmic problems

New rhythmic problems are taught as they appear in the song material. For plans of teaching refer to Chapters VI, VII, VIII and IX.

4. Two- and three-part singing

Part singing should not begin until the children sing and read one part well. Plans for teaching are found in Chapters VI and VII.

5. Songs in minor keys

Songs in minor keys may be taught in the following order; natural, harmonic, melodic, and mixed. These songs should not be attempted unless the children sing unison songs well in major keys. Plans for teaching are found in Chapters VI, VII and VIII.

6. The study of music theory

Music theory should be taught incidentally through the song material sung. Even though it is not necessary to teach the names of the lines and spaces in order to have the children learn music reading, it is advisable to do so. If there are boys in the room whose voices have begun to change, teach the names of the lines and spaces in the bass clef also. The point is especially important if the children are beginning the study of instrumental music, either through melody bands, class piano, or band and orchestra instruments.

7. Playing melody instruments

Playing melody instruments is an additional means of developing music reading. Tonettes and song flutes have been the most popular instruments up to the present time. Recorders are excellent, but they are rather expensive. For materials and methods of teaching see Chapter V.

8. Using the class piano
Every child can participate in the use of the class piano, while children who have pianos in their homes can accomplish a great deal. As with melody instruments, the class-piano activity should not replace singing. Methods of teaching are found in Chapter V.

9. The listening program
There are many worth-while radio programs. Occasionally one of them may be used for a listening lesson. There will be many opportunities to correlate the listening to good music with the topics discussed in social studies, English, science and other subjects. Consult previous chapters for recommended records and suggested teaching plans listed for the fourth grade and up.

10. Suggested cycle of activities for the week
It is impossible to outline for the upper grades a daily program that will work in all schools, since there are many variable factors such as the number of grades, the number of pupils in each grade, and the ability of the children. The program given below may serve as a model for other programs. Each section, a-e, indicates the work to be given on any one day of the week.

It must always be kept in mind that singing should comprise at least one-half of the entire music program and that the child should be given a chance to sing during the day whenever the opportunity presents itself in other subject-matter fields.

a. There should be much singing of well known songs —patriotic, seasonal, and religious songs, songs for fun and the like.

b. Follow the plan for the study of music reading as outlined in this chapter for the upper grades in the one-room school, or refer to Chapters IV and V.

c. Teach new rote songs with books in the hands of the pupils; also continue the unfinished reading problems previously begun.

d. Use the melody band or class piano, or continue the rote-singing and music-reading program, if the instrumental program is not developed.

e. Divide the time between listening to the radio and the phonograph.

11. Suggested basic texts.

Note: Other books from the lists compiled for grades four through eight may be used for supplementary material. Good community song books may be selected from the list compiled for the one-room school in this chapter.

Beattie, J. W. and others. *American Singer*, combined grades. American Singer Series. American Bk., 1947.

Hood, M. V. and others. *On Wings of Song*. World of Music Series. Ginn, 1945.

————. *Singing Days*. World of Music Series. Ginn 1944.

C. Music in the One-room School

1. Time Allotment

The amount of time to be given to the teaching of music in a one-room school has always been a problem. Most administrators and successful teachers agree that not less than twenty minutes a day should be devoted to music. The basic problem in the rural program is to make more time available for music. The most progressive rural teachers have found that, by planning their work in social studies, language arts, and other activities so that some subjects are correlated, additional time will be gained. Appropriate grade combinations and the grouping of pupils according to ability levels will give added time.

2. Suggested Cycle of Activities for the Week.

It is impossible to outline a model music program for every school. Assuming that the period is twenty minutes long, the weekly program could be arranged in several ways. The program adopted should be one which will fill the needs of the particular group.

In the outline given below, each of the sections *a-e* indicates the work to be given on any one day of the week.

a. Have the entire school sing in unison to develop a repertory of well-known community songs—patriotic, folk, religious, seasonal, and holiday.

b. Divide the work for the lower and upper grades as follows:

1. *For the lower grades*

Note: If the children in the fourth grade are well advanced in singing, they should be with the upper group; if slow, combined with the lower group.

a. A review of the rote songs learned previously for enjoyment and relaxation.

b. The learning of new rote songs, with books in the hands of the pupils, as outlined in Chapter IV.

Occasionally there should be exercises in developing reading readiness as outlined in Chapter IV. The nonsingers should be given special help.

2. *For the upper grades*

Correlation of the music with other subjects as opportunities are presented during the day.

c. Divide the work for the lower and upper grades as follows:

1. *For the lower grades*

Correlation of the music with other subjects during the day.

2. *For the upper grades*

a. The singing of rote songs

The plan for teaching rote songs will be found in Chapter V.

b. Music reading

In this weekly period the children learn the mechanics of music reading. All of the activities listed below cannot be engaged in on one day of the week, therefore the teacher should if possible find another period in the school program for the acquiring of these skills.

1. Songs for analysis

   The study of music reading may be begun by using this plan as outlined in Chapter V.

2. Reading songs

   Children are taught to read new songs by using the tonal-pattern approach. Follow the plan outlined in Chapter V.

3. New intervals and rhythmic problems

   When a new problem arises it should be taught as a part of a new song. Follow the plan as outlined in Chapter VII.

4. Two-part songs

   The reading of two-part songs in the upper grades should not be begun until the children can read unison songs well. The plan for teaching two-part songs is found in Chapter VI. Occasionally the younger children can sing the melody or upper part of a two-part song.

5. Three-part songs

   Three-part songs should not be taught until many two-part songs have been sung. The plan for teaching is found in Chapter VIII. If there are boys in the group whose voices have changed, three-part songs having soprano, alto, and baritone parts should be taught occasionally.

6. The study of music theory

   Music fundamentals should be taught as an outgrowth of the song material and not as isolated facts. The teacher should acquaint the pupils with the following theory facts,

however, and should teach them in this
order:

a. The staff
b. Leger lines
c. Clef signs
d. Bars and double bars
e. Measure
f. Names of lines and spaces
g. Sharps and flats

Note: Natural signs, double sharps, and double flats are taught only if
they appear in the song material.

h. Rules for finding *do*
   Refer to Chapter V.

i. Time signatures and values of notes as
   they appear in the songs sung.

j. Rests as they appear in the songs sung.

k. Scales
   1. Major scale
      See the Song for Music Analysis,
      Chapter V.
   2. Chromatic scale: ascending and de-
      scending.
      See Chapter VI.
   3. Minor scales: natural, harmonic, me-
      lodic, and mixed.
      See Chapters VI, VII and VIII respec-
      tively.

   1. Common tempo markings and terms of
      expression as found in the songs studied
      See Common Music Terms and Expres-
      sions.

7. New rhythmic problems
   New rhythmic problems should be taught as
   they appear in the songs which are sung.
   See previous chapters for methods of teaching.

d. Provide for rhythms and instrumental study.
   This period will have to suffice for the study of instru-
   ments unless other periods of the day can be used.
   It is suggested that the entire period be used for one

group, upper grades and lower grades alternating on different days, rather than to divide the time into two short periods. The following activities should be taught:

1. Rhythm band in the lower grades
   Directions for teaching will be found in Chapter III.
2. Class piano
   Consult Chapter V.
3. Rhythmic response
4. Melody band in the upper grades
5. Folk dancing
6. Singing games

e. Provide for listening and creating

1. Recordings
   Sometimes lessons may be arranged so that the entire school may take part. At other times, particularly when the lesson is being correlated with other subjects, it is better to teach each group—upper and lower—separately. Records may be selected from the different grade levels listed in previous chapters. Those to be used for primary grades may be selected from records recommended for the first three grades and those to be used for upper grades, from the record lists for grades four and up.

2. Radio
   By securing advance announcements of educational broadcasts from the large networks, the teacher can arrange a series of interesting listening lessons.

3. Demonstrations should be done by high-school pupils or adult performers to foster appreciation

4. Audio-visual aids

5. Creative activities
   Consult previous chapters in regard to procedures for creative activities and adapt them to individual needs.

Note: Often during discussions in social studies, English, or other classroom activities, occasions will arise when the teacher or children will discover a music activity that will fit the subject under discussion. While studying the Revolutionary War period, for instance, the class can listen to the recording of *A Ballad for Americans,* sung by Paul Robeson. The minuet and other folk dances of that period may be learned and songs such as *Yankee Doodle* may be sung. Rhythm instruments imitating the instruments of that period are also usable. The music period is flexible and is put into the daily program whenever a certain activity is suggested.

3. Suggested Materials
   Basic texts

Note: Phonograph records for rote singing are available for most of these books. Teachers who cannot sing should make sure that records are available before texts are purchased.

Beattie, J. W. and others. *American Singer,* combined grades. American Singer Series. American Bk.,

Burns, S. T. *Come and Sing.* American bk., 1938.

Dykema, P. W. and others. *Happy Singing.* Singing School Series. Birchard, 1947.

Dykema, P. W. and others. *Music in The Air.* Singing School Series: Birchard, 1947.

Fullerton, C. A. *New Elementary Music,* a one-book course. Follet, 1936.

Hood, M. V. and others. *On Wings of Song.* World of Music Series. Ginn, 1945.

————. *Singing Days.* World of Music Series. Ginn 1944.

McConathy, Osbourne and others. *New Music Horizons,* one-book course. New Music Horizons Series. Silver (in preparation).

b. Supplementary texts

1. Community song books

Clark, K. S. *Keep on Singing.* Paull-Pioneer Music Corp., 1933.

Freeman, W. S. and Leavitt, H. E. *Songs to Sing.* Ginn, 1943.

Frey, Hugo, ed. *America Sings.* Robbins Music Corp., 1935.

Oberndorfer, Marx and Oberndorfer, A. S. F. *New American Song Book.* Hall & McCreary, 1941.

Smith, Fowler and others. *Songs We Sing.* Hall
& McCreary, 1941.

Surette, T. W. and Davison, A. T. *Home and Community Song Book.* E. C. Schirmer, 1931.

2. Books about music and musicians
Refer to previous chapters in this book. To make
more books available to the teachers in the county,
. a cooperative library could be formed. To finance
the project each school could be charged a small
fee, which would preferably be paid by the school
district.

4. Classroom Equipment
A well-tuned piano
A good combination radio-phonograph
A good pitch pipe
A staff liner
Blackboard
Rhythm band and melody instruments

Note: The autoharp and a set of melody bells, while more expensive
than some melody instruments, are worth-while investments for
a rural school.

Cardboard keyboards
A good supply of phonograph records
A practical plan is to develop a cooperative library having all the schools in the county pay a certain amount
per school into a fund. The county superintendent may
then appoint a committee of teachers to purchase the
records for the county library. Each teacher will be per-
mitted to draw on this library of records for her school.
Check back to previous chapters for suggestions. The
RCA Victor educational records provide excellent teaching material for listening lessons. They are unbreakable
records, slightly more expensive, but worth the difference
in cost.

Note: These unbreakable records and the albums are arranged to cover the
following: singing activities, listening activities, rhythmic activities,
patriotic songs, Christmas songs, singing games, music of American
Indians, and music for rhythm bands.

5. Long-Term Planning in the Rural Music Program
It is impossible to cover in one-year's time all of the ac-

tivities suggested in the one-room rural-school program. Long-term planning is essential. Many activities can be alternated every other year; e.g., tonettes and class piano.

Evaluating the Music Program

1. **Some Definite Goals Which Have Been Attained**

   a. Every child enjoys singing and contributes wholeheartedly.

   b. That uncomfortable self-conscious feeling about singing has been lost.

   c. As a group, the children know what an acceptable tone quality is for both individual and group singing.

   d. They are able to sing as a chorus in part or in unison, using good tone and correct expression, and to follow their director.

   e. With a few exceptions each child is able to acquit himself creditably if asked to sing alone or as one of a trio or quartette.

   f. Through singing and playing musical instruments all of the children have found a means of self-expression that will give them lasting enjoyment.

   g. A desire has been created to continue with the work begun, both vocal and instrumental.

   h. The children have become acquainted with some of the world's best music and through this knowledge have gained a standard by which to judge new music.

2. **The New Attitude Toward Music**

   Music is no longer looked upon as something in which only a few gifted persons can excel; nor is it considered as a pastime for girls or sissies. It is a natural means of expressing our feelings. Through music we can show our love for our country or our sympathy for the Volga boatman; we can share the fun of Halloween or express our deep reverence for the Christmas story. This is music as we have learned to know it, and it will go with us wherever we go.

6. **The County Musical Festival**

   The main purpose of the county music festival is the promotion of good music in the county. Children of one school who hear performances of the various types of music activities in other schools will be very anxious to have such activities in their own school.

They will also receive great satisfaction from singing in a large massed chorus under a competent director.

a. Organizing and planning the festival

If there is a county music supervisor, he should organize the festival; but, if there is no supervisor, the initiative must come from the county superintendent. He should appoint a committee of the best teachers of music in his county to plan the festival and select the music to be performed. This planning should be done early in the year. It is customary for the committee to select first a topic around which to build the program. Such topics as The United Nations, One World, Foreign Lands and Peoples, Our Home, Our Country, have been used successfully.

The program should be mimeographed and sent to each teacher in the county early enough for each school to learn the music thoroughly. In planning the program the committee should keep in mind that only one activity of a kind should be presented; for example, one number by a rhythm band, one group of songs by each level—upper and lower, one vocal solo. The songs selected should be those from books most widely used in the county and found on phonograph records so that teachers who cannot sing but use the phonograph for teaching will be able to present the materials to their groups. Also, the songs definitely should be used in the classroom so that the program will be an outgrowth of regular classroom work.

The entire program should not exceed *one hour in length* and should be so well planned that it will move ahead smoothly.

b. Teacher participation in the program

The teachers themselves might present a group of songs as a part of the program, using only those num-

bers, however, which will be within their abilities.[1]
This participation in the festival is excellent training
for teachers, who are often called upon to assist with
4-H choruses and with community singing at social
functions.

c. Resumès of successful festivals held in three counties[2]

1. Douglas County

The county superintendent of schools, Miss Olga L.
Peterson, reports that for a number of years con-
tests had been carried on with only talented pupils
participating. Her aim when she took over her
duties was to have every child participate in various musical activities, learn good music, and, above
all, enjoy singing. Consequently, the contest plan
was abandoned and the festival idea adopted. The
change, however, was made slowly and cautiously.
The county was divided into four groups, each
group being responsible for a certain number of
songs. There was no competition; each group
was given a job to do, the best that group could
do. This was their beginning.

Each year since then they have had a program with
a theme. Occasionally they have pantomimed
songs in which one group sings while another group
does the pantomiming. The pupils plan with the
teacher the costumes and stage settings for each
pantomime. In a recent festival a mass tonette
and flutophone band was presented.

The festivals are held in the Alexandria High-School
auditorium in the afternoon. No admission is
charged. The rehearsal is held the morning of
the festival when teachers and pupils gather. Their
accompanists and directors are from their own
group of rural teachers.

Miss Peterson feels that the level of music instruction
has been definitely raised and that the children are

[1] Miss Clarissa Bergquist, while county superintendent of Becker County, organized and directed a very successful teachers' chorus.
[2] From material collected by Mrs. Pyne and Miss Kennedy, rural school supervisor, State Department of Education.

getting a fine knowledge and true appreciation of music.

2. Yellow Medicine County

Miss Clara Thorpe, the county superintendent, reports that county music festivals have been held in her county since 1938. They are held in the Granite Falls High-School auditorium. The themes used the last few years for their festivals are as follows:

1941—Music Around the World.

1942—America Sings.

1943—Keep the United Nations Singing.

1944—Holidays Through the Years.

1945—Musical Moments Among Good Neighbors
This festival was in the nature of a fiesta with the children gaily costumed.

1946—A Musical Trip on the Victory Ship.

1947—Ring Ye Bells of Freedom.

This program was an outgrowth of the unit on Inter-cultural Relationship.

Narrators are used to explain carefully the theme to the audience.

Miss Thorpe states that participation in music festivals has greatly improved the quality of music in the rural schools of her county. The children have gained confidence, poise, and a sense of community pride from these experiences. The annual music festival is the culminating activity of the music program in each school.

3. Big Stone County.

Miss Agnes F. Nelson, the county superintendent, reports that there have been county music festivals in her county since 1932. Some of the themes which have been used are:

Folk Songs and Dances of European Nations.

Songs of the American Continent (Indian, Mexican, Negro, mountaineer and cowboy songs and songs of Stephen Foster).

Patriotic Songs in Different Periods of History (Discovery of America, Revolutionary War, War of 1812, Civil War, Spanish-American War, World War I, World War II).

Our Holiday in Song.

Parade of the Allied Nations.

Songs of Home (Infancy, childhood, youth, career, home, old age).

Seasonal Songs.

The festival director early in the year works with the teachers to familiarize them with the songs. They hold several district get-to-gethers during the year.

Their festival is given in the Ortonville High-School auditorium in the evening; a practice is held on the afternoon of the festival.

Miss Nelson feels that the festival has created greater interest in music in the schools of her county.

7. Instrumental Music in the Rural School

Many of the problems connected with the teaching of instrumental music in the one-room rural school are almost insurmountable. In spite of this, some counties have developed remarkable programs of instrumental instruction. First steps consist of appointment of traveling instrumental instructors, who visit a number of schools at least once a week and provide opportunity for massed playing experiences on Saturday in some central location. When annual music festivals are held more pupils become interested, and the activity grows in size and effectiveness.

Individual groups from small towns and consolidated schools can combine in appointing instrumental-m u s i c teachers who have the organizational abilities and the special knowledge and aptitude required for such positions. Each group will have its own way of working out the details; success will depend on the effectiveness of the cooperation among interested and supporting laymen, school officials, and the instrumental teacher.

A Program Which Might Be Used For a County Festival
"Music Around the World"

I

May Day Carol................................English Folk Song
Big Corral................................American Cowboy Song
Song of a Garden....................French-Canadian Folk Song

Massed Chorus

II

Folk Dance, Norwegian Mountain Dance

III

Shortnin' Bread........................American Plantation Song
The Slumber Boat..Gaynor
Sing a Song of Sixpence................................Old Air

Lower Grades

IV

Rhythm Band

V

Goin' to Shout................................Negro Spiritual
The Papaya Tree............................Filipino Folk Song
Chiapanecas................................Mexican Folk Song

Upper Grades

VI

Tonette Band

VII

Piano Solo

VIII

Star Lullaby................................Polish Folk Song
Czecho-Slovakian Dance Song....................Czech Folk Song
Heighol Maid of the Mill......................Welsh Folk Song

Small Ensemble

IX

Vocal Solo

X

Battle Hymn of the Republic..............................Steffe
Once to Every Man and Nation..................Welsh Melody
Praise to the Lord......................................Melica

Massed Chorus

Professional Bibliography
Books not listed within the text of this chapter

1. Book listed in the Professional Bibliography for the first grade (Chapter III) and good also for the rural school.

   Brooks and Brown. *Music Education in the Elementary School.*

2. Additional books for the rural school.

Annett, Thomas. *Music in the Rural School.* Boston music, 1938.

Hood, M. V. and others. *Music Procedures for Consolidated and Rural Schools.* Ginn, 1937.

Kinscella, H. G. and Tierney, E. M. *Music in the Small School.* Univ. of Nebr. extension division, 1939.

McConathy, Osbourne. *Music in Rural Education.* Silver, 1937.

Music Educators National Conference. *Music Education Curriculum Committee Reports.* 64 E. Jackson blvd., Chicago: The Conference, 1945.

——————. *Music Education Source Book;* edited by Hazel N. Morgan, 64 E. Jackson blvd., Chicago: The conference, 1947.

National Society for the Study of Education. Thirty-fifth yearbook, Pt. 2: *Music Education.* A music program for rural schools by Marguerite V. Hood. Blooming: Pub. School Pub. Co., 1936.

Appendix

SUPPLEMENTARY MATERIALS FOR CLASSROOM USE
Anvil Chorus from Il Trovatore—Verdi V 19879

From the opera Il Trovatore, written by Verdi, comes the well-known song, *The Anvil Chorus*. The story tells of a band of soldiers travelling from one country to another.

While journeying they spent one of their nights in the camp of some friendly gypsies. As the shadows of night were passing away, with the dawn in the offing, the gypsies began their day's work. In the famous *Anvil Chorus* they hammer as they sing. The swinging tune is accompanied by the ring of blows on the anvil, the rough voices of men, and the sound of their hammers, making an impressive musical picture.

Guiseppi Verdi (1813-1901)

Verdi was born in Italy of humble parents. The village organist gave him his first lessons upon a rickety little spinet, which his father bought for him. While he was still a young boy, he became organist of his village church.

The people in his little town of Busseto thought he had such great promise as a musician that they offered to give him the necessary education to attain that goal.

He turned to the field of opera and found he was very successful. Some of his well known operas are Rigoletto, Il Trovatore, La Traviata, and Aida.

The Arkansas Traveler—American Traditional V 20638

Late one rainy afternoon in the frontier days of the West, a traveler on horseback followed a narrow trail through the Arkansas wilderness. The rider looked anxiously for the cabin of some settler, but saw only a lean wolf sulking among the underbrush.

At last his ears caught the sound of a fiddle. His eyes brightened, for he was a fiddler himself. New friends around a hearth fire would be welcome after a lonely day. Then he noticed that the music never went on to a finish; there was just one little part of a tune played over and over. But the traveler said to himself, "Half of a fiddle tune is better than the whole of a lean wolf," and he jogged along with a smile on his face. When he reached the clearing in the wilderness, his smiled disappeared.

Before him was a miserable shanty of a "squatter family," as the shiftless type of early setttler was called. The open door hung from one hinge and the rain dripped from the half-shingled roof into the darkness of the dreary cabin. Dogs and children tumbled over each other in the dooryard. Seated upon an empty barrel, the man of the place sawed away at an old fiddle tucked under his chin.

The traveler stopped his horse and gave a friendly greeting. The dogs and the children stood and stared. The fiddler, after one careless glance, went on playing the same part of the tune over and over. He repeated his greeting and asked for night's lodging.

The fiddler shook his head. "Roof leaks," he answered. "Why don't you stop the leaks?" "Bin rainin' all day." "Why not mend it in dry weather?" "Don' leak then." "But there must be dry spots in your cabin." "We sleeps in 'em." The fiddler never even looked up.

The traveler decided that he might as well go on. He asked, "How far to the next house?" "Don' know, stranger, never bin thar." "Can you tell me where this road goes?" "Stranger, it never goes no whar, it's allers thar when I gits up in the mawnin'!" "Well, how far to where it forks?" "It don' fork, it splits." Still he fiddled the same bit of tune over and over. The traveler had an idea. "Why don't you play the balance of that tune?" he asked. "This chune 'es got no balance." "I mean why don't you play the whole of it?" The traveler explained. The squatter began to show signs of interest. "Here, I'll show you how." The traveler took the violin and played the tune the squatter had been fiddling. He then added to it a "turn of the tune" which made the squatter's bit of music into a merry jig. The man stood spellbound 'till the traveler finished, then doffing his coonskin cap he made a low bow and cried, "Friend, 'light your hoss and get yourself down." He turned to the family—"Stir yourselves, all of you, quick now, and make the gentleman welcome. Dick, you kerry the traveler's hoss around to the shed and give him all he'll eat. Sall, you go down to the holler where I killed that buck an' get the best meat an' cook it up tasty. Jane, you climb into the loft an' find that rag thet's got the sugar tied up in it and brew him a cup o' tea. Stir yourselves, all ev ye, like a six-hoss team in a mud-hole, an' make this gentleman feel to hum." He turned to the stranger. "Friend, you set down an' you can stay just as long as you please. Thet thar dry spot's yourn, an' we got a plenty fur you to eat an' drink."

The stranger was Colonel Faulkner, a wealthy plantation owner, and a famous story teller. After this experience, his favorite story was how he fiddled for a night's lodging. As he told the story Colonel Faulkner always played his fiddle, repeating the one little strain over and over. As he finished the tale he would finish the tune with the merry jig which he himself had added.

The story was repeated wherever frontier people gathered. The tale and tune were called The Arkansas Traveler. Many a night its jolly strains have set shanty, sod-house, or log cabin shaking with merriment. *The Arkansas Traveler* is a real American pioneer.[1]

The Beautiful Blue Danube
Johann Strauss V-15425

The Danube is one of the most important rivers in Europe. It was used by the crusaders as they journeyed to Jerusalem. It is still used by both European and Asiatic countries, so it may be truly said to "link land unto land."

The Danube has its beginning in a small spring near a palace in the Black Forest of Germany, and it grows wider, deeper, and stronger as it meanders through Europe on its way to the Black Sea. Many curious customs belong to the people who live in its valley. There are several different languages spoken along its banks, and many charming stories might be told about old castles, about ruined towers and walls that it passes, and about things which have taken place upon its waters and upon its shores.

One of the large cities that the Danube passes is Vienna, which was for so many years the home of Johann Strauss, the musician, whose composition *The Beautiful Blue Danube* has made it the most sung-of river in the world. It was written first as a song, then arranged for orchestra.

Johann Strauss (1825-1899)

The people of Vienna, where Strauss was born, were very fond of dancing. The dance which they liked best of all to do was the waltz. Famous composers like Beethoven called the people "waltz mad." He said they would rather dance than attend one of his concerts.

It is believed that Strauss must have inherited much of his father's musical ability, for Johann, the elder, wrote a great deal of music and conducted court orchestras. It was Johann, the son, however, who wrote so many fine waltzes that he was called "The Waltz King." Besides the *Beautiful Blue Danube,* he wrote *Tales from the Vienna Woods, Southern Roses Waltz,* and *Thunder and Lightning Polka.*

[1] Buchanan, Fannie R. Stories of American Music. Follett Publishing Company, New York.

By the Waters of Minnetonka
Thurlow Lieurance C 7569M

This is an old Indian love melody. It was played on the flute by young Indian braves.

The legend tells of a young Indian chieftain from the Sun tribe who fell in love with a very beautiful Indian maiden of the Moon Tribe.

It was a tribal law that members of different tribes could not inter-marry. This made the chieftain and the princess very sad, but he still wooed her by playing the flute to her. They knew they could never marry, so they decided that they would rather die together than to live and be apart.

One day they walked hand in hand into Lake Minnetonka and never returned. We are told that on certain days of the year the rays of the sun embrace the rays of the moon, which means that the two lovers are together and happy in the "Land of the Blessed Spirits."

Thurlow Lieurance (1897-   )

Lieurance was born in Oskaloosa, Iowa. He became interested in the life and music of the Indians when he was at one time visiting his brother, a physician at an Indian reservation in Montana. He spent several months learning their songs, dances, and tribal rituals. He received a Ph. D. from Fountainbleu, France, in recognition of his work with the Indians.

He was employed by the Smithsonian Institute, at which time he visited 33 tribes, learning their songs, dances, languages, and customs.

Dixie—Dan Emmett—V 21950

Jolly Dan Emmett (1818-1904) who was born in Ohio, earned his living by being funny. He was in a minstrel show and was the funniest man in the show. He would set the audience into roars of laughter, which is why the songs they sang were called "hooray songs."

But one season Dan Emmett just couldn't be funny, and when his manager told him one Saturday night that they needed a new hooray-song for Monday morning, Dan wondered how he could ever write one.

As he went shivering along the streets of New York, all he could think of was that he wished he were down in Dixie. He kept thinking of Dixie and even saying to himself, "I wish I was in Dixie." His lips puckered into a whistle. The hooray song! He had it! "To live and die in Dixie!" That would make a hooray song worth singing!

Monday morning at rehearsal the men of the troupe pronounced the new song a rouser. "I knew you could do it," the manager said.

Monday night Dan Emmett with banjo and bones sang Dixie for the walk-'round, and the people cheered, just as people have ever since whenever and wherever Dixie is heard.

Folk Music from Many Lands

The music of every country is greatly influenced by geographical locations and climatic conditions. Each country's music is distinguished by respective rhythms and melodic qualities.

I. Great Britain

A. England

The people in early England danced and chanted to drive away evil spirits, famine, or sickness. These tunes later became folk lore for May Day or other celebrations. The music showed love of country, freedom, and action.

One of the earliest composers of English music was Purcell (1658-1695.) He introduced Italian musical signs and expression marks into England. One of his best known songs is *Passing By*, V2179.

Some well known English songs are: *Drink to Me Only with Thine Eyes*—V 4322, *Sweet and Low*—V 21949, and *Shepherd's Hey*—V20802.

In the composition *Shepherd's Hey* there is really only one theme, but it is repeated so many times in various ways that there seem to be several themes. The strings introduce the theme; then the woodwinds take it up; next come the brasses —and finally the whole orchestra.

Dancing is an important pastime in England among the country folks. "Hey" is an old form of English country dance.

B. Ireland

Many people believe that Irish folk music is the most human, the most varied, the most poetic, and the most imaginative in the world. Many of the Irish songs are rich historically; the tunes are rich and imply sympathetic sensitiveness. Some well known Irish tunes are *Pat on the Railway*, *Wearing of the Green*, and *Last Rose of Summer*.

C. Scotland

The music of the Scotch Highland dates back to centuries ago. The Highlander playing his bagpipe and dressed in plaids and kilts is a common sight in Scotland. Scotch music is different because of a queer little trick of rhythm called a "snap", in which a note of short value is followed by a dotted note of a longer value.

Robert Burns' poems have been set to music. He saved old songs and gathered remains of unpublished songs. In his own words, he said, "I have collected, begged, borrowed, and stolen all the songs I could meet with." Some well known Scottish airs are: *Comin' Through the Rye—V* 2055, *Robin Adair, Blue Bells of Scotland*, and *Loch Lomond—V* 10-1301.

II. Scandinavia

The Scandinavian countries are rich in folk music. They have many songs and dances reflecting their mode of life.

A. Norway

Edvard Grieg did much to glorify the music of his country. His *Norwegian Dance No.* 2—22171, is similar to the *Halling* dance, which is typical, energetic dance music of Norway. Perhaps the greatest violinist Norway produced was Ole Bull, with whom Grieg at one time studied.

B. Sweden

Jenny Lind, the Swedish Nightingale, publicized Sweden and her music perhaps more than anyone else. The *Swedish Wedding March—V* 20805, by Sodermann, and the *Ace of Diamonds—V* 20989, dance are typical of the country.

C. Finland

To think of Finland, is to think of Jan Sibelius, (1865-   ) and his composition *Finlandia—V* 7412.

In Finnish folk music there is almost always a tinge of sadness and loneliness. Sibelius distinctly felt an essence of sadness while writing, for his people would become depressed and discouraged, and those emotions would seep into his music.

The hymn-like theme of *Finlandia* has been adopted by Finland as its national anthem.

III. Russia

The national Russian instrument is the Balalaika, which is a quaint old instrument of the guitar family. It has three strings which are plucked. There are several different sizes and each plays a different part: soprano, alto, tenor, bass.

The Russians are a singing people; they sing when they work, they sing when they play. Their music has a mournful quality because of their constant struggle against poverty, their political difficulties, and their long, bitter cold winters.

The Volga Boatman is a well known folk song. Composers with some of their contributions are:

Tschaikowsky: *Nutcracker Suite*—V-DM 1020.
Rachmaninoff: *Prelude in C♯ Minor*—V 11922.
Prokofieff: *Peter and the Wolf*—C-MM 477.
Stravinsky: *Firebird Suite*—VDM-933.
Shostakovitch: *Symphony No. 1*—VDM-192.

IV. Spain

In Spain are found many gypsies, whose music reflects their carefree life of singing and dancing. There are many changes of mood in Spanish music: at one moment it is slow and dreamy, the next it is boisterous and fiery and very emotional.

Tambourines, guitars, and castanets are the widely used instruments to accompany singing and dancing. Several common Spanish dances are the bolero, the rhapsody, and the fandango.

All of these tendencies are felt in Bizet's opera *Carmen*, the two most popular arias of which are *Habanera*—V 14419, and the *Toreador's Song*—V 8124. Carmen is a gypsy, reckless and bewitching. She breaks hearts wherever she goes, and yet people are drawn to her. Her life ends tragically, however, for a lover whom she has scorned, in a fit of jealousy stabs her to death.

V. Germany

The folk songs of the Germans are the backbone of the great classical and romantic periods of the 18th and 19th centuries, which made Bach, Brahms, Beethoven, and Wagner, the music masters of the world.

As early as the 14th century, collections of these songs had been made, the subjects of which were mostly historical. By the 16th century, music had grown so much that every sentiment of the human heart and every occupation of life had its own song. The spirit and power of the folk tunes supplied melodies for chorales and hymns. Every town had its own band, called the "town pipers." The peasant boys played fiddles, and the shepherds, oboes. Every festivity was accompanied by song and dance.

Nothing before or since has equalled the music which the masters from Germany have given us. To list everything great which has come to us from Germany would be impossible. The following composers, however, should be mentioned: Bach, Handel, Beethoven, Mendelssohn Schumann, Wagner, and Brahms.

VI. American Music

A. Music of the American Cowboy

In the days before the Middle West and West became too thickly settled, the cowboy tending cattle on the prairie was a familiar figure. At night the cowboys met at the ranch house or around a fire in the open and sang and told stories. Usually their songs were of their own experiences. Sometimes they made up new tunes, other times they substituted words to familiar tunes. A cowboy usually sang when he was on the trail.

Cowboy songs everyone enjoys singing are: *Home on the Range, Put Your Little Foot,* and *Big Corral.*

B. Music of the American Indian

The Indians had music which they sang and music which they played. They had lullabies, spinning songs, work songs, songs for fasting, praying, and indeed, songs for every important act in life.

They used rattles, drums, gourds, whistles, and flutes for instruments to help emphasize the rhythm.

Pure Indian melodies, such as *The Omaha Ceremonial*—VE-89 and *Winnebago Lullaby*—VE-89 used the whole tone scale which seems to have given it a certain eerie quality.

C. Negro Music

The Negro spiritual tells of their trials and tribulations during their years of slavery.

The Jubilee was more joyous than the spiritual and was often accompanied by the clapping of hands.

Examples of the spiritual are: *Were You There?*—V 1966, *Swing Low Sweet Chariot*—V 2168.

Good examples of the jubilee are: *Every Time I Feel the Spirit* — 2032, and *Dere's No Hidin' Place Down Dere.*

D. Modern American Music

Some of the modern music which Americans have composed is written in syncopation, as for example: *The Rhapsody in Blue* by Gershwin—C-MX251, *On the Trail* from the Grand

Canyon Suite by Grofe—C 7390 M, *From the Canebrake*—V 21750, and *The Juba Dance* by Dett—V 21750.

Other composers who should be mentioned are Sigmund Romberg and Victor Herbert, both of whom have written appealing light operas.

Funeral March of a Marionette—Gounod, C 7374

A marionette is something like a puppet, only it is made of wood. Its body is strung with wires that can be pulled to make the marionette walk or bow or shake its head. It can do many strange and funny things!

Once upon a time two marionettes were having a bad argument. They quarreled and quarreled and grew very angry; in fact, in the scuffle, the nose of one of them was broken, and he died.

All of his friends decided to go to his funeral. The day was very warm, and, as they trudged up the hill, they became hot and tired, and they were sad, too, that their friend was no longer with them.

They passed an inn and decided it would be a fine idea to stop and get a cool drink. "What a good suggestion," one marionette said to another, nodding his little wooden head.

And so they had a cool drink and talked a great deal about their departed friend. Their tongues wagged and their heads bobbed up and down in their excitement. They almost forgot about the funeral until one marionette, looking at his watch exclaimed, "Boys, we'll have to run for it if we're going to get there, on time!"

There was a scurry of wooden feet. Click, clock, click, clock! The dust flew as they ran along as fast as ever their wooden feet would carry them.

They arrived just in time for the funeral—wiped the dust off their feet and the perspiration off their brows, and stood sadly as their good friend was buried.

Charles Gounod (1818-1893)

Gounod was a Frenchman who wrote beautiful melodies. His opera *Faust* was perhaps his best known work.

Golliwog's Cake Walk—Debussy, C 68962D

Claude Debussy (1862-1918) was a famous French composer. He wrote a series of short musical stories called *The Children's Corner*. Among them are *The Little Sheperd, Serenade for a Doll, Jumbo's Lullaby,* and the *Golliwog's Cake Walk*. These he dedicated to his small daughter. Debussy never visited America, but he was much interested in American dance music, so he wrote the story as his idea of ragtime, but to Americans the rhythm of the cakewalk is more like jazz than ragtime.

A golliwog is a French doll made of black rags; it has large feet, glass beads for eyes, and a thatch of black, wooly hair. When you listen, notice the humorous, jerky movements and remember it is danced by a spineless doll. Sometimes it sounds as if the golliwog is stepping along fast doing a fine little dance. Then, all of a sudden, it seems he stumbles over his own feet—falls down—picks himself up with a few running steps, and off he goes into his dance again!

Hansel and Gretel—Humperdinck, CM 424

Hansel and Gretel were children of a poor broom-maker and his wife. These children preferred singing and dancing to working. Their mother one day became angry and sent them out to the woods to gather berries.

The children lost their way; night came on and the forest sounds were terrifying. The sandman came to shake sand in their eyes, and they fell asleep. After a night of dreams in which fourteen angels guarded their sleep, the little Dew Fairy awakened them.

A wonderful little house made of gingerbread cakes and candy appeared before their eyes. At first they were afraid, but soon they became completely entranced.

As they began to nibble on the house of gingerbread, an ugly witch opened the door and cast a spell over the two children with her magic wand as she said, "Hocus-pocus elder-bush, rigid body loosen, hush." This is the witch who rode her broomstick at night, and in the daytime enticed little children into her house and made gingerbread of them.

Hansel was locked in the barn, but Gretel released him. The witch, not knowing of Hansel's release, asked Gretel to look into the oven to see if the cakes were done. Gretel told the witch she did not know how to look into the oven, and as the old woman was showing her how, Gretel pushed her into the oven.

The oven fell apart and many children, who had been turned into gingerbread, came back to life amid great rejoicing.

To this happy scene came the parents of Hansel and Gretel. Finding their children safe from harm, they thanked God who had protected them.

Engelbert Humperdinck (1854-1921)

Humperdinck was a German composer who loved children and children's stories. In the opera *Hansel and Gretel*, he achieved much popularity. He has a fine imagination and his ideas show originality.

Hark! Hark! the Lark[1]—Schubert, V-P39

To Franz Schubert (1797-1828) the Austrian musician, a beautiful poem always suggested music. He was never so happy as when fitting words and music together. In the thirty-one years of his short life, Schubert wrote more than six hundred songs, both great and small, but all beautiful. Some of his best songs were written to words by famous poets.

One day he was seated in a restaurant reading Shakespeare's *Cymbeline*. He came to the lines where the lover sings an aubade or morning song beneath his lady's window. Turning to a friend, Schubert said, "If I had a bit of paper, I could write this out for a song." Finding none, he turned over the menu, drew on it the lines of the staff, and there at the time he finished *Hark! Hark! the Lark*, one of his loveliest songs.

"Largo" from Xerxes—Handel, C 9143

The action of this opera takes place in Egypt. For days the Egyptian soldiers in combat had difficulty holding their fort. It seemed impossible, in fact, that they could carry on even for another day. Then one day, almost as if by magic, they were able to push back their enemies.

So grateful were they, that the entire company knelt down and thanked God for his favors toward them. "Largo" was their song of thanksgiving. It also implored their Master's continued help.

George Frederick Handel (1685-1759)

Handel was born in Germany, but travelled extensively throughout Europe. He was stricken with blindness, which in turn paralyzed his hearing, but that seemed not to hinder his composing, for he was a real genius.

He is best known perhaps, for his oratorio *The Messiah*. In addition, he wrote several operas—among them *Xerxes*, and orchestral music, of which his *Water Music* is best known.

[1] Buchanan, Fannie R. How Man Made Music. Follet Publishing Company, New York.

March of the Caucasian Chief—Ippolitov-Ivanov, V 1335

Michael Ippolitov-Ivanov (1859-1935), a modern composer, wrote this vivid, musical story describing the approach of a victorious tribe with their chieftain at the head.   These are not soldiers in the usual sense, but a band of half savage brigands in continual warfare with other tribes in the Caucasian Mountains.

The first melody is played by the piccolo.   Then in the second section, the music loses some of its fierce, military character, and a whirling oriental melody that the piccolo had in the beginning is played. Then the brasses come in, giving an effect of a brillant procession, with fluttering banners: and gay costumes in a triumphal mood.

March of the Little Lead Soldiers—Pierne, V 4314

There are three important instruments in this composition: the trumpet, the drum, and the piccolo.

Thomas was a little boy who loved to play with his toy soldiers. After he had played with them all of one day, when he went to bed that night he dreamed that his twenty-four soldiers hopped out of a box when the three officers, Major Trumpet, Captain Drum and Lieutenant Piccolo called for a drill.   They go through the drill, marching one way, then another, and soon go hopping back into their box, one by one, followed by the three officers.

Henri Pierne

Henri Pierne was born in France in 1863.   He loved little children and wrote many songs and pieces for them.

March of the Tin Soldiers—Tschaikowsky, V 22168

There is an interesting "toy" effect found in this stiff, precise little march.   Trumpets lead the way in true military fashion, and children at once fall into step with rigid arms, stiff knees, and eyes straight ahead.

Let the children imagine they are carrying their guns, wearing red coats, visored caps, and blue striped breeches as they march in time to the music.

The Messiah—Handel

Handel was 56 years old when he wrote *The Messiah*.   The music was written in 24 days.   Someone asked him how he could write such beautiful music and he replied: "I thought I saw all Heaven before me and the great God Himself."

The *Hallelujah Chorus*—V 11825, is probably the best known

chorus in *The Messiah*. When it was sung the first time in London, the King was present, and he was so impressed with the great beauty and sublimity of the music that he rose and stood with bowed head. The audience followed his example. From that time on, the custom has been established that the audience stands during the chorus.

Some well known choruses and arias from this great oratorio are:

Behold the Lamb of God........................ V 11824
Glory to God in the Highest...................... V 11824
Pastoral Symphony .... V 7316
He Shall Feed His Flock .... V 18324
I Know That My Redeemer Liveth............... V-DM927

Overture to Midsummer Night's Dream—Mendelssohn, CM-504

Mendelssohn wrote many beautiful compositions, but in none of them is found more charm and beauty than in the dramatic story of Fairyland and its tiny people. Queen Titania and her retinue, King Oberon and Puck, are pictured in the great forest dancing, singing, flying, and scampering about.

There are human beings in this story too: Duke Thesius and his court, and heavy awkward tradesmen who rehearse a dance.

Listen to the four magic chords which take us into Fairyland. Next enters the Duke and his hunting party. Then the French horn tells in a tender melody of the four lovers and their troubles.

Finally, we hear again the fairy horns playing the magic chords.

Felix Mendelssohn (1809-1847)

Mendelssohn was born in northern Germany of wealthy parents. He displayed real talent while he was yet a boy. At the age of nine, he made his debut as a concert pianist, and by the time he was eleven years old, he had written more than fifty compositions. *The Midsummer Night's Dream* he wrote when he was only seventeen, and it was one of the best things he ever did. He also wrote, among other things, *The Spring Song,* and *On Wings of Song.*

Mignon—Ambrose Thomas, V 20443

The opera *Mignon* was written by a French composer, Ambrose Thomas (1811-1896). He wrote few compositions besides this opera.

It tells the story of a beautiful girl, Mignon, who, when a baby, was stolen by gypsies. She has been reared by these gypsies and wanders with them through the country dancing to make money for her unkind gypsy master.

One day her master threatens to beat her because she says she is too weary to dance.

William Meister, a kind young man who is passing by, takes pity on Mignon in her distress, and buys her from the gypsies.

Among the people who have gathered during the scene are some strolling players who invite Mignon and William to join their company. In this company is Filina, a very gay and handsome actress, who sometimes teases Mignon and makes her very unhappy. The melody of Filina's brilliant song, which you hear in the overture, well represents her gaiety.

Mignon cannot remember her father and mother from whom she was stolen, but she seems to recall a beautiful country in which she once lived. One day as she is dreaming of it, she sings to William the beautiful song, *Knowest Thou the Land,* in which she describes the wonderful country, and asks him if he has ever seen it. The melody of this song is one which you hear in the overture.

At the end of the opera Mignon finds her father, who is a wealthy nobleman, and the story ends happily.

Narcissus—Ethelbert Nevin, V 20443

Echo was a beautiful wood nymph who lived long ago. She was very pretty, but had one great fault. She talked too much and always wanted the last word.

For this, June, the queen of the Gods, decided to punish her. She said, "You may still have the last word, but you shall have no power to speak first."

Not long afterwards it happened that Narcissus, who was a noble young man, was out hunting and became separated from his companions. Echo saw him and wanted to say something to him, but of course she could not speak. Narcissus called out "Who's there?" and Echo replied softly, "Here." He looked around but saw no one. He called again, "Come!" Echo answered, "Come." She hurried to him, but could not speak to him.

Narcissus could not understand her strange actions, so he walked away leaving Echo broken-hearted. In time she faded away and there was soon nothing left of her but her voice. Even to this day, she will reply to anyone who calls her.

Because Narcissus was cruel to the nymph, he was punished. While looking for his companions, he came upon a lovely pool. He stooped down for a drink and saw his own image staring up at him. He liked his image so much that he stayed there for hours, then days—admiring his curly hair, his rosy cheeks, and his bright eyes. He soon grew pale, however, and died.

The elves had heard him and came to find him, but all they found was a lovely white flower, which they called Narcissus in memory of him.

Ever since that day the Narcissus has grown in a shady place by a quiet pool, where it stands looking at its own image in the water.

Ethelbert Nevin (1862-1901)

Ethelbert Nevin was born near Pittsburgh, Pennsylvania. His parents were both very musical. They were good friends of the family of Stephen Foster. Nevin wrote many songs—among them: *The Rosary* and *Mighty Like a Rose*.

The Nutcracker Suite—Tschaikowsky, V-DM 1020

There was a little girl whose name was Marie. She received many beautiful Christmas presents, one of them being a wonderful silver nutcracker. She also received many pretty dolls. One of them was a Russian doll dressed in a bright blouse and heavy boots. There was an Arabian doll who wore a colored veil, gold bracelets and bangles. There was a pig-tailed Chinese doll, too, who was dressed in a satin jacket, trousers, and skull cap. But of all her presents, Marie liked her silver nutcracker best.

During the evening as the children played with their new toys, Marie's brother tried to crack too large a nut and the nutcracker was broken. Marie felt very sorry about this and so, before she went upstairs to bed, she wrapped up the nutcracker very carefully and laid it on the mantel with her dolls, her brother's tin soldiers, and some other toys.

After she went to bed, Marie could hardly sleep because she was so excited about her new toys and about the beautiful Christmas tree with sugar plums (candy) hanging from it.

When she went to sleep, Marie had this wonderful dream:

She went downstairs to look again at the Christmas tree, and while she was sitting on the bottom step looking at it, the tree began to grow and grow. The sugar plums and the toys (which hung on it) all came to life—even her favorite toy, the nutcracker.

Suddenly the cracks in the floor began to open wide and an army of mice sprang through them. They rushed into the room after the sugar plums.

The tin soldiers leaped down from their place on the mantel and began to fight.

The king of the mice and the nutcracker had a terrible battle. The king seemed to be winning and the nutcracker was in great danger. Marie, fearing what would happen, took off her slipper and threw it with all her might at the king of the mice. This killed the king and the other mice scampered off.

The nutcracker was then changed, as if by magic, into a handsome prince. He thanked Marie for saving his life and led her into a wonderful land called the "Land of the Sugar Plum Fairy." Here Marie was treated just like a princess. The dolls, tin soldiers and other toys which she and her brother received for Christmas, did a march for her; the Sugar Plum Fairy herself did a lovely dance for her; the toy flutes danced a jerky little polka; the Russian doll, the Arabian doll, and the Chinese doll danced; even the flowers had come to life and waltzed gracefully.

As she watched, her eyes grew wider and wider until at last they opened very wide indeed as she found herself back in her little bed on a sunny Christmas morning, and "The Land of the Sugar Plum Fairy" was nothing but a dream.

Peter Ilyitch Tschaikowsky (1840-1893)

The music of Tschaikowsky, a famous Russian composer, follows closely the traits of the Russian people—savage gaiety and profound melancholy, strange and varied rhythms and a taste for strong color.

His parents wished him to become a lawyer, so Tschaikowsky first attended law school, but he soon realized that he was better adapted to the study of music. As a result he enrolled as a music student at the St. Petersburg Conservatory. Upon his graduation, he taught music at the Moscow Conservatory and began composing.

Many of his compositions were not received favorably (particularly in his own country) until near the time of his death. He wrote mostly for the orchestra.

Some of his well known compositions are: *The Nutcracker Suite,*

Symphony No. 6 in E Minor (Pathetique), Romeo and Juliet, The Sleeping Beauty (a ballet), and many others.

Of a Tailor and a Bear—MacDowell, V 20153

There was once a tailor, who, each day worked very hard in his shop. He spent many hours making suits and coats. He was a happy man, though, because he liked music so well. He played the violin, and whenever he had sewed a long time and had become tired, he would get down his violin, tune it, and then for a little while he would play the songs he liked best. That would make him forget how tired he was.

One day, while he was busy at work, he heard a noise in the doorway. What could it be? He looked up and there stood a great big bear. The tailor was very frightened, but he suddenly remembered that bears like music.

He went over to get his violin. The bear growled and the tailor quickly tuned his violin. Again the bear growled. Then the tailor began to play a pretty tune, and as he was playing, the bear came into the shop and started to dance. All the while the bear danced, he growled, but not because he was angry. That was his way of telling the tailor how much he liked the music.

Soon the bear became tired of dancing, so he backed out of the door and went down the street. If you listen, you can hear at the end of the piece, where the bear growls "goodbye" to the tailor.

Peer Gynt Suite—Grieg, V-DM 1100

Peer Gynt was a tall, strongly-built youth of twenty who lived with his mother, Ase, in a broken-down farmhouse in Norway. Peer's father, after throwing away the family fortune, had died. Ase struggled on, attempting to look after the farm, forever scolding Peer for being such a lazy fellow.

Peer liked nothing better than to lie on a wooded hillside and dream mighty dreams of quest and power. In the record "Morning," the calmness of early morning, with Peer dreaming his dream, can be felt. He with his wild stories of impossible deeds, was the laughing-stock of the whole countryside.

One time he went to a wedding celebration and there fell in love with a beautiful girl named Solveig. Her parents did not approve of Peer, and forbade his seeing her. So Peer, very angry, wandered off to the mountains where he met the Troll King's daughter, who took Peer to her father.

The Troll King, short and ugly, sat upon a throne with a crown upon his head and a scepter in his hand. Troll imps, ugly, brown little creatures, and Troll witches surrounded him. Peer was the guest of the King and the Trolls for several weeks, until he did something to displease them. Then the king turned him over to the Trolls, who danced around him and tormented him. Peer sought to escape down the mountain, but the Trolls swarmed around him and tripped him, so that he fell and was buried in a heap of Trolls. Just then came the sound of church bells in the valley below and the Trolls took to flight with yells and shrieks. This is depicted in *The Hall of the Mountain King*.

Next Peer built himself a little hut in the forest. He fastened a reindeer's horns over the door, and was working on a huge wooden bar to keep out the Trolls. It was winter and the snow was deep on the mountains. As he stood hammering, Solveig came toiling up the path on snowshoes. In spite of all the stories she had heard of Peer's lies and laziness, she believed in him.

But Peer, thinking of his life of laziness, felt how unworthy he was of Solveig's love, and determined to go out into the world to make something of himself. Solveig promised to stay in the little hut in the forest and wait for him. She sings *Solveig's Song* to him.

Then followed strange adventures for Peer. Through many distant lands, he traveled and finally, in far off Morocco, he became a wealthy merchant. From there he set sail for Greece, but was forsaken by the crew on a lonely desert island.

Wandering on the desert, he found a beautiful white horse and a bundle of gorgeous robes which had been stolen from an Arab chief. Donning the robes and mounting the horse, he rode afar and was taken for a prophet. Peer had not forgotton how to tell marvelous stories and the Arabs believed him and treated him like a king. Beautiful Arabian girls danced for him; Anitra, the chief's daughter, was the most lovely dancer of all. So graceful was she that Peer, before he journeyed on, gave her all his gold and jewels. This story is told in *Anitra's Dance*.

And so for many years Peer wandered over the world, until, an old man, he turned toward home.

During his absence his mother died: *Ase's Death.* Poor and bitterly disappointed to return empty handed, he dragged himself up the mountain path to his little hut in the woods. Alone in the world, forgotten by everyone, Peer thought only of getting to his empty hut to die.

But as he he drew near he heard singing, and through the door with the reindeer horns above it, came Solveig. She was old now, had white hair, but was still waiting in the forest for Peer. As he came up the path to the hut she was singing *Solveig's Song*. Through all the years, she had believed him and waited for his return.

Joyfully she greeted him, and, at peace with the world, Peer died.

Edvard Grieg (1843-1907)

Grieg was born in Norway. He loved his country very deeply, and used native folk songs in many of his writings. After having studied in Germany, he did quite a bit of composing, some of his best known works being *Norwegian Dances, Piano Concerto in A Minor,* and the *Peer Gynt Suite.*

Snow White and the Seven Dwarfs—Disney, VY-17

Snow White was a little girl who lived in a castle near the woods. Her stepmother was a beautiful woman but she was very wicked. As Snow White grew up, she became more beautiful than the queen. This made the queen very angry, so she decided Snow White must not be allowed to live. She asked a hunter to take her to the woods and kill her.

Snow White begged him not to kill her. So he left her alone in the forest. She was frightened, but the animals didn't harm her. They were her friends.

She found a lovely little cottage near the edge of the woods, but no one was at home, so she walked in. Imagine her surprise to see a table set with seven plates, and seven spoons and seven mugs! Upstairs she found seven beds. She climbed up into one of them and was so tired that she fell fast asleep.

When the seven dwarfs, who lived in the cottage, came home, they gasped with surprise to see the beautiful Snow White. They asked her to stay with them to keep their house clean and to cook their meals while they were out digging for copper and gold each day.

One day while the dwarfs were at work, the wicked queen came. She was dressed as a peddler, so Snow White did not recognize her. She tried to sell Snow White a velvet belt, and the wicked old woman pulled the belt tighter and tighter around Snow White's waist until Snow White fainted.

When the dwarfs came home, they revived Snow White, but warned her she must indeed be careful of strangers.

The next day the witch returned, this time dressed as an apple peddler. She urged a poisoned apple on Snow White, but Snow White was suspicious. The old woman, to prove the apple wasn't poisoned, ate from the half of the apple which she had not poisoned. When Snow White saw this, she bit into the poisoned part of the apple and fell down dead.

The dwarfs, all seven of them: Grumpy, Doc, Sneezy, Happy, Dopey, Bashful, and Sleepy were very sad. They buried her in a beautiful glass coffin.

One day a handsome prince came riding by. When he saw Snow White, he fell in love with her and wanted to take her with him. As they were riding, the piece of poisoned apple fell out of her throat and she woke up. How happy she was!

The prince lifted her onto his horse and rode away with her. They lived happily ever after.

The Song of the Volga Boatman[1]—Russian Folk Song, C 4276M

In the days of Old Russia, the heavy freight boats on the Volga River were hauled by men who were harnessed like draft animals to the tow lines. These men toiled along the towpath, tugging and straining at loads often far too heavy for them. To encourage one another, and to time the pull at the line, the men called out the Russian words which mean "yo-heave-ho."

After a time, this call of "yo-heave-ho" became a kind of chanting call in which the pull on the line marked the accent. Then other words were added and the men sang together to ease the hours of panting toil. A less burdened and brighter strain of music was added, perhaps to be sung as the men neared a place where they could rest or the work was less hard.

This song of the Volga Boatman, with its chanting call and contrasting, brighter strain, has grown into one of the most remarkable of all work-songs. It is begun softly to give the feeling of distance. The tone increases in volume as though singing men were drawing nearer. The great climax seems to bring the barge and struggling men before our very eyes, and then it dies out gradually as the singers vanish about a bend.

[1] Buchanan, Fannie R. How Man Made Music. Follett Publishing Company New York.

The Star Spangled Banner—Key, C 17217

In 1814, England and the United States were at war. After the English army and fleet burned the city of Washington, they advanced against Baltimore. But Fort McHenry guarded the city of Baltimore, and it was necessary to destroy this fort before the city could be taken. For this purpose, the best ships of the British fleet sailed up Chesepeake Bay, dropping anchor opposite Fort McHenry.

On the British flagship, a doctor who was an American citizen was being held as a prisoner of war. A young lawyer of Washington, Francis Scott Key, and a friend, embarking in a small boat, rowed out to the British flagship to plead with the admiral to release the doctor. It happened that the fleet was then ready to begin firing on Fort McHenry. Key and his friend were forced to remain during the night aboard the British ship, guarded by English sailors.

All night long they heard the loud booming of the guns on the ships and the answering thunder of the cannon in the fort.

The minutes seemed hours, and hours seemed days, as they anxiously watched and waited. With the first gray light of dawn, they fixed their eyes upon the fort, hoping to get a glimpse of the flagpole. Through the smoke and mist, they saw the Stars and Stripes still waving in the breeze. Unbounded was their joy when they realized that the fort had withstood the bombardment and that the British had met defeat. In his wild enthusiasm Key pulled an envelope from his pocket and wrote on the back of it the first stanza of *The Star Spangled Banner*.

The British admiral ordered Key, his friend, and the doctor to return to shore. On the way back, while his two companions handled the oars, Key wrote the remaining stanzas of the song.

Several days later handbills of the poem were printed and distributed through the town. A week later a newspaper, the *Baltimore American*, printed it with instructions to sing it to the tune of *Anacreon in Heaven*, a jolly old English song which everyone knew.

Before long, people in all states were singing this spirited song, which soon became the best known of all the patriotic airs. It has become the national anthem, to be played whenever the colors are raised or lowered.

Francis Scott Key (1779-1843)

Francis Scott Key was an American lawyer who wrote the *Star Spangled Banner.* He had no paper on which to write the words, so he used an envelope which he had in his pocket.

The Stars and Stripes Forever—Sousa, V 35805

On the deck of a great steamer some forty years ago, a famous American band leader paced back and forth. His eyes were upon the top of the flagstaff where in the morning sun the Stars and Stripes rippled proudly in the sunshine. As he walked, the right hand of the band master moved as though it held the time-beating baton. Under his breath, he whistled a new tune, a tune which today is familiar to every sailor and to every citizen. It was John Philip Sousa (1856-1932) who came to a halt, still gazing up at the flag and speaking to himself. It will be a wonderful march," he said, "a wonderful march!" He whistled the new tune again. "I shall call it 'The Stars and Stripes Forever'. Yes, the 'Stars and Stripes Forever'!"

The famous march was born with the roll of the ocean in its compelling rhythm, the light of the sky in its singing melodies, and the thrill of the floating flag in its clean, crisp chords. Yet even Sousa, himself, little dreamed of the dramatic scenes through which he and his wonderful music would be marching together. There was that inauguration in Washington when throngs of loyal people gave a great cheer for the new President, and then a great cheer for John Philip Sousa and the U. S. Marine Band, as with pipes and horns and drums the music of *The Stars and Stripes Forever* filled the air.

There was that day in the London palace when King Edward and his court gathered to hear Sousa in a command performance. Royal feet were tapping the floor in time to the music of a democracy. Royal heads were nodding to the rhythm of tunes which American newsboys whistled on their beats. And then King Edward was speaking his thanks and bestowing the medal of the Victorian Order upon John Philip Sousa, the first American musician to receive an English decoration. "The March King," he was called.

Steal Away—Negro Spiritual, V 2211

Many Negro songs are called "spirituals" because they sing of his spiritual life. The Negro sang about his thoughts, beliefs, and longings.

An aged Negro in explaining how the spirituals grew said, "When the slaves wanted to steal away from their cabins to hold a prayer meeting, the word had to be passed from one to another by a sort of code. In the cotton field perhaps a leader would sing, "Steal Away to Jesus." Nearby workers, understanding would take up the refrain. As it rolled along from group to group, some would vary it by singing alto, others tenor, and still others might add a bass part. Perhaps at the meeting, the middle part would be added by the leader and later sung by all in unison.

The Swan—Saint-Saëns, V-M 0785

The famous composer Camille Saint-Saëns, (1835-19921) wrote an unusual group of numbers called *The Carnival of Animals,* in which tried to describe the actions and habits of certain birds and animals. in this suite is the beloved melody *The Swan.*

The remaining numbers of the suite were never published during the life of the composer because he was afraid they might be misunderstood, but after his death in 1921 they were found and published.

The music to *The Swan* describes the majestic bird as he sails slowly over the smooth lake with the silence broken only by small ripples of water.

Through the Looking Glass—Deems Taylor, CM 350

Part I—Dedication

This is the story of a little girl whose name is Alice. On a warm summer's day, Alice has grown tired of playing, and she is sitting in her backyard resting. She becomes very sleepy; soon her head starts nodding, and before long she is fast asleep.

While asleep, a fairy comes to Alice and takes her to a Wonder Land—Land of the Looking Glass.

While listening to this record, notice its "sleepy" quality. Toward the end, it can be plainly heard that Alice is now sleeping.

Part II—The Garden of Live Flowers

The first place Alice visits in Wonder-Land is the Land of Flowers. Here she sees all sorts of lovely flowers, but the thing about them which most delights her is their size, for each flower that she sees is not its usual size, but it is as large as she, Alice, is!

She goes to a tiger-lily and says: "Tiger-lily, I wish you could talk to me."

And to her surprise the tiger-lily can talk, and answers, "Many people aren't worth talking to. But you are a nice little girl, Alice, and I like talking to you."

Then all of the flowers begin talking to Alice, and what a chatter! They sing and dance for her, too.

But she knows she must leave her flower friends and see what else she may find in Looking Glass Land.

The tiger-lily at the very end of the record says, "Good-bye, Alice!"

In the first part of the record, listen first to Alice talking, then to tiger-lily answering, then to all the flowers talking at once.

Part III—Jabberwocky (First Part)

As Alice is walking through the forest she comes upon a Brave Man who is looking for a fierce monster called JABBERWOCKY. He searches and searches and for a time it seems as if Jabberwocky has again escaped. Soon, though, Brave Man sees the bad creature a short way off, but at that moment Jabberwocky sees the Brave Man, too, and scurries off.

Part IV—Jabberwocky (Continued)

The monster and Brave Man keep going around in circles. It seems at first as if one will win, and then the other.

Finally, though, Brave Man is able to slyly sneak upon Jabberwocky —his blade goes "snicker-snack" and Jabberwocky is dead!

Part V—Jabberwocky (Conclusion)

The people cheer as this bad creature is no longer in their midst to frighten and torment them. The church bells ring and hurrahs are heard.

But this is not the end of Jabberwocky, for the ghost of that miserable fellow returns to haunt the people.

Part VI—Looking Glass Insects

As Alice continues her way to Wonder-Land, she sees all sorts of insects, but they aren't their usual size, either. For the June bugs, lady bugs, mosquitoes, and ants aren't the tiny little fellows that we know, but they are as big as Alice! They can talk, too, in bug language, but Alice can understand them, for she is in Wonder-Land!

Listen to the insects buzzing and talking to Alice.

Part VII—The White Knight— (First Part)

Alice next sees a fine looking knight on a beautiful white horse. The knight is a proud sort of fellow who has a good opinion of himself, but Alice likes him anyway!

He tells her how well he rides, and is waving his arms to illustrate when he loses his balance and falls out of his saddle!

The Knight climbs back into the saddle and begins all over again. But, alas! He waves his arms at the wrong moment, and, bump!—he is on the ground again.

Listen to prancing horses in the background.

Part VIII—The White Knight— (Concluded)

The horse, because it is in Wonder-Land, can talk, too, and he tells Alice of his master's bravery.

The Knight tells Alice he must go, but that he will be back one day to give her a ride on his steed. The horse speaks and nods agreement.

Alice is sad that he is going, but the Knight tells her to watch him go, and when he comes to the bend in the road, he will wave to her and she is to wave her white handkerchief at him.

Alice promises, and off the horse ambles. He reaches the turn, she waves; he rounds the turn and is gone.

Deems Taylor 1885-

Deems Taylor is an American composer, music commentator, and writer. His best known composition is *Through the Looking Glass*—an adaptation of a fairy tale. He is, at present, musical adviser to the Columbia Broadcasting Company.

To a Wild Rose—Edward MacDowell, C 4279M

The music of Edward MacDowell should be known to every boy and girl, for he was one of our best liked American composers.

For several years, his teaching and concert appearances as a pianist forced him to spend much time in cities, but he loved the quiet of the country and found in the beauty of nature, inspiration for much of his work.

In the last years of his life, he owned a farm in Peterborough, New Hampshire. So that he could write his music where he would be undisturbed, his wife built for him a small cabin in the woods a short distance from their home.

Each day his wife brought his lunch to him and, if he was busily working, she would leave the basket on the doorstep and slip quietly away. One day when she came with his lunch, Mrs. MacDowell found that her husband was very discouraged with his morning's work. His wastebasket was filled with songs which he had written and thrown away because he thought they were not worth keeping.

Mrs. MacDowell went to the wastebasket and picked out a scrap of paper with a tune on it, and she began to hum it.

"Why, this is lovely," she said. "It reminds me of a wild rose blooming in the woods."

Mr. MacDowell agreed that he liked it also. He called the tune *To a Wild Rose,* and included it in a series of pieces which he called *Woodland Sketches.*

Since his death Mrs. MacDowell, with the help of many friends, has kept the farm at Peterborough as a memorial to her husband. It is open to musicians, poets, painters, and other artists who wish to live and work in the beautiful surroundings which MacDowell loved.

Edward MacDowell (1861-1908)

Edward MacDowell was born in New York City. He began to study piano at the age of eight, and, when 15 he entered the Paris Conservatory where he was a fellow student with Debussy.

He was a concert pianist and also taught piano in Boston. While much of his music is not profound, he was one of the first Americans who wrote music of distinction. He gave confidence for composing to many of his successors.

He wrote mostly for the piano, but composed also a few orchestral works, and several songs. Some of his best known compositions are: *Woodland Sketches* and *Indian Suite.*

The Toy Symphony—Haydn V 20215

Franz Joseph Haydn was a famous musician in Europe. At that time there were no large, wonderful orchestras which played for all of the people. Every orchestra was owned by a wealthy nobleman. Haydn was employed by a man named Prince Esterhazy. He conducted the Prince's orchestra and wrote most of the music played by the orchestra.

Once when he was visiting in another city, he saw in a store some bird whistles, tambourines, triangles, and other toy instruments. He decided it would be great fun to write a little symphony about them. Listen to the way the toy instruments and bird whistles sound.

The Waltzing Doll—Poldini V 1981

There was a little girl, Frances, who had been ill for many weeks. For a time it seemed that she could not get well.

Then her uncle who had been abroad, came to visit Frances and brought a gift for her. When Frances opened her present her eyes danced with joy, for indeed it was a lovely gift. There was a crystal ball with stars on it, and atop the ball was a tiny, but beautiful doll. Her dress was of satin with a very full skirt. Her hair was yellow and she had blue eyes. As the ball moved, beautiful music came from it, and the doll, with tiny steps, waltzed in time to the music.

Frances spent hours watching her doll waltz. It seemed the more she watched her, the stronger she became, and it wasn't long until she was entirely well. How happy the waltzing doll made Frances. Perhaps it will make you happy too, listening to it.

This song was written by Edward Poldini, a Hungarian.

Overture to William Tell—Rossini V-DM 605

An overture is sometimes called a door leading into what is to follow. Operas have overtures so that the listener may feel the mood of the opera music to follow.

This overture has several sections, as follows:

I. At Dawn

Day break in the Alpine Mountains is here pictured musically. The feeling of peace and quiet in the village of Altdorf, where the story takes place, is felt. Toward the end of this section may be heard a low rumble of thunder, which foretells the approach of the storm.

II. The Storm

This is a musical description of the great storm which overtook William Tell and the boatload of soldiers as they were rowing on Lake Lucerne. Perhaps the feeling of tenseness often experienced during a storm can be noticed in this music.

III. The Calm

The wonderful feeling of joy, release from strain, calmness, and peace experienced when a storm is spent, can be easily detected. The chirping of the birds and the Herd Boy's Song are heard.

IV. Finale

The mood of The Calm is suddenly displaced by music which sounds martial and militant. It is an omen of the war to come, with troops assembling and warfare a certainty.

Gioachino Rossini (1792-1868)

Rossini was born in Italy. He learned to love music at an early age and could sing well even as a small boy. His father played a trumpet and his mother was a fine singer. Young Rossini learned to play a horn and when he was only ten years old, he played with a group of strolling musicians who travelled through the country during the summer months.

He became interested in composing as he grew up, and wrote a number of operas, some of which we enjoy today: *The Barber of Seville, Otello,* and *William Tell.*

Assignments

1. Study these stories to become very familiar with them when presenting a listening lesson.
2. Plan a listening lesson for at least ten of these records with accompanying stories, making the stories the basis for each lesson.
3. There are records mentioned throughout the book which have story possibilities. Select five records and write a story (not found in this appendix) about each one.

BIBLIOGRAPHY

Buchanan, Fannie R. *Stories of American Music.* Follet Publishing Company, New York.

Cross, Donzella. *Music Stories for Boys and Girls.* G. Schirmer Co., New York, 1926.

Hartshorn, William. *The Pilot.* Ginn and Co., Chicago, 1940.

GOOD BOOKS FOR THE READING SHELF

Grades 1-2

Kinscella, Hazel G. *Storyland.* University Publishing Company, 1939.

Suitable Stories for the Teacher to Read to the Children

Berry, Erick. *One String Fiddle.* Winston Publishing Company, Chicago, 1939.

The teacher may read many stories for her first and second grades from the 3-4 grade reading shelf.

Grades 3-4

Buchanan, Fannie R. *How Man Made Music.* Follet Publishing Company, Chicago, 1936.

Commins, Dorothy B. *Making an Orchestra.* The Macmillan Company, New York, 1931.

Dearborn, Frances R. *How the Indians Lived.* Ginn and Company, Boston, 1927. Pp. 182-189.

Kinscella, Hazel G. *The Man in the Drum.* University Publishing Company, 1939.

Kinscella, Hazel G. *Folk Tales from Many Lands.* University Publishing Company, 1939.

Stearns, Theodore. *The Story of Music.* Harper and Brothers, New York, 1931.

Wheeler, Opal and Deucher, Sybil. *Joseph Haydn, the Merry Little Peasant.* E. P. Dutton and Company, New York, 1936.

Grades 5-6

Barber, Grace E. *The Wagner Opera Stories.* Public Schools Publishing Company, Bloomington, 1916.

Buchanan, Fannie R. *How Man Made Music.* Follet Publishing Company, Chicago, 1936.

Buchanan, Fannie R. *Magic Music.* Wallace Publishing Company, Des Moines.

Commins, Dorothy B. *Making an Orchestra.* Macmillan Company, New York, 1931.

Kinscella, Hazel G. *Conrad's Magic Flight.* University Publishing Company, 1939.

LaPrade, Ernest. *Alice in Orchestralia.* Doubleday, Doran and Company, New York, 1940.

Stearns, Theodore. *The Story of Music.* Harper and Brothers, New York, 1931.

Wheeler, Opal and Deucher, Sybil. *Curtain Calls for Joseph Haydn and Sebastian Bach.* E. P. Dutton and Company, New York, 1935.

Wheeler, Opal and Deucher, Sybil. *Mozart, the Wonder Boy.* E. P. Dutton and Company, New York, 1934.

Grades 7-8

Barber, Grace E. *The Wagner Opera Stories.* Public Schools Publishing Company, Bloomington, 1916.

Browne, C. A. *Our National Ballads.* Thomas Y. Crowell, New York, 1916.

Buchanan, Fannie R. *How Man Made Music.* Follet Publishing Company, Chicago, 1936.

Burch, Gladys. *A Child's Book of Famous Composers.* A. S. Barnes and Company, New York, 1939.

Commins, Dorothy B. *Making an Orchestra.* Macmillan Company, New York, 1931.

Faulkner, Anne S. *What We Hear in Music.* Victor Talking Machine Company, Camden.

Kinscella, Hazel G. *History Sings.* University Publishing Company, Lincoln.

LaPrade, Ernest. *Alice in Orchestralia.* Doubleday, Doran and Company, New York, 1940.

Wheeler, Opal and Deucher, Sybil. *Curtain Calls for Joseph Haydn and Sebastian Bach.* E. P. Dutton and Company, New York, 1935.

Wheeler, Opal and Deucher, Sybil. *Curtain Calls for Mozart.* E. P. Dutton and Company, New York, 1941.

Wheeler, Opal and Deucher, Sybil. *Mozart, the Wonder Boy.* E. P. Dutton and Company, New York, 1939.

Musical Terms

A Cappella — Vocal music without accompaniment.

A Tempo — In time. Usually a return to the original tempo.

Accelerando — *(accel.) Gradually faster.*

Accent — Stress or emphasis.

Accidental — A sharp, flat, or natural sign placed before a note to change its pitch.

Adagio — A slow tempo, slower than Andante, not so slow as Lento.

Air — The melody, or tune.

Allegretto — A moderately fast tempo, faster than Moderato, slower than Allegro.

Allegro — A quick, lively tempo, faster than Moderato, slower than Vivace.

Alto — The lowest of the women's voices. Also Contralto.

Andante — A moderately slow tempo, faster than Adagio, slower than Moderato.

Andantino — Slightly faster than Andante.

Animato — Animated, lively.

Anthem — A religious choral composition.

Arco — With the bow.

Aria — A solo vocal form, part of an opera or oratorio.

Arpeggio — A broken chord, distinguished from a simultaneous chord.

Art Song — An artistic song in which the music closely fits the words.

Augmented — A term applied to major and perfect intervals enlarged by one-half step.

Ballad — A narrative song.

Ballet — An artistic group dance, usually expressing a story in pantomime.

Barcarolle — A boat song, usually having a smoothly flowing melody.

Baritone — A male voice, between tenor and bass in pitch. Also an instrument.

Bass — The lowest male voice. Also an instrument.

Berceuse — A lullaby, or cradle song.

Binary — A two-part song form.

Bridge — A support for the strings of stringed instruments.

Cadence — A harmonic ending.

Cantata — A composition with choral and solo parts, built around a central theme.

Carol — A festal folk-song, usually on a Christmas or Easter theme.

Chaconne — A dance-like form, of Spanish origin.

Chamber music — Music for a small group intended for a small room.

Chant — A religious song, with groups of words sung on the same pitch.

Choir — A group of singers, usually for a church service.

Chorale — A hymn-like type of music, usually sacred.

Chord — Three or more tones sounded together harmonically.

Chromatic — Progressing by half-tone intervals.

Classic — Music written with adherence to a strict pattern or form.

Coda — An extended ending of a composition.

Coloratura — A specialized type of high soprano voice.

Composer — One who writes music.

Composition — A piece of music; the art of writing music.

Con — An Italian prefix meaning "with."

Concert — A public musical performance.

Concerto — A composition for solo instrument with orchestral accompaniment.

Con fuoco — With fire.

Con moto — With motion.

Consonance — A chord or combination of sounds pleasing to the ear. Opposed to dissonance.

Con sordino — With mute. (Applies only to stringed instruments.)

Contralto — The lowest woman's voice. Also alto.

Contrapuntal — Relating to counterpoint.

Counterpoint — The setting of one melody against another.

Crescendo — *(cresc.)* Increasing in loudness.

Da Capo — *(D. C.)* To the beginning.

Dal Segno — *(D. S.)* Literally, from the sign.

Descrescendo — *(decresc.)* Decreasing in loudness.

Diatonic — Progressing by scale intervals.

Diminished — A term applied to minor and perfect intervals made smaller by one-half step.

Diminuendo — *(dim.)* Gradually softer.

Dissonance — A combination of sounds unsatisfying to the ear. Opposed to consonance.

Duet — A song for two solo voices or instruments.

262

Embouchure — Tongue and lip control in instrumental tone-production.

Ensemble — Together, a group of players playing together.

Etude — A musical study or exercise.

Fantasia — A free and fanciful form of composition.

Finale — The last part, or close of a composition.

Fine — A term indicating the termination of a composition.

Flat — A Symbol (♭) indicating that a tone is to be lowered in pitch one-half step.

Folk-song — A song characteristic of a people or nation.

Forte — (f) Loud.

Fortissimo — (ff) Very loud.

Forzando — (sf) Strongly accented. The same as sforzando (sfz).

Fugue — A common form of contrapuntal composition.

Fundamental — A term applied to the lowest note of a chord in normal position.

Gavotte — A dance form.

Glee — A choral composition for three or four voices.

Grave — A slow and solemn movement. The slowest tempo in music.

Harmonics — Overtones obtained on instruments or voice; usually applied to stringed instruments.

Harmony — Combinations of tones into chords and chordal progressions.

Hexachord — A scale or system of six tones.

Hymn — A common form of religious song, intended to be sung by the congregation.

Intermezzo — An instrumental interlude.

Interval — The distance between two tones.

Intonation — The act of production of tone in exact tune or pitch.

Invention — A short composition in free contrapuntal style.

Inversion — A change in position from normal of an interval or chord.

Key — A system of tone relationships following the pattern of a recognized scale.

Largo — A very slow tempo.

Legato — Connected.

Lento — A slow tempo, slower than Adagio, faster than Largo.

Libretto — The text or words of an opera or oratorio.

Madrigal — A secular part song developed during the sixteenth century.

Major — Greater, when referring to intervals or scales. Opposed to minor.

Marcato — Marked; accented.

March — A military air or composition.

Mass — A choral composition performed at the celebration of High Mass.

Mazurka — A dance form of Polish origin.

Measure — The space between two bar lines on the staff.

Melody — A pleasing succession of tones, usually having a pleasing rhythm.

Meno — Less.

Meno mosso — Less motion; slower.

Mezzo-forte — (mf) Medium loud.

Mezzo-piano — (mp) medium soft.

Minor — Less, when referring to intervals or scales. Opposed to major.

Minuet — A dance form. The court dance of France in the 18th and 19th centuries.

Modes — Kinds of scale patterns, as minor and major modes.

Moderato — A moderate, average tempo.

Modulation — The process of moving harmonically to a different key.

Monody — For one voice, as opposed to polyphony.

Morendo — Dying away; gradually diminishing the tone and the tempo.

Motet — A sacred choral composition, usually in contrapuntal style.

Muted — Softened, by means of a mute.

Natural — A symbol (♮) used to cancel the effect of a sharp or a flat.

Neumes — A type of notes used in the middle ages.

Nocturne — A night song.

Notation — The representation of tones by written or printed characters.

Obligato — An instrumental part usually accompanying a vocal solo.

Octet — A composition for eight voices or instruments.

Opera — A musical drama.

Opera comique — Comic opera.

Operetta — A light musical drama with spoken dialogue.

Opus — Literally, a "work." A musical composition or group of compositions.

Oratorio — A sacred musical drama in concert form.

Overtones — Complementary harmonic sounds present in all musical tones.

Overture — An introductory part to an opera or oratorio; a musical form sometimes a separate form.

Passion — A sacred composition depicting the suffering of Christ.

Pastorale — A musical picture of scenes from rural life.

Pentatonic — Five-tone.

Percussion — Referring to instruments which are played by striking.

Pianissimo — (pp) Very soft.

Piano — (p) Soft. Also the pianoforte.

Pitch — The rate of vibration of any given tone.

Piu — More.

Piu Mosso — More motion; quicker.

Plainsong — The name given to the earliest form of religious chant.

Pizzicato — (pizz.) Plucking. Opposed to arco (bowing).

Poco a poco — Little by little.

Polka — A dance form of Bohemian origin.

Polonaise — A Polish dance form.

Polyphonic — Many-voiced. Opposed to monophonic.

Prelude — Introductory movement of a composition. A musical form.

Prestissimo — As fast as possible.

Presto — Very fast.

Prima donna — A principal woman singer in opera.

Program (music) — Descriptive music. Opposed to absolute or pure music.

Quartet — A composition written for four voices or instruments.

Quintet — A composition written for five voices or instruments.

Rallentando — (rall.) Gradually slower.

Recitative — Musical declamation usually introducing an aria.

Recital — A form of musical program usually by one artist.

Repertory — A list of compositions which any artist has ready for performance.

Rhapsody — An instrumental fantasia usually based on national melodies.

Rhythm — A periodic recurrence of accent; regular pulsation.

Ritard — (rit.) Slower.

Romantic — Referring to the period in music between the classic and modern.

Rondo — A musical form wherein a principal theme recurs several times.

Round — A short song in two or more parts sung at different time intervals.

Rubato — Robbed time. Time taken from one note and given to another.

Scale — The succession of tones upon which music is built.

Scherzo — A piece of a lively, sportive character.

Schottische — A dance form in rather slow tempo.

Score — The musical notation of a composition. The conductor's score.

Secular — Worldly, as opposed to religious.

Semitone — Half-tone.

Senza — Without.

Septet — A composition written for seven voices or instruments.

Serenade — A nocturnal love song.

Sextet — A composition written for six voices or instruments.

Sharp — A symbol (♯) used to raise a tone one-half step in pitch.

Signature — A group of sharps or flats indicating the key of a composition. Figures indicating the meter of a composition.

Slur — Passing smoothly from one tone to another without break.

Solmization — The practice of applying syllable names to scale tones.

Solo — A composition for one voice or instrument.

Sonata — An extensive instrumental composition, of three or four movements.

Soprano — The highest female voice.

Sordino — A mute.

Sostenuto — Sustained.

Spiritual — A type of religious folksong peculiar to the American Negro.

Staccato — Detached; Notes played sharply separated from each other. Indicated by dots (...) over notes.

Staff — The five parallel horizontal lines on which musical notes are written.

Strain — A portion of a composition, separated by a double bar. A period.

Stringendo — Faster.

Suite — A series of short related compositions under one title.

Symphonic Poem — An extensive orchestral work usually in one movement.

Symphony — A composition of several movements for full orchestra, based on the sonata form.

Syncopate — To place the accent on an unconventional beat.

Tacet — Silent.

Tango — A dance form originating in Argentina.

Tenor — The highest male voice.

Tenuto — Held. Sustained for full time value.

Ternary — A three part song form.

Tetrachord — A group of four notes, the basis of the Greek scale system.

Theme — A musical subject. Contrasted with *development*.

Toccata — An old form of composition for organ requiring great technique.

Tone — A musical sound of definite pitch.

Transposition — The process of performing in another than the written key.

Treble — The upper part; the highest voice.

Tremolo — A trembling or quivering. A shaking of the tone.

Triad — The common chord, consisting of a root, third, and fifth.

Trio — A composition for three voices or instruments.

Tutti — All; used after a solo passage to mean all instruments or voices.

Unison — Two or more tones having the same pitch.

Vibrato — A tremulous effect, akin to tremolo but less marked.

Virtuoso — An accomplished artist.

Vivace — Lively, briskly.

Vivo — Animated, lively.

Waltz — A dance form, of German origin.

SELECTED RECORDS

Academic Festival Overture—Brahms CX-200
Ace of Diamonds, The . . . . V 20989
Achieved is the Glorious Work, from The Creation—Haydn. . . . V 11960
Adagio and Rondo—Mozart . . . . V 11-9570
A Dream—Bartlett . . . . V 4367
Air de Ballet—Gretry . . . . C 71330
Air de Ballet—Jodassohn . . . . V E-72
Air for G String—Bach . . . . V 7103
Allemande, from French Suite in E Major—Bach. . . . . V 14384
All Through the Night . . . . V 1558
Amaryllis—Ghys . . . . V 21938 or V 20169
America the Beautiful—Smith-Carey . . . . V 21972 or 45-5082
A Mighty Fortress is our God,
   from Hymns of All Churches Album . . . . V P-162
Andante Cantabile (string quartet) . . . . V 6634
Andante and Rondo—Haydn . . . . C 70106D
Arioso—Bach . . . . V 11-8236
Arkansas Traveler, The . . . . V 20638
Ase's Death, from Peer Gynt Suite—Grieg. . . . . V DM-1100
At the Brook—Boisdeffre . . . . V 20344
Ave Maria—Schubert . . . . V DM-1020
A Wandering Minstrel, from The Mikado—Gilbert & Sullivan. . . V 36148
Away for Rio . . . . 2175 A and B
Babes in Toyland—Herbert . . . . V 12592
Baby's Boat—Gaynor . . . . V 24534
Badinage—Herbert . . . . V 20164
Battle Cry of Freedom . . . . V 45-5082
Battle Hymn of the Republic . . . . V 45-5082
Beautiful Savior—Christiansen . . . . V 15644
Bee, The—Schubert . . . . V 20614
Begone Dull Care . . . . 2175 A and B
Behold the Lamb of God, from The Messiah—Handel. . . . . V 11-824
Believe Me If All Those Endearing Young Charms. . . . . V 10-1247
Bendemeer's Stream . . . . 2175 A and B
Berceuse—Godard . . . . C 4212M
Billy Boy . . . . 2175 A and B
Blow the Man Down . . . . 2175 A and B
Bluebells of Scotland . . . . V 10-1301
Blue Danube Waltz—Strauss . . . . V 15-425
Bourree, from French Suite No. 6 in E Major—Bach. . . . . V 14384
Bourree, from Suite No. 2 in B Minor. . . . . V 6915
Butterflies—Schumann . . . . V E-73
By the Waters of the Minnetonka—Lieurance. . . . . V 21972
Canaries . . . . V 25-0001
Carnival of Animals—Saint-Saëns . . . . V MO-785
Chant of the Eagle Dance—Hopi . . . . V E-89
Columbia, the Gem of the Ocean—Becket. . . . . V 22083

Minuet—Bach .... V 20079
Minuet—Boccherini .... V 7256
Minuet—Gluck .... V 20440
Minuet—Mozart .... V 20440 or V 45-5012
Minuet from Eine Kleine Nacht Music .... V DM-1163
Minuet in G—Beethoven .... V 20164
Moment Musical—Schubert .... V M-684
Morning, from Peer Gynt Suite—Grieg.......... V DM-1100 or V 19926
Music Box, The—Laidow (woodwinds) .... V 19923
My Native Land, from Aida—Verdi..................... V-8994
Narcissus—Nevin .... C 414
Nocturne—Tschaikowsky .... V 20614
Norwegian Dance—Grieg .... V 22171
Nutcracker Suite—Tschaikowsky ....V DM-1020
Of a Tailor and a Bear—MacDowell ....V 20153
Oh! Hall of Song, from Tannhauser—Wagner (Helen Traubel).. V 17268
Ol' Man River, from Showboat ....V 25376
Old Folks at Home—Foster ....V 1825
Omaha Ceremonial ....V E-89
One Fine Day, from Madame Butterfly—Puccini...... V 6790 or V 71320
On the Trail, from the Grand Canyon Suite—Grofe.......... C 7390M
O Rest in the Lord, from Elijah—Mendelssohn ....V 18325
Overture of 1812—Tschaikowsky ....V DM-515
Overture to Egmont—Beethoven ....V 7291
Overture to Marriage of Figaro—Mozart ....V 11242
Overture to Tannhauser—Wagner .... C MX-123
Passepied from Bergamesque .... C 70406D
Passing By ....V 2179
Papillon—Grieg ....V 18153
Papillons, No. 8—Schumann .... V 45-5008
Parade of the Wooden Soldiers—Jessels .... C 35719
Pastoral Symphony—Beethoven .... V 7316
Pavanne—Byrd-Stokowski .... C 7046D
Pavanne, from The Sleeping Beauty—Ravel................... V E-81
Peer Gynt Suite—Grieg .... V DM-1100
Pee Wee, the Piccolo ....V Y-344
Peter and the Wolf—Prokofieff ....VCM-566 or CMM-477
Piano Concerto in A Minor—Grieg .... V DM-900
Piano Concerto No. 5 (Emperor)—Beethoven............... V DM-989
Pictures at an Exhibition—Moussorgsky .... V DM-706
Pledge to the Flag—Malotte .... V 4535
Poem for Flute and Orchestra—Griffes ....V 11-8349
Polka and Fugue, from Schwanda—Weinberger ....V 12-0019
Polka from The Bartered Bride—Smetana ....V 8694
Pomp and Circumstance .... V 6648
Pop Goes the Weazel ....V 20151
Prelude in D♭—Chopin ....V 6847
Prelude in C♯ Minor—Rachmaninoff ....V 11922

Prelude in Act III of Lohengrin—Wagner .... V 7386
Prize Song, from Die Meistersinger—Wagner.................. V 7105
Pueblo Lullaby .... V E-89
Quadrille 22991
Reflections on the Water—Debussy .... V 6633
Rendezvous—Aletter .... C 418M
Rhapsody in Blue—Gershwin .... C MX-251
Ride of the Valkyries, from The Valkyrie—Wagner.......... C 11987D
Robin Adair.. V 10-1301
Rockabye Baby... V 20174
Rockabye Parade—de Leath..................... V Y 16 or C 4212M
Run, Run, Run—Concone.................................. V 20162
Rustle of Spring—Sinding .... V 18153
Rusty in Orchestraville.............................. Cap. BC 35
Sarabande, from French Suite No. 6 in E Major—Bach........ V 14384
Semper Fidelis—Sousa.................................... V 18-0053
Serenade for the Doll—Debussy........................... V 7147
Sextette, from Lucia di Lammermoor—Donizetti............. V 10000
Scherzo, from 3rd Symphony—Beethoven.................... V 45-5026
Scherzo, Sonata, Op. 26—Beethoven....................... V 45-5042
Shawnee, Indian Hunting Dance—Skilton.................... V E-89
Shepherds Christmas Music, from Christmas Oratorio—Bach.... V 7142
Shepherd's Hey .... V 20802
Shuffling Feet—Sioux..................................... V E-89
Silent Night... V 45-5070
Skaters Waltz, The—Waldteufel........................... V 45-5012
Skipping .... V 22765
Skipping, Running.. V 22767
Snow White—Disney...................................... V Y-17
Sonata for Flute, Harp, and Viola, No. 2—Debussy.......... V DM 873
Sonata in C Minor—Beethoven............................ V 16250
Sonata in A Major—Mozart.............................. V 11593
Song of the Volga Boatman.............................. C 4276M
Songs of the Zoo .... V Y-337
Soldiers' Chorus, from Faust—Gounod..................... V 45-5015
Soldier's March—Schumann.............................. V 22168
Sourwood Mountain............................. 2175 A and B
Spanish Guitar................................. 2175 A and B
Spinning Song—Mendelssohn............................. V 20195
Spring Song—Mendelssohn.............................. V 20195
Stars and Stripes Forever—Sousa........................ V 35805
Star Spangled Banner, The—Key-Smith .... V E-91
Storm, The, from William Tell Overture................ V DM-605
Sunrise Call, The—Zuni................................ V E-89
Swan, The—Saint-Saëns................................ V MO 785
Swan Lake, The—Tschaikowsky........................... V DM 1028
Swedish Wedding March, The—Sodermann .... V 20805
Sweet and Low.. V 45-5024

INDEX

INDEX